AGAINST
THE
HORIZON

Recent Titles in
Contributions in Women's Studies

New Dimensions of Spirituality: A Biracial and Bicultural Reading of the
Novels of Toni Morrison
Karla F. C. Holloway and Stephanie Demetrakopoulos

Women and Music in Cross-Cultural Perspective
Ellen Koskoff, editor

Venomous Woman: Fear of the Female in Literature
Margaret Hallissy

Hard News: Women in Broadcast Journalism
David H. Hosley and Gayle K. Yamada

Faith of a (Woman) Writer
Alice Kessler-Harris and William McBrien, editors

The Language of Exclusion: The Poetry of Emily Dickinson
and Christina Rossetti
Sharon Leder with Andrea Abbott

Seeing Female: Social Roles and Personal Lives
Sharon S. Brehm, editor

A Disturbance in Mirrors: The Poetry of Sylvia Plath
Pamela J. Annas

Women of Exile: German-Jewish Autobiographies Since 1933
Andreas Lixl-Purcell, editor

The Biosocial Construction of Femininity: Mothers and Daughters in
Nineteenth-Century America
Nancy M. Theriot

Good-bye Heathcliff: Changing Heroes, Heroines, Roles, and Values in
Women's Category Romances
Mariam Darce Frenier

The Compassionate Memsahibs: Welfare Activities of British Women
in India, 1900-1947
Mary Ann Lind

AGAINST
THE
HORIZON

Feminism and Postwar
Austrian Women Writers

Jacqueline Vansant

Contributions in Women's Studies, Number 92

GREENWOOD PRESS
New York • Westport, Connecticut • London

Library of Congress Cataloging-in-Publication Data

Vansant, Jacqueline, 1954-
    Against the horizon : feminism and postwar Austrian women writers
/ Jacqueline Vansant.
        p.   cm. — (Contributions in women's studies, ISSN 0147-104X ;
no. 92)
    Bibliography: p.
    Includes index.
    ISBN 0-313-25863-5 (lib. bdg. : alk. paper)
    1. German fiction—20th century—History and criticism.   2. German
fiction—Austrian authors—History and criticism.   3. German
fiction—Women authors—History and criticism.   4. Feminism and
literature—Austria.   5. Women in literature.   I. Title.
II. Series.
PT3818.V36   1988
830'.9'352042—dc19   87-24951

British Library Cataloguing in Publication Data is available.

Library of Congress Catalog Card Number: 87-24951
ISBN: 0-313-25863-5
ISSN: 0147-104X

First published in 1988

Greenwood Press, Inc.
88 Post Road West, Westport, Connecticut 06881

Printed in the United States of America

The paper used in this book complies with the
Permanent Paper Standard issued by the National
Information Standards Organization (Z39.48-1984).

10 9 8 7 6 5 4 3 2 1

Copyright Acknowledgments

The author and publisher gratefully acknowledge permission to use excerpts from the
following:

Simone de Beauvoir, *The Second Sex*, edited and translated by H. M. Parshley, New York:
Random House, 1974. Permission courtesy of Alfred A. Knopf, Inc. for U.S., Canadian, and
open market rights. British Commonwealth rights courtesy of Jonathan Cape, Ltd. and the
estate of Simone de Beauvoir.

Contents

Acknowledgments

I am indebted to Professors Barbara Becker-Cantarino, Janet Swaffar, Lynda J. King, Elke Frederiksen, Jane Marcus, and Katherine Arens, who read and commented on my manuscript in its original dissertation form. They offered invaluable suggestions. I would also like to thank Professor Walter D. Wetzels for his useful comments on translations.

Barbara Frischmuth, Elfriede Jelinek, and Brigitte Schwaiger deserve my heartiest thanks for their time, in addition to their literature. I cannot thank them enough.

I am grateful to the Fulbright-Hays Program, the Austrian Ministry of Science and Research, and the Austrian Ministry of Art and Education for their generous financial support from fall 1982 to summer 1985, without which my stay in Vienna would have been impossible. My three years in Vienna were so valuable due to the assistance of scores of individuals, only a few of whom can be mentioned here. I particularly want to thank Professor Schmidt-Dengler for his critical eye in reading the first drafts of my manuscript. I would also like to thank Dr. Robert Pichl for facilitating access to the Bachmann manuscripts. The Austrian Bureau of Women's Affairs supplied me with valuable information. Johanna Dohnal, State Secretary for Women's Affairs, was kind enough to respond in detail to my questions, in the form of a letter and interview. I also want to thank Dr. Stella Klein-Löw for her personal interview. Without the kind help of those at the *Nationalbibliothek*, the *Dokumentationsstelle für neuere österreichische Literatur*, the *Phonothek*, and the *Renner-Institut*, my work would have been much more difficult and the results less exciting.

Hamilton College deserves my thanks for the financial support of the final editing of the manuscript. However, without the advice of University of Texas computer consultant, James Taylor, the manuscript would still be a prisoner in the University of Texas computer system.

I certainly do not want to forget all my friends during the seemingly never-ending process of researching and writing. Unfortunately the majority will go unnamed because of lack of space. However, I especially want to thank Pieter Judson and Diane Shooman for our long discussions at the *Nationalbibliothek*; Sharon Alley and Sandy Gliboff for use of their computer, an item hard to come by in Vienna; University of Texas secretary Ingrid Huskey for her instruction on the UT computer system; and Ron Garrett for typing and proofreading services—all given without remuneration.

Last but not least I would like to thank Ron Garrett, Gwynedd Cannan, and Cynthia and Hegel Wood for creating a supportive and humorful atmosphere during the last months I was working on my manuscript.

Jacqueline Vansant

Hamilton College
Clinton, New York
November, 1987

AGAINST
THE
HORIZON

1

Against the Imaginary Line

> "Otherwise, future generations would assume the countryside to be depopulated if there is nothing which stands out against the imaginary line called the horizon."
>
> Elfriede Jelinek, *Die Bienenkönige*
> (The Bee Kings), p. 46.[1]

Feminism in Austria

Because the recent feminist movement has had minimal impact on conservative Austrian society and on the Austrian consciousness, Austria and feminism appear to many a contradiction in terms.[2] However this does not preclude a literature possessing feminist elements. The conflicts and contradictions existing in women's lives that became the focus of the feminist movement in the late sixties and seventies are central themes in the works of Marlen Haushofer (1920-1970), Ingeborg Bachmann (1926-1973), Barbara Frischmuth (1941), Elfriede Jelinek (1946), and Brigitte Schwaiger (1949), the five Austrian writers who are the subject of this study.

Despite the widespread use of the term in literary criticism as well as in popular culture, the definition of feminism has been by no means stable. The implications of the term have varied from extremely negative to positive depending on who defined it and when. Luise Pusch, a German linguist, traces the change in the definition of feminism in the German dictionary, the *Duden*, from 1929 to the present and points out that much of the implicit anti-feminist sentiment had its roots in National Socialist thought/ideology, which attributed to it a "corruption" of a perceived appropriate patriarchal social structure. Thus in the 1929 *Duden* feminism was "emancipation of women; emphasis on the feminine," but after the Nazi takeover (*Duden*, 1934) feminism changed to "exaggerated emphasis on the feminine; predominance of the non-masculine."[3] The negative definitions remained in the dictionary long after 1945; as late as 1973 anti-feminism persisted in the seventeenth edition of the *Duden*, in which it was defined as "femininity in men; overemphasis of the feminine."[4] Only in the eighteenth edition of 1980 was the definition revised to "aspect of the women's movement which strives for a new self-awareness in women and abolition of traditional sex roles."[5] With the rebirth of the women's movement came a positive reevaluation of the word feminism that included the political and social dimensions of the word.

Similar to the *Duden* definition of 1980 are those of American historian Linda Gordon and Romanists Elaine Marks and Isabelle de Courtivon. Gordon defines feminism as "an analysis of women's subordination for the purpose of figuring out how to change it."[6] For Marks and Courtivon feminism is essentially the same: they define feminism as "an awareness of women's oppression-repression that initiates both analysis of the dimension of this oppression-repression, and strategies for liberation."[7] So defined, feminism implies recognition, analysis, and change.[8]

The feminist movement has had an impact on all disciplines, and the study of literature is no exception. One aspect of such study has been to focus on literature that is either explicitly or implicitly feminist.[9] Such works are assessed as a provocative literature that challenges the status quo, a literature that is in part a reconstruction of female history.[10] Thus Evelyn Beck and Biddy Martin describe the literature as follows: " 'Women's literature' (*Frauenliteratur*) exposes the myth of a general human culture lacking gender in that it brings to light the reflections, hypotheses, and experiences of femaleness which traditional forms of representation negate."[11] In sum, literature implicitly or explicitly feminist rejects the notion of a general sex-neutral cultural experience and seeks to change consciousness about women's status by criticizing the status quo as well as presenting alternatives.

Feminism and Austrian "Feminist" Writers

The degree to which writers have been hailed by feminist critics as feminist, or to which they identify themselves and their writing with the movement, varies greatly from country to country.[12] In the German-speaking countries writers have identified themselves with feminism to a much lesser extent than have those in France or the United States, probably due in large degree to lingering anti-feminist sentiment from the Nazi Period.[13] In addition the writers wish to avoid being labelled writers of *Frauenliteratur*, sentimental trivial literature for consumption by a purely female readership.[14]

Of the five Austrian writers I have chosen to write about, only one unequivocally calls herself a feminist. However this does not mean that the writers' literature is devoid of strong feminist elements. In order to understand this apparent contradiction, it is essential to consider the period and atmosphere in which they wrote. Haushofer and Bachmann both died before the movement had a strong impact.[15] The message of their work is not any less perceptive nor is their critique of women's position in society any less appropriate. Their literature broke a long-held silence about women's experience in a male-dominated society with a message many were not ready or not able to hear. Although they did not have the option or opportunity to call themselves feminists in the new sense of the word, their works provide an articulation of women's experiences and a critique of a male-centered world. In her book *Woman's Consciousness, Man's World* Sheila Rowbotham explains the necessity of self-articulation for a heretofore unrepresented group, characterized by the accomplishments of Haushofer and

Bachmann:

> In order to create an alternative an oppressed group must at once
> shatter the self-reflecting world which encircles it and, at the same
> time, project its own image onto history. In order to discover its
> own identity as distinct from that of the oppressor it has to become
> visible to itself.[16]

This articulation of problems and assertion of an identity separate from the
accepted stereotype place in question the validity of the stereotype and the
system that produces it. Haushofer's and Bachmann's works are examples of
articulation that many were not ready to hear: their literature was either
misread or reached only by a small audience.[17] However with the rising
interest in literature written by women, these works are enjoying a
renaissance among both the critics and the general population. Many of
Haushofer's books, long out-of-print, are being reissued both in hardbound
and paperback editions. As of fall 1986 her novels *Die Wand* (The Wall),
Die Tapetentür (The Wallpapered Door), *Eine Handvoll Leben* (A Handful of
Life), and *Die Mansarde* (The Attic); her novellas *Himmel, der nirgendwo
endet* (Never-Ending Sky) and *Wir töten Stella* (We're Killing Stella); and
her collection of short stories *Schreckliche Treue* (Terrible Fidelity), have
been reprinted. She has also gained renewed critical attention, although not
to the same degree as Bachmann, whose life and works have been the topic
of numerous articles, panel discussions, and literary conferences in recent
years.[18]

Among the younger Austrian women writers the stance on feminism
and the women's movement varies. The range extends from Schwaiger's
rejection of "feminist" as a suitable label for her, through Frischmuth's
conditional acceptance of the label to describe herself, to Jelinek's pronounced
political feminism. Schwaiger's and Frischmuth's views on feminism contain
contradictions fostered by the popular perception of feminism and by their
own views on women's issues. While denying alignment with feminism per
se, Schwaiger perceives "natural," i.e. biological, distinctions, whereas
Frischmuth sees socioeconomic disparity as the core problem. In an
interview Schwaiger states that she is not a feminist—as a writer she cannot
allow herself to be—but she is certainly not the opposite.[19] She points out
that she has been greatly influenced by the classics of the women's
movement, particularly by Simone de Beauvoir's *The Second Sex*. Although
she does not consider herself a feminist, she maintains, "I am all for it that
there are feminists, but I wouldn't describe myself as one" (April 8, 1983).
She sees the necessity of feminism, but her personal position is far removed
from mainstream feminism, which seeks total legal equality for women.
Schwaiger claims, "I am simply not in favor of women having the same
rights in every respect because men are different from women" (April 8,
1983). Her concept of a natural difference rather than one arising from
societal conditions comes out much more in personal conversation than in
her writing.

Frischmuth does consider herself a feminist and locates her feminism in
the social sphere. In an interview with this author, she states, ". . . I'm a
feminist as far as laws are concerned, and above all in all those matters
which can be taken care of through legal means" (February 25, 1983). She

clarifies her statement:

> On the other hand, the expression "feminist" is also so dangerous
> because its definition is subject to such ups and downs. For the
> most part it stands for whatever slogans some group of feminists
> happens to be using at the time. I just can't declare myself in
> solidarity with a large part of this. In no case is feminism for me
> separatism. (February 25, 1983)

Frischmuth's core concerns as a feminist are for legal equality and for equal
opportunities for women. She rejects separatism and believes that both men
and women are needed to bring about social change.

Although Schwaiger and Frischmuth differ in their personal stances
toward feminism, both view it as imbued with a strong man-hating
component, which they reject.[20] When asked specifically where man-hating is
present in the movement, the writers point to the use of certain slogans. To
Frischmuth man-hating slogans represent the separatism she personally
rejects, and to Schwaiger, slogans like "off with their pricks" are an
expression of the man-hating element in the feminist movement; she similarly
objects to generalizations about men, stating, "Sure there are men who rape
women, but that's not all men. There are men who suffer from the fact
that men do it. Not every man is a pig" (April 8, 1983). Schwaiger
believes that such slogans are offensive and too global, and lead to a
repression of pluralistic views.

The media play a major role in labelling the women's movement as
man-hating. A report in the conservative Viennese newspaper, *Die Presse*,
owned by the city Chamber of Commerce, contains one example of the
media's coloring of events:

> Those women's libbers are concerned with neither moral
> sentiments as such nor the social perniciousness of pornography.
> The fight against sexism is simply a fight against the world of men,
> a fight against what these women's groups see as the given fact of
> discrimination against the entire female sex in a society whose power
> structures in their opinion cement the exploitative domination of
> men over women.[21]

The paper trivializes the women's protest against pornography by
labelling them "libbers" (*Emanzen*) and by suggesting that the fight against
sexism is directed individually against men. The article does not address the
women's criticism of pornography, but uses emotionally charged words to
sway its audience against feminists.

Both Frischmuth and Schwaiger agree that the media portrayal of
feminists plays an important role in the perception of the movement as
man-hating; however, both authors appear to have been negatively influenced
by the media's presentation.[22] A general confusion has arisen whether a
critique of a male-centered world that questions the structure of society, or
the idea of man-hating, should be the basis for a movement. The press
exploits the confusion to discredit a potentially powerful movement.[23]

The third of the younger writers, Elfriede Jelinek, does not, as a

Marxist-feminist, believe that legal reform alone will result in needed changes, nor that patriarchal structures will be eliminated by a restructuring of capital. In an article in the *Volkstimme*, the newspaper of the Austrian Communist Party, Jelinek writes:

> The fact, however, that with the abolition of private ownership of the means of production and class domination and exploitation, in short with the radical change of the existing society, the deep gulf between the sexes, the well-worn tracks of male domination and phallo-centrism will simply not fall on their own or by sleight of hand. Patriarchy retains its norm-building function.[24]

Jelinek's article critiques both patriarchy and capitalism, and she appears to be little affected by the media's portrayal of feminism. She has been active within the movement and has written several essays in the feminist journal *Die schwarze Botin* (The Black Messengerwoman). In these essays Jelinek is very critical of the "new femininity" and the tendency to turn away from political action.

The relationship of the women's movement to the authors' writings varies considerably between authors. Haushofer and Bachmann, both of whom died in the early seventies, were never confronted with the issue of their relationships to the women's movement. Had they lived longer, they surely would have been confronted by it because of their popularity among women interested in women-related issues. The three writers of the younger generation respond to the women's movement in the following ways: Schwaiger strongly believes that the effect on her writing has been negative, serving more as a censor rather than as possible affirmation of her work (April 8, 1983). Since her first novel about the dissolution of the narrator's marriage and her struggle for independence, Schwaiger has moved toward other themes (her relationship to her father, critique of middle-class narrow-mindedness) and has not continued in the direction expected by many. Frischmuth does not see a direct connection between her writing and the movement, but believes that knowing there is an interest in a woman-centered perspective has allowed her to feel more confident in exploring this territory (February 25, 1983). Jelinek adamantly states that she gains strength from the knowledge of the existence of a group of like-minded people (September 19, 1983).

Just as the feminist movement itself has no single definition, these Austrian writers also defy facile categorization. Haushofer and Bachmann died before the women's movement, and one can only conjecture whether they would have considered themselves feminist writers. Schwaiger does not consider herself a feminist, and Frischmuth locates her feminism in a call for legal equality. Only Jelinek unequivocally calls herself a feminist. However the work of all five authors is implicitly feminist, in that they write against clichés, work toward a new identity for women, and attack women's subordinate position in a male-centered world. Their literature constitutes a body that "stands out against the imaginary line," i.e., against projections of femininity, thereby placing the male-centered constellation in question.

Criteria for Selecting Writers

To narrow the scope of this study, I chose writers who published for the first time after 1945. The end of the Nazi era is a logical point of departure, since there were breaks both in literary traditions and progressive women's movements at that time. The second step was to consider works that contain a critique of male-centered society from a woman's perspective. Moreover I looked for writers who have published more than one book from a critical woman's perspective or who have made an impact as indicated by the sale of any one book, as in the case of Schwaiger's *Wie kommt das Salz ins Meer* (Why Is the Sea Salty).[25] The literature of Haushofer, Bachmann, Frischmuth, Jelinek, and Schwaiger represent five different approaches to the same theme—women's subordinate position in society. In addition the generational difference between the two older writers and the three younger writers allows for further comparisons of the impact of fascism on the older generation and the impact of the changing status of women and the women's movement on the younger generation.[26]

Organization of this Study

Rather than examine the foregoing five writers individually, I have organized my study around the major themes in their works. Before examining the literature, I look in chapter two, "Austrian Women's Struggle for Autonomy," at the changing status of women in Austria since they received the vote, concentrating on legislation, party policies, and women's position in society. The historical background provides a picture of the society in which the writers grew up. Understanding this background is essential to interpreting their works, because their fiction is anchored in their experiences growing up female in Austria and it confronts and criticizes the patriarchal nature of Austrian society.[27] The second part of the study consists of an analysis of the texts centered around the major themes in the works. The major foci of both explicitly and implicitly feminist writing are women's identity and their subordinate position in relation to men. This can be seen specifically in: 1) the difficulty of self-expression and search for an identity and 2) women's relationships to persons and institutions. These topics will be dealt with in chapters three through five. Chapter three, "Beyond the Mirror," looks at women's struggle for self-definition and the difficulty of achieving it in a male-dominated society. In a world in which women are defined by men and through the men to whom they are attached, it is not surprising that love and marriage are a main focus of the writers' texts. Chapter four, "War, Violence, and Struggle in Love and Marriage," is the central part of this study and examines works in which the primary figure's relationship to a man plays a major role. The relationships with men are portrayed almost without exception as negative experiences; however the women gradually reject total male control and gain some autonomy. In contrast to the great number of male-female relationships, there is a marked lack of female-female friendships and love relationships. Chapter five, "Only Contrasts," focuses on the dearth of female friendships and lesbian relationships. Only as the protagonists gain respect for themselves do they identify themselves positively with the female sex and find themselves capable of forming strong attachments to women.

Because the focus of this study is women and Austria's social realities and their representation in literary form, questions of a female aesthetic extending beyond perspective and a discussion of women's place within the symbolic order receives little attention.[28]

Notes

1.   Translations of the German texts, unless otherwise stated, were done by the author and Ronald E. Garrett.

2.   Unless otherwise stated, when I use the terms women's movement or feminist movement I am referring to the movement rising out of the student movement of the sixties and centered around the abortion issue. For those interested in the earlier women's movements in Austria see Edith Rigler, *Frauenleitbild und Frauenarbeit in Österreich* (Vienna: Verlag für Geschichte und Politik, 1976), Sozial- und Wirtschaftshistorische Studien, Alfred Hoffmann and Michael Mitterauer, eds., Vol. 8.   This study includes an extensive bibliography.

3.   Luise F. Pusch, "Zur Einleitung: Feminismus und Frauenbewegung—Versuch einer Begriffserklärung," in Luise F. Pusch, ed., *Feminismus* (Frankfurt am Main: Suhrkamp, 1983), p. 16.

4.   Pusch, p. 16.

5.   Pusch, p. 16.   Cf.   Herrad Schenk, *Die feministische Herausforderung* (Munich. Verlag C. H. Beck, 1980), p. 107.

6.   Cited in Hester Eisenstein, *Contemporary Feminist Thought* (Boston: G. K. Hall & Co., 1983), p. xii.

7.   Elaine Marks and Isabelle de Courtivon, eds., *New French Feminisms* (New York: Schocken Books, 1981), p. x.

8.   For a discussion of the different directions feminist theory has taken in the U. S., see Hester Eisenstein, *Contemporary Feminist Thought*.

9.   Barbara Becker-Cantarino, "Stimmen des >zweiten Geschlechts<: die neue Politik und Literatur der Frauen," in *Propyläen Geschichte der Literatur: die moderne Welt 1914 bis heute* (Berlin: Propyläen Verlag, 1982), VI, pp. 416-439.

10.   Renate Möhrmann, "Feministische Trends in der deutschen Gegenwartsliteratur," in Manfred Durzak, ed., *Deutsche Gegenwartsliteratur* (Stuttgart: Reclam, 1981), p. 338.

11.   Evelyn Torton Beck and Biddy Martin, "Westdeutsche Frauenliteratur der siebziger Jahre," in Paul Michael Lützeler and Egon Schwarz, eds., *Deutsche Literatur in der Bundesrepublik seit 1965*, (Königstein/Ts.: Athenäum, 1980), p. 136.

12.   For an overview of feminist literature in the FRG and GDR and of the direction that the literature has taken see Wolfgang Emmerich's article "Identität und Geschlechtertausch. Notizen zur Selbstdarstellung der Frau in der neueren DDR-Literatur" in *Basis: Jahrbuch für deutsche Gegenwartsliteratur*, 8 (1978), pp. 127-154 and Evelyn Beck and Biddy Martin's "Westdeutsche Frauenliteratur der siebziger Jahre," in *Deutsche Literatur in der Bundesrepublik seit 1965*, pp. 135-149.   Emmerich briefly describes major directions of the West German women's movement and literature and compares them to those of women's literature in the East using three texts to illustrate his point. He writes that the West German movement and literature sets up a male-female dichotomy, which equates male with bad and female with good, and places women outside the historical process (p. 130).   He then uses Christa Wolf's "Selbstversuch,"

Sarah Kirsch's "Blitz aus heiterem Himmel," and Irmtraud Morgner's *Leben und Abenteuer der Trobadora Beatriz* to illustrate the emphasis in women's literature in the East:

> Images of the emancipation of woman to woman, which distinguish themselves by their emphasis on the right to individual happiness and a fundamental frankness of its conception, are delineated. The simple equalization of man and woman is not recommended, neither is the existing difference between the two sexes laid down in a polarizing manner, nor is a fundamental distancing of woman from man argued in order to achieve a woman's identity, in contrast to what appears so frequently in Western literature. Rather the women authors have the courage not to dogmatize the "masculine" and "feminine" of the future, but to let diverse possibilities of thinking and doing remain in the testing stage.

In the East German writers' refusal to define "masculine" and "feminine" and their desire to break down the categories lies the utopian moment in the literature, and this, according to Emmerich, sets them apart from their West German counterparts. However, it should be added that Alice Schwarzer, editor of the West German feminist monthly *Emma*, for example, views female differences as historically founded, but at the same time as a positive model for change. In Evelyn Beck and Biddy Martin's article the authors provide a wide range of examples of West German texts that describe female experience; they focus on the works of Margot Schroeder, whom they view as most far-reaching in her criticism of a male-centered society while at the same time providing models for change through political involvement. Another informative article discussing West German women's literature, including some Austrians, is Sigrid Weigel's two-part article " 'Woman Begins Relating to Herself': Contemporary German Women's Literature," *New German Critique*, 11, No. 1 (Winter 1984), 3-94, and "Overcoming Absence: Contemporary German Women's Literature," *New German Critique*, 11, No. 2 (Spring-Summer 1984), 3-22. For an article dealing specifically with Austrian counterparts see Ingrid Cella's article " 'Das Rätsel Weib' und die Literatur: Feminismus, feministische Ästhetik und die neue Frauenliteratur in Österreich" in Herbert Zeman, ed., *Studien zur österreichischen Erzählliteratur der Gegenwart* Amsterdamer Beiträge zur neueren Germanistik 14 (Amsterdam: Rodopi, 1982), pp. 189-228. Although her article is mainly a description and criticism of the second women's movement and of theory arising from it, in the last eight pages Cella briefly summarizes literature by women, focusing on women since 1945. She writes, "It is characteristic of the new Austrian women's movement and women's literature that the ideas of radical feminism have hardly gotten a response here" (pp. 220-221). According to Cella, the Austrian feminist writers are not as radical as the German feminists. However Cella equates radical with man-hating (p. 222) and thereby overlooks a far-reaching critique of a male-centered society, not to be confused with man-hating.

    13.   Evelyn Torton Beck and Patricia Russian, "Die Schriften der modernen Frauenbewegung," in Jost Hermand, ed., *Neues Handbuch der Literaturwissenschaft*, (Wiesbaden: Akademische Verlagsgesellschaft Athenaion,

1979), p. 375. Beck and Russian write:

> However, a closer look at the area of literature confirms that
> feminism has had a minimal influence on the literary institutions in
> the Federal Republic of Germany up until now. Authors such as
> Tillie Olsen and Adrienne Rich in the USA and Christiane
> Rochefort and Monique Wittig in France prove that a feminist
> perspective is developing among respected writers; there is   nothing
> comparable in Germany.

Beck and Russian offer the following explanation for the situation: "An
essential factor is that the professional women writers hardly feel themselves
addressed by the feminist activities because the early women's movement
itself is only marginally interested in the mutual relationship between the
women's question and culture" (p. 375).   Luise Pusch writes of the
anti-feminist sentiment on page 16 of her introduction to *Feminismus*: "Nazi
rule may have ended in 1945, but not its massive anti-feminism."

    14.   Beck and Russian, pp. 375-376.
    15.   Although Haushofer died before the women's movement became a
force in Europe, she was influenced by the theories of Simone de Beauvoir.
Dagmar C. G. Lorenz, in her article "Marlen Haushofer—eine Feministin aus
Österreich," *Modern Austrian Literature*, 12, No. 3/4 (1979), 171-191, draws
parallels between the two women, discovering a change in Haushofer's work
after the appearance of the German translation of *The Second Sex* in 1951.
"A significant point in Haushofer's literary production must be fixed around
1951, before the publication of her longer prose, when Simone de Beauvoir's
The Second Sex appeared in German.   De Beauvoir's theories confirmed
Haushofer's implied considerations and radicalized her feminist point of view"
(p. 176).
    16.   Sheila Rowbotham, *Woman's Consciousness, Man's World*
(Middlesex: Penguin, 1973), p. 27.
    17.   Lorenz, in her article in *Modern Austrian Literature*, pp. 172-173,
discusses the reception of Haushofer's works and points out that although the
books were well-received when they were first published, they were by no
means best-sellers, and the critics found fault with the narrow world
Haushofer describes:

> One group of critics considered Haushofer's choice of themes too
> narrow and of negligible general interest, "typically female."   This
> criticism implicitly denied her contemporary significance.   "However
> readable and competent, this is scarcely a rich or a definite
> presentation of a woman's world," Marjorie L. Hoover maintains,
> and ". . . perhaps typically a woman's novel," Marianne Bonwit.

Ellen Summerfield, in her book *Ingeborg Bachmann: Die Auflösung der
Figur in ihrem Roman* Malina (Bonn: Bouvier Verlag Herbert Grundmann,
1976), p. 1, provides the first clear summary of reviews and criticisms of
Malina written before 1976 and points to the writers' misunderstandings and
devaluation of Summerfield's text. A reassessment of the significance of the
works of both authors has taken place subsequent to the women's movement
as a result of issues raised and of the growing body of involved feminist

critics in academia.

A striking example of the shift in appreciation can be seen in the attitude change between the two Bachmann *TEXT + KRITIK* volumes, the first published in 1971 and the second in 1984. The first volume was largely negative, particularly toward Bachmann's prose (*TEXT + KRITIK*, 6 [1980, 4th printing]). The 1984 edition was a special volume entitled: *TEXT + KRITIK: Ingeborg Bachmann* (Munich: edition text + kritik, 1984). Sigrid Weigel, the guest editor of the 1984 volume, offers the following explanation for the Bachmann renaissance:

> The greatly improved availability of the texts brought about by the publication of the *Werke* can not alone take credit for the Bachmann renaissance. Rather the development of the social movements and theoretical discourses of the seventies contributed to closing the gap between Bachmann's literature and expectations of the readers. A "rethinking" (*Umzug im Kopf*), a term which she herself used to describe her changing of genres, obviously took place in other heads as well in the previous decade. The initial stimulation of feminist cultural criticism and poststructuralism were necessary for Bachmann's later works to be understood and the radical dimension of her written work comprehended. And only on the basis of the disappointments with the political and autobiographical literature of the seventies does it seem possible to accept her prose without measuring her against a predefined concept of "political relevance" or "emancipation." (p. 5)

18.   1983 marked the tenth anniversary of Bachmann's death, which was commemorated by the publishing of Bachmann's interviews and a Bachmann album. In 1983, and 1984, and 1985 there was a Bachmann panel at the annual meeting of the Modern Language Association. An international Bachmann conference took place in Rome in October of 1983, and in May of 1984 at the University of Basel a seminar entitled "Ingeborg Bachmann—*Der Fall Franza*: Weibliche Ästhetik" was held with guest speakers from Austria, the Federal Republic of Germany, and Poland. The articles and books published on Ingeborg Bachmann in recent years are witness to the renewed interest.

As stated earlier, Haushofer has not enjoyed the same amount of interest as Bachmann, but the very fact that her works are being reprinted indicates a growing interest in her works. In addition, she is gradually receiving more attention via articles, radio programs, and academic work. Most recently the book >>*Oder war da manchmal noch etwas anderes*<< (Frankfurt a.M: Verlag neue Kritik, 1986) is proof of the increased interest in Marlen Haushofer, particularly outside scholarly circles. The book includes new articles about Haushofer, interviews with her, an excerpt from her diary, and reprinted articles. It makes no pretense of being a scholarly book; rather, the goal of the book is to acquaint the reader with Haushofer. The most useful article for scholars is Regula Venske's review of Haushofer's reception, " 'Vielleicht, daß ein sehr entferntes Auge eine geheime Schrift aus dem Splitterwerk enträtseln könnte . . .' Zur Kritik der Rezeption Marlen Haushofers," pp. 43-66.

19.   Personal interview with Brigitte Schwaiger, April 8, 1983. I also

conducted personal interviews with Barbara Frischmuth, February 25, 1983, and Elfriede Jelinek, September 19, 1983 and April 10, 1985, and will place further references to these interviews in the text.

20.   Jutta Menschik, in *Feminismus* (Cologne: Paul-Rugenstein Verlag, 1977), pp. 52-53, points out that the man-hating component of the women's movement is very small.   It would therefore seem that the press has played an important role in discrediting the women's movement and feminism.

21.   Arbeitsgruppe Frauenmaul: *Ich hab' Dir keinen Rosengarten versprochen . . .: Das Bild der Frau in vier österreichischen Tageszeitungen—eine Dokumentation* (Vienna: Frischfleisch und Löwenmaul, 1978), pp. 104-105.

22.   Compare with Ingrid Cella's discussion of the anti-male element in the women's movement in her article "Das Rätsel Weib," in which she states, "There exists throughout such a strong fixation on the 'enemy' man that the various directions of feminism can be categorized according to the degree of this fixation" (pp. 195 and 197).   She centers the women's movement around the "enemy" man. To illustrate her point she draws a circle with one pole being coexistence with men and the other as the total opposite and locates feminist theories around the circle (p. 196).   She concludes, "This 'circle of feminism' shows that only about three-eighths of the different directions are not anti-male.   All others advocate attitudes of antagonism, separatism, or androgyny to the point of the abolition of gender differences altogether" (p. 197).   Cella does not clearly define "anti-male" and places Valerie Solanas and Phyllis Chesler on the same pole, not distinguishing between them and their critiques of society.   The lack of distinctions in her illustration is similar to the contradictions embodied in Schwaiger's and Frischmuth's stances.

23.   This appears similar to "lesbian baiting."   Hester Eisenstein, in *Contemporary Feminist Thought*, pp. 48-57, writes of the phenomenon of "lesbian baiting" as one of the methods of splitting the women's movement. She describes the political effectiveness of such labelling: "The fear of the label 'lesbian' among women who sought to establish a powerful and effective force for changing the status of all women was ironic testimony to the power of the label to isolate and to silence those to whom it was applied" (p. 48).

24.   Elfriede   Jelinek,   "Frauenbewegung   und   Frauenkultur," *Volksstimme* (22 July 1978), n. p.

25.   The following figures for numbers of books sold by the individual authors as of November 1984 were made available by Suhrkamp, Rowohlt, Deutscher Taschenbuch Verlag, and Claasen publishing houses:

Marlen Haushofer (figures for post-1983 reprints)

Himmel, der nirgendwo endet	10,000
(Never-Ending Sky)	
Die Mansarde	10,000
(The Attic)	
Die Wand	15,000
(The Wall)	

Ingeborg Bachmann

Das dreißigste Jahr	12,000
(The Thirtieth Year)	

Der Fall Franza (dtv)	6,000
(The Case Franza)	
Der Fall Franza. /Requiem	
für Fanny Goldmann (Suhrkamp)	1,500
(The Case Franza. /Requiem for Fanny Goldman)	
Malina (various editions)	131,000
Simultan	6,300
(Simultaneous)	

Barbara Frischmuth

Amy oder die Metamorphose	1,400
(Amy or the Metamorphosis)	
Bindungen	2,000
(Bonds)	
Haschen nach Wind	1,088
(Chasing the Wind)	
Kai und die Liebe zu den Modellen	1,500
(Kai and the Love of Models)	
Die Mystifikationen der Sophie Silber	1,977
(The Mystification of Sophie Silber)	

Elfriede Jelinek

Die Klavierspielerin	10,100
(The Piano Player)	
Die Liebhaberinnen	14,000
(Women in Love)	
Michael. Ein Jugendbuch für die Infantilgesellschaft	7,200
(A Youthbook for Infantile Society)	

Brigitte Schwaiger

Lange Abwesenheit	34,000
(The Long Absence)	
Mein spanisches Dorf	70,000
(My Spanish Village)	
Wie kommt das Salz ins Meer	350,000
(Why is the Sea Salty?)	

The publishing houses Piper (Bachmann), Zsolnay (Schwaiger and Haushofer), and Residenz (Frischmuth) did not disclose numbers of books sold.   Therefore only the numbers for Elfriede Jelinek are complete. Although not complete, the figures offer a vague idea of the general market popularity of the authors' works.   None approach the figures of the paperback edition of Schwaiger's first novel, *Wie kommt das Salz ins Meer.* A book of such popularity focusing on the development of a female consciousness merits closer scrutiny.

26.   Hilde Spiel and Jeannie Ebner, two older writers who published before 1945 and whose writing does not foreshadow the more radical conclusions of postwar feminist writing, were eliminated.   See Ingrid Cella's article " 'Das Rätsel Weib,' " p. 222.   She writes:

Hilde Spiel as well as Jeannie Ebner represent in their novels

Fanny von Arnstein (1962) and *Figuren in Schwarz und Weiß* (1962) an emancipation in the sense of the first women's movement. Spiel makes her case for an emancipation in the spirit of the best and most worthwhile ideas of the German Enlightenment and classical period, while Ebner, with the fate of Theres Meinhart, portrays the problematic of a professionally independent women torn between the desire for dependence and the demand for emancipation, and suggests a solution in the balance between emotion and intellect. (p. 222)

Another obvious omission is Ilse Aichinger, a major writer of the postwar and contemporary period. Although her protagonists are often female and her works contain a critique of Western society, her style and approach to themes do not lend themselves to a comparison with the works of the other writers. Christa Gürtler, in her *Schreiben Frauen Anders?: Untersuchungen zu Ingeborg Bachmann und Barbara Frischmuth* (Stuttgart: Akademischer Verlag Hans-Dieter Heinz, 1983), also does not include Aichinger in her study, noting, "In her case, the thematization of the women's problematic plays a subordinate role even though the main protagonists of her works are women . . ." (p. 66). Examples of other writers and works critical of women's position in society are: Marianne Fritz (*Die Schwerkraft der Verhältnisse*), Marie-Thérèse Kerschbaumer (*Der weibliche Name des Widerstands* and *Schwestern*), Elfriede Hammerl (*Vater-, Mutter- und Geburtstag: 3 Erzählungen*), Christine Haidegger (*Zum Fenster hinaus*), and Waltraud Anna Mitgutsch (*Die Züchtigung*).

27. In his article "What Is Austrian Literature? The Example of H. C. Artmann and Helmut Qualtinger," in Reinhold Grimm, Peter Spycher, and Richard A. Zipser, eds., *From Kafka and Dada to Brecht and Beyond* (Madison: The University of Wisconsin Press, 1982), pp. 63-83, Egon Schwarz places in question the use of the term Austrian literature as "the unchangeable expression of a disembodied Austrian 'spirit' that leaves all political, social, and economic matters behind . . ." (p. 69). It is exactly those political, social, and economic factors that shape the literature. He affirms "there is an Austrian literature because there is an Austrian historical reality. Every work of literature emerging from this reality reflects it in some way and is bound to be impregnated with elements of the Austrian experience." (p. 80) The purpose of chapter two is to draw the connection between political, social, and economic factors and literature. For those interested in the debate surrounding the definition of Austrian literature, the volume containing the German version of Schwarz's article offers an informative discussion. See also Norbert Weber's *Das gesellschaftlich Vermittelte der Romane österreichischer Schriftsteller seit 1970* (Frankfurt am Main: Peter D. Lang, 1980) for a critical overview of the discussion through 1970. His book also includes an extensive bibliography on the subject. For an even more recent discussion on the subject see *Modern Austrian Literature*, 17, No. 3/4 (1984).

28. Critics have increasingly used the theories of Julie Kristeva, Hélène Cixous, and Luce Irigaray to elucidate the works of Ingeborg Bachmann. For an overview of such articles see the first footnote of Ritta Jo Horsley's "Re-reading 'Undine geht': Bachmann and Feminist Theory," in *Modern Austrian Literature*, 18, No. 3/4 (1985), 234-235.

2

Austrian Women's Struggle
for Autonomy

"That women are hardly interested in politics has its roots in a
certain resignation. Politics is something which is practiced over
our heads and in almost every case against our interests. There is
no party which represents the concerns of women."

Marlen Haushofer, *Die Tapetentür*
(The Wallpapered Door), p. 95.

1918 is a logical starting point for a discussion of women in Austria, for it
marks the dissolution of the Austro-Hungarian Monarchy and the founding of
the First Republic. It was at this time that women, who had heretofore
been disenfranchised, gained the right to vote. The boundaries of
present-day Austria were decided after World War I, and the new
constitution, on which the present constitution is based, established
democracy in the former monarchy. The struggle for women's autonomy in
Austria from 1918 to the present has been marked by continued conflict and
contradiction in both politics and the reality of women's lives.

Women's Position in Society:
A Political and Legal History

Always closely tied to the economic situation and the configuration of
the country's political parties, legislation and party policies directly affecting
women have gone through three phases since the establishment of the First
Republic. An initial progressive period from 1918 to the early twenties was
followed by a reactionary period. This second phase reached its high point
with the policies of the Austro-Fascists and the National Socialists. However
it did not stop with the end of the Third Reich, but continued into the
fifties and early sixties. The seventies witnessed the beginning of the third
phase, a second progressive period, which continued into the eighties.

Initial Progressive Period: 1918 to Early Twenties

The initial progressive period coincides with the control of the government by the Social Democratic Party (SDPÖ, renamed SPÖ after World War II—the Socialist Party) under the chancellery of Karl Renner from 1919-1920.   During the two years of the Social Democratic majority, wide-sweeping reforms, several of which concerned women, were pushed through.[1] After Renner's coalition government fell apart in 1920 the Social Democrats never regained national power, and for all practical purposes the brief period of social reform was over.

On November 12, 1918 it was proclaimed that in the next   national elections women would gain both passive and active voting rights, i.e., both the right to vote and the right to be elected to public office.   They practiced their newly gained rights in the elections of   1919.   The second substantial legal improvement for women was the inclusion of an Equal Rights Statute in the Constitution of 1920.   It states, "All citizens are equal before the law.   Privileges of birth, sex, status, class, and religion are forbidden."[2]   However, from the inception of the Equal Rights Statute, Austria's Supreme Court (*Verfassungsgerichtshof*) openly admitted that the amendment would not necessarily result in absolute equal treatment of women before the law because of the range of possible interpretations.[3] In the Equal Rights Statute men and women are viewed as having the same worth as human beings, but by the nature of the difference of their sex are to receive different treatment.   Theoretically the Constitution of 1920 guaranteed sexual equality.   However, as a practical matter, equality was and still is subject to interpretation by judges who are in turn influenced by public opinion and who as historical beings cannot be impartial.   Although there was much talk about reforms and about women's role in society, the public consciousness necessary to institute sweeping reforms did not exist.

Nonetheless, a segment of society maintained strong support for the legal improvement of women's status.   At the forefront in progressive women's issues, the Social Democrats put forth the most radical demands for reform in the party program of 1926.   The *Linzer Programm*, the last party platform written before the party went underground in 1934, is filled with the radical idealism of the twenties.   The platform involves a radical utopianism pointing to the desire for and the belief in revolutionary change, although the consciousness of most party members was not so progressive.[4] Major demands were: 1) the removal of all laws that discriminated against women, 2) equality for women in civil service positions, 3) coeducation by teachers of both sexes in public schools, 4) the opening of all professions to women except those that could be harmful to the reproductive organs, 5) equal pay for equal work, 6) facilities for easing women's domestic responsibilities through the building of communal living spaces, and 7) the establishment of daycare centers to ease mothers' work loads.[5] The most radical feature of the program was the family planning and abortion section. It specified that family planning clinics and birth control be paid for by the state health insurance.   The Social Democrats believed that such measures would cut down on the need for abortions.   Abortions were to be legalized and patients provided with counseling and financial support from the government.   Abortions were to be available on demand if performed in a hospital or clinic under one of the following conditions: 1) if the mother's life were endangered, 2) if there were indications that the child had birth defects, and 3) if the birth of the child would endanger the financial existence of the mother, her professional advancement, or her ability to raise children she already had. According to the *Linzer Programm* the operation was to be paid for by the State.[6]

However widesweeping the reforms were, they still demonstrate the belief that childcare and housekeeping are women's responsibilities. Through communal living and state-run daycare centers mothers gainfully employed were to be relieved of some of their domestic duties. Their burden would be eased by the State and not through a restructuring of the family unit. In effect these policies were the party's attempt to adjust to women's continued involvement in the work force.

The Social Democrats were not alone in addressing the changing role of women in society. The conservative Christian Socials (the People's Party or ÖVP after World War II), also, made room in their party platform for issues concerning women. In 1919 the platform's first demand was as follows:

> The Viennese Christian Social Party decisively supports the demands of Christian women. Therefore, it demands that the legal equality of women with men be carried out in fact in public bodies and offices. The changed position of women should be taken into account in the reform of civil and criminal law.[7]

If this acknowledges women's involvement in public life, the other demands represent an effort to slow or guide the change along very conservative lines. Believing that the family should be protected, the Christian Socials demanded that large families should be subsidized and due special consideration for state and city housing. In line with their desire to protect and support the family and indicative of their close relationship to the Catholic church was the Christian Socials' outspoken stance against birth control and sex education. In response to women's involvement in the work force, the party also wanted the State to develop more industries for women that complemented their natural abilities, thereby reinforcing traditional sex roles.[8] The tone was already set for the policies introduced in the reactionary period.

Reactionary Period: Twenties to 1945

After Renner's coalition government fell apart in June 1920, the conservative leadership took over, and in the elections of October 1920 the Social Democrats were replaced by the Christian Social Party, which became Austria's leading political force in the years following. As historian Karl Stadler writes:

> . . . except for a twelve-month period in 1929-30, it was this party which between 1922 and 1938 provided the *Bundeskanzler* or head of government as well as the key Ministers in every cabinet. Since it never had an absolute majority, it was compelled to enter

into coalitions with the other anti-socialist parties or groupings represented in Parliament . . . . .[9]

From this point on Austria moved slowly but surely in the direction of fascism due in part to the severe economic problems facing the country. Christian Social Engelbert Dollfuβ, chancellor from May 20, 1932 until his assassination on July 25, 1934, suspended Parliament (*Ausschaltung des Parlaments*) on March 4, 1933 and took command of the government by calling on an emergency decree intended for use during wartime. "His aim was the substitution of an authoritarian corporate state for parliamentary democracy, and for this purpose political parties were not needed: the 'Fatherland Front' which he proclaimed in May was to be the only body with political powers for all patriotic Austrians."[10] In addition to suspending Parliament, he eliminated official opposition by outlawing opposing political parties. In May 1933 he banned the Communist Party and in June, the National Socialist Party. His most dramatic act was in February 1934 when he outlawed the Socialist Party, after groups of ill-equipped Socialists made an unsuccessful attempt to fight the fascist government in the short-lived Civil War.

Neither the political nor the economic situations of the twenties and thirties allowed for reforms. Indeed reactionary policies and attitudes toward women typify the political policies of this time. Plagued with economic problems such as high unemployment and inflation, the government sought any possible way to alleviate the problems. From 1921 onward unemployment rose at a frightening rate. The following chart shows the jump from 1.4% unemployment in 1921 to 26% unemployment in 1933.

Unemployment in Austria, 1921-1933

Year	Total number of unemployed	Percent of work force
1921	28,000	1.4
1922	103,000	4.8
1923	212,000	9.1
1924	188,000	8.4
1925	220,000	9.9
1926	244,000	11.0
1927	217,000	9.8
1928	183,000	8.3
1929	192,000	8.8
1930	243,000	11.2
1931	334,000	15.4
1932	468,000	21.7
1933	557,000	26.0

Note: Figures are yearly averages.

Source: Weinzierl and Skalnik, *Österreich 1918-1938* (Graz: Verlag Styria, 1983), pp. 367 and 369.

The financial instability of the Austrian population caused by the economic problems reflected in the unemployment figures of the above chart had serious repercussions and led to reactionary policies and attitudes toward women, typical for a period of economic instability. By 1934 the slogan "woman back into the home" (*Frau zurück ins Haus*) was the basis of the State's policies toward women.[11] Women working as civil servants were one of the first groups affected by laws passed to take women out of the work force. At the end of February 1934 a law went into effect that forced women employed as civil servants and married to civil servants who earned monthly incomes of more than 340 Schillings to quit.[12] If a woman were to marry while employed she could be fired. Those exempt from the ruling were postmistresses, actresses, and female workers at the state tobacco monopoly (*Tabakregie*).[13] It was made virtually impossible to get around the new law. If a couple lived together without getting married, this could be cause for dismissal.[14] As Edith Rigler states:

> The ordinance which had been promulgated as a fight against "two-income families" represented in reality discrimination against women; it in no way affected individuals with a double or multiple income, but it was directed solely against women. Criteria such as education or professional qualifications were not taken into consideration; only the person's sex was essential. The law thus created a "special privilege" for the female sex which, as the Chamber of Commerce ascertained, stood in direct contradiction to the Equal Rights Statute of the Constitution.[15]

Rigler establishes a contradiction between the law's ostensible goal, to eliminate two-income families, and its actual impact, which was to force women out of the work force.

The government hoped to get women back into the home not only with the help of legislation, but with the aid of a "proper" education. New schools and new curricula were introduced which gave young women a foundation in the subjects required before study at the university and provided them with courses designed to enhance their "natural" qualities:

> In the Secondary School Ordinance of 1934, two types of girls' secondary schools were introduced, the *Oberlyzeum* and the already established *girls' grammar school* (*Frauenoberschule*). Fundamentally, their goals resembled each other and also the curriculum of the girls' grammar school of 1927. The *Oberlyzeum* offered Latin in addition to two modern foreign languages. Otherwise, it was identical to the girls' grammar school. The girls' grammar school did not offer Latin in addition to the two living languages, but instead the following subjects: childcare, home health care, needlework, complemented with sewing and dressmaking, cooking and housekeeping.[16]

The *Oberlyzeum* was also structured to facilitate the easy transfer of girls with university-oriented backgrounds to the more home and family-oriented girls' grammar schools.[17] Girls were to be trained for their future profession of wives and mothers; if they did not marry, they would possess all the skills needed for a woman's profession (*Frauenberuf*).

The Austro-Fascists prepared the way for the even more drastic measures of the National Socialists.[18] After the unification of National Socialist Germany with Austria in 1938 (*Anschluß*) women were confronted with policies that were more reactionary and more aggressive in their effort to push and shut women out of the public sphere and lock them into the home.   Policies particularly aimed at barring women from white-collar positions included the continuation of policies directed against married female civil servants.   In addition women could not serve as judges or lawyers during the Third Reich.   The number of female teachers was reduced greatly and a *numerus clausus* limited female students to ten percent of the total student population.[19] Female doctors had a difficult time finding hospitals to do their residencies; they usually ended up taking the most unattractive positions in homes for the elderly and in psychiatric clinics.[20]

Nazi educational policy was built on the groundwork laid earlier by the Austro-Fascists.   After 1938 girls in Austria had one only choice of school:

> For girls there was a single school type, the "girls' grammar school"; English was taught in the beginning years, and the upper-classes were divided into a homemaking and a language branch.   In the language branch, a second modern foreign language and Latin were added, one as a requirement, and the other as an elective.   In isolated cases girls could also attend a liberal arts secondary school. In areas where there were no girls' grammar schools, they attended the grammar schools for boys, but in their own classes and with their own curriculum.   Coeducation was not desired.[21]

The educational differences further institutionalized discrimination against women.   Women were edged out of professions through laws and inferior education and coerced into agriculture and domestic work.[22]

Women were also required to do a year of "in-service" (*weibliches Pflichtjahr*) in someone's home or on a farm.   Women under twenty-five who had not completed the year were barred from other employment.[23]

With the advent of the war the day-to-day reality contradicted Nazi ideology as women were drawn into war industries and positions vacated by men serving in the military.   Women once again filled lower-level service jobs and university positions formerly closed to them.[24] However, the ideology did not change; women involved in those occupations were only filling a temporary need.

Reactionary Period: 1945 to the Sixties

The end of the Nazi Regime did not bring about radical changes in policies concerning women, in part due to the other tasks facing the country after the destruction of the war.   Austrians were faced with the challenge of rebuilding their country and reestablishing democracy in a land that had experienced eleven years of fascism.   Already before the end of World War II provisional governments were being formed by the Resistance in all parts of

Austria.   The groups desired to work together with the Allies to restore democracy and hoped to avoid further bloodshed by ousting the National Socialists before the Allied troops marched into Austria, thereby removing possible armed opposition.   In the eastern part of the country Dr.   Karl Renner, first chancellor of the Austrian First Republic, negotiated with the Russians an Austrian government autonomous from the occupation forces. The Russians installed Renner as chancellor of the Second Republic with the task of forming a provisional council, which was approved by the Allies on October 20, 1945.   The first elections were held on November 25, 1945 with the following results: eighty-five seats for the conservative People's Party (*Österreichische Volkspartei*, ÖVP), seventy-six for the Socialists (*Sozialistische Partei Österreichs*, SPÖ), and four for the Communist Party (*Kommunistische Partei Österreichs*, KPÖ).   The People's Party and the Socialist Party formed a coalition government that lasted until 1966 under various leaderships.   The new government was faced with the tasks of negotiating with the Allies for reestablishment of a free and autonomous state, restoring democracy to a country that had been under Austro-Fascism for four years (1934-1938) and Nazi rule for seven years (1938-1945), and rebuilding the economy of a country devastated by war.   The first goal was achieved on May 15, 1955 when the Austrian president and representatives of the Allied nations signed the Austrian State Treaty (*Staatsvertrag*).   October 26, 1955, after the last foreign soldier had left, Austria declared itself a neutral country with Switzerland as its model.

As a consequence of this comparatively slow and complex period of reconstruction, the fifties and sixties witnessed a general conservatism, which extended to society's attitudes towards women and women's role; it manifested itself both in legislation and party policy.   The idea that women's primary role should be that of mother served as the impetus for much legislation in the postwar years.   On March 13, 1957 the Mother Protection Act (*Mutterschutzgesetz*), which had been introduced by Socialist Wilhelmine Moik, was passed.   Women working outside the home were required to remain home six weeks prior to and six weeks after the birth of the child. Basically the same law introduced by the Nazis in 1942, it would ideally encourage population growth and accommodate women in the work force unwilling or unable to give up their positions.   On April 1, 1974 the mandatory leave was raised to a total of sixteen weeks, eight weeks before and eight after the birth.[25]

In 1960 a bill supported largely by Catholic women's groups was passed, allowing women to take additional leave after the mandatory leave. Women who wanted to take pregnancy leave or vacation, as the German word *Karenzurlaub* implies, originally could remain at home for an additional ten months with payments allotted according to the family income, and with the guarantee that their exact same positions would be waiting for them upon their return.   After April 1, 1974 the payments received were made independent of family income.   Female government workers now have the option of remaining home an additional two years without pay, but with job security.   In a time of rising unemployment such measures ease the strain on the job market to a certain extent.

No matter how progressive the laws appear, the measures encourage women to be the major caregivers of children, thus cementing women into certain roles.   While women are absent on maternity leave, their male colleagues are gaining more experience and are being promoted.   Because women have children and the exclusive right to maternity leave, businesses and organizations often use this as an excuse not to hire women.   One example of such discrimination is at the Vienna Philharmonic.   When asked if the Philharmonic had an active policy against the hiring of women in the orchestra, Dr. Gottfried Heindl, director of the Austrian Federal Theater Administration, replied, "No, but women have babies."[26]

In 1981 an effort to introduce paternity leave was met with large opposition from the unions, powerful bodies in policymaking in Austria; much of the union opposition came from within the female ranks.[27] By 1983 the SPÖ and the ÖVP, the two major political parties, had adopted a call for paternity leave as part of their party programs.   However, because the two parties could not agree on the conditions under which paternity leave would be granted, it has yet to become law.   It came the closest to being passed into law during the SPÖ-FPÖ coalition government.   Passed in the National Council in 1986, it was blocked in the Federal Council, where the conservative People's Party has the majority.[28] But even if such legislation were passed, it is doubtful whether many fathers would take advantage of it. Because the male typically earns more, many families would be neither willing nor able to give up the larger income.   But as Johanna Dohnal, state secretary for women's affairs, stated, "Although I don't believe that a great number of men would take advantage of it, the consciousness-raising effect of such measures cannot be valued highly enough."[29] In other words, by stressing equality of responsibility in child rearing, the adoption of such a measure could nonetheless have an effect on public consciousness.

Party programs were no exception to the conservatism of the postwar years.   Expected of the conservative People's Party, the successor of the Christian Socials, it is all the more striking in the policies of the Socialist Party, particularly in comparison with the revolutionary fervor of the twenties.   The Socialist Party Program of 1947 (*Aktionsprogramm der Sozialistischen Partei Österreichs*) was considerably abbreviated in the areas of women's issues in comparison with the *Linzer Programm* of 1926.   It contained neither the explicit demands for the removal of discriminatory laws, more coeducation, and equal educational opportunities, nor the establishment of daycare centers and other facilities to ease the burden of the working mother.   The Socialists did, however, add a demand for family protection in their list which read, "Full appreciation of woman as mother and housewife, recognition of motherhood as a social accomplishment," pointing to their view that the realm of the family was closer to the lives of women than to those of men.[30]

Population policies were also considerably weakened in the new platform; demands that birth control be available through socialized medicine and that abortions be given free on demand were deleted.   However the program stated that abortion was not to be combated with threat of a prison term.[31]

During the fifties the party platforms reflected the Socialists' desire to improve relationships with the Catholic church and to avoid alienating Catholic voters.[32] In 1952 no mention of women's issues was made, and in 1958 the party put forth a policy on women, which was conservative on issues of family and birth control, with the exception of the demand for a revision in family law.[33] The 1958 policy is totally devoid of such controversial issues such as family planning and abortion, whereas the wording on the social significance of the family was at the same time strengthened.   Although the Socialists recognized the social and economic necessity of the work of women outside the home, housework was still considered the woman's responsibility.   Again, as earlier, the State should step in and ease women's "double burden."   In the sixties this policy continued in abbreviated form along the same lines.[34]

The one progressive party adjusted to outside pressures and overlooked a component within the Socialist Party itself that the male leadership felt to be expendable, the women.   Time and time again the leadership modified the demands of the women within the party in order not to alienate the conservative public.[35] This is particularly the case after World War II.   The practical experience of living through Austria's fascist regime and National Socialism sobered the revolutionary spirit of the Socialists, who decided to be cautious on certain issues, that, in their opinion, could be overlooked without sacrificing votes.   The women in the party were not always in agreement with the more conservative policies espoused in the programs.   As Johanna Dohnal stated in a letter to this author:

> One must establish from the outset that women have always had to fight long and vehemently for their rights, even within the socialist movement.
>
> I'd just like to remind you that the demand for women's suffrage was deferred at the beginning of the century in order not to jeopardize universal male-suffrage.[36]

The demands of the women within the party have often been overlooked for what the leadership felt were more pressing demands or issues, such as economic problems in the eighties and the decline of the prominence of the Socialist Party.   Dohnal contends that the blame lies not totally with the men, but on the lack of solidarity among the women.   In 1983 in a speech she remarked, "The necessary solidarity of women required for the achievement of women's demands is also, however, hindered by the fact that the women in the SPÖ of course don't represent a united group, however essential that may be!"[37] However, according to Dohnal, as the demands of the women within the Socialist Party continue to be overlooked, the tendency towards solidarity within the party is growing.[38]

It is not surprising that the two conservative parties, the People's Party and the Freedom Party (die Freiheitliche Partei), had very conservative programs, particularly on women and family.[39] Despite their basic conservative ideologies, those parties also became aware of outside pressures and in the seventies developed policies that were more progressive.

The ÖVP programs of 1945 and 1947 contain no statements on the women's question; in the program of 1958 demands are made on women's behalf for the first time since World War II.   The postwar party platforms of the ÖVP consistently stated that the conservative party viewed the family as the cornerstone of a healthy society.   Their position vis-à-vis women and the family was consistent with the ideas of the Catholic church.   Their anti-abortion policy continued and renewed the Christian Social's stance of the interwar period. For example families in which the mother was gainfully employed were to receive subsidies so that the mother could return to her family, and both big and fatherless families should receive aid from the State. The measures were drawn up to protect an institution the party felt to be threatened by modern society.[40]

The platform in 1965 reiterated the support of the People's Party for the family, but it was modified somewhat due to women's continued involvement in the work force:

> It [the People's Party] advocates a further development of the Family Compensation Act, through which mothers would be given back to their many children. The family policy of the Austrian People's Party includes support of gainfully employed women and mothers who contribute substantially to a thriving economy.[41]

The conservatives realized that Austria needed women working outside the home for economic growth, but they viewed the work away from children and family as a necessary evil and not a choice a woman would make if she had other options—again a position espoused by their First Republic counterparts.

One of the most striking demands during the interwar period, missing from the ÖVP postwar platforms, was the elimination of the call for schools that specifically trained girls in female professions.[42] Although this signaled a move in a more progressive direction, the People's Party's policies concerning women were consistent with its conservative stance. The Freedom Party (FPÖ) first addressed the women's question at length in 1957 in the section on family and women's policies. Formerly the extent of their women's policies had been to encourage young marriages and large families.[43] But in 1957, this and additional demands formed the basis of the policy statement "Guidelines of Freedom Party Policies" (Richtlinien freiheitlicher Politik). The family was viewed as the carrier and reproducer of Austria's folk and cultural heritage, and as such essential for the education and socialization of the young.[44] Although the party did state that it viewed the patriarchal family as outdated because of women's increased involvement in the work force, it nonetheless supported policies which would help perpetuate a patriarchal society. For example, Freedom Party ideologues believed that the State should make it possible for women who would otherwise be forced to work outside the home because of financial difficulties, to stay at home if they so desired. The party also supported sexual equality in the sense that women are "equal but different" from men. "We support the granting of equal rights to women in professional and general legal matters. We do not, however, place weight on a purely formal pseudo-equalization, but on full satisfaction of mutual legal demands, taking into consideration the differences between the sexes."[45] The Freedom Party's policy, then, viewed women and men as having equal worth, but belonging to different spheres.

Because of the problems arising after the end of World War II and because of the transition from fascism to democracy, the postwar period did not witness an immediate change in legislation and policies for women. Indeed the first twenty-five years after World War II, with respect to women's issues, can be characterized as reactionary. The Socialist, the

People's, and the Freedom Parties placed particular significance on the social value of the family and of its intimate relationship to women. During these years lawmakers and policymakers viewed women primarily in terms of their potential to bear children.

Progressive Period: Seventies to the Present

Just as the socialists yielded to pressure to modify their radical policies in the first twenty-five years after World War II, the conservatives yielded to pressure to alter theirs in a more progressive direction. The platform of 1972 (and of the 1980 program) which supported marriage based on partnership, necessitated a change in their attitude toward the role of wife and husband in marriage, anticipating the 1975 reform in marriage law. The ÖVP also called for equal educational and professional opportunities for women but continued in their belief that women with familial responsibilities should be able to choose whether they wanted to work outside the home or to devote themselves totally to their families.[46] The party also adopted a more liberal position on birth control, supporting women's right to choose the use of birth control. However it remained consistent on its anti-abortion policy.[47]

The women's movement of the People's Party, which was basically a charity organization, was upgraded to involve its members in the political process. Thus the ÖVP yielded to a liberalization that was being experienced by society as a whole, and the party can serve as a barometer of change.

The economic prosperity of the seventies allowed for progressive political changes. After the election of 1972 when the Socialists gained the absolute parliamentary majority, they set about passing laws that had been on and off their agenda since the First Republic. Sweeping changes in laws concerning the status of women were approved.

Previous to the revision of the laws in the areas of marriage, property and divorce, abortion and family planning, and equal pay for equal work, the public consciousness was more progressive than the antiquated laws; but with the sweeping changes the public consciousness did not make a commensurate leap, and it continues to lag behind.[48] The pre-1975 laws controlling marriage set down in the *Allgemeines bürgerliches Gesetzbuch* (*ABGB*, Civil Code) define male and female roles in a marriage in very traditional, patriarchal terms. The *ABGB* of 1948 states, "The husband is the head of the family. In this capacity it is above all his duty to direct the household; he is above all obligated to provide his wife with a decent living according to his means, and to represent her in all public matters."[49] The head of the household had the right to determine how the family was to be run and was responsible for the financial needs of the family. Through marriage the wife assumed the name of the man and enjoyed the rights of his class. In addition the patriarchal law states:

She is bound to follow her husband in his place of residence, to assist him according to her abilities in the household and his profession, and, insofar as domestic order requires it, to follow the rules laid down by him, as well as to see that they are followed by others. (1) The common residence is determined according to the will of the man.[50]

The pre-1975 marriage laws placed extreme restrictions on women's personal freedom.   Legally a husband could force his wife to follow him if he were transferred, for example.   If she refused to go, this would be grounds for divorce.   The housework was seen as the duty of the housewife, whereas the husband was to provide for the financial security of the family.   If an Austrian woman married a foreigner, she automatically lost her citizenship and took on that of her husband, as did their children, a reflection of the fact that women and children were to be defined by and through their husbands.   If a woman was being mistreated by her husband and moved out of the house without first obtaining a court order, this was grounds for divorce regardless of the fact that her life might have been endangered.   The husband also had the right to forbid his wife to work outside the home if he felt that she was neglecting her domestic duties.

    The reformed marriage law provides the legal basis for marriage based on partnership, with spouses having equal responsibilities and rights.   The man is no longer head of the household, as the revised *ABGB* states, "Insofar as another provision of this section does not provide otherwise, the rights and duties of husband and wife are the same."[51] Decisions are to be made jointly and not solely by one partner or the other, and both partners are legally responsible for providing for the family.[52] If the wife has good reasons, for example professional or familial reasons, for living separately from her husband, this is legal and no longer grounds for divorce.[53] However the reformed marriage law cannot dictate consciousness, but can only provide the legal framework for equitable marriages.   If only one spouse chooses to work outside the home, the other is by law responsible for the household.[54] Practically speaking, the person to remain home is the wife.   In addition spouses, and this traditionally means wives, are required to help as much as possible in the businesses of the other spouses.   They cannot, however, be denied the right to remuneration or insurance, a clause which is particularly crucial in case of divorce.[55]

    Not only were patriarchal marriage laws removed, but divorce laws were amended.   Previous to 1978 divorce by mutual consent did not exist, and there either had to be a guilty party or one had to be fabricated. Since 1978 divorces have been granted if both parties wish or if, after a separation of six years, the guilty party desires a divorce despite protest from the injured party.[56]

    Over the opposition of the Catholic church and the People's Party to abortion and the Church's opposition to family planning, extensive family planning services and the liberalization of abortion proceeded in the mid-seventies.   In 1974 the law for the promotion of family counseling (*Familienberatungsförderungsgesetz*) called for the establishment of family planning centers all over Austria, including not only state-run organizations, but also church and political groups.[57] Since this time the services these centers should offer are: 1) partner counseling, 2) family counseling, 3) information concerning birth control, and 4) counseling for pregnant women by social workers and doctors.[58]   Women receive very different messages from the state-run and church-supported organizations, particularly concerning the option of abortion. The effectiveness of the centers can be questioned; according to statistics quoted in a 1981 survey one out of every two children is not planned, and 40% of the children born to married parents are conceived before the parents marry.[59]

On January 1, 1975 abortion became a legal option for women when performed during the first three months of pregnancy by a doctor after counseling in either a hospital or a clinic.[60] Then and now, any doctor has the right to refuse to perform the operation, just as hospitals may forbid the performance of abortions on their premises, with the exception of cases in which the mother's life is endangered. For women living outside of Vienna, particularly in the more conservative provinces, it is often difficult to obtain an abortion. Women desiring abortions often must travel to Vienna, which involves not only extra inconvenience, but also extra expense, since the operation is not paid for by state-run medical insurance. However despite the expense and inconvenience the number of abortions performed yearly is estimated at between 30,000 and 100,000.[61]

In 1979 the Parliament passed the Equal Treatment Act (*Gleichbehandlungsgebot*), a provision demanding equal pay for equal work in an attempt to fight discrimination. However the basis for further discrimination is contained in the provision itself. The act states, "In the establishment of salaries no one may be discriminated against on the basis of sex; 'discrimination' is each disadvantageous differentiation which is undertaken without material justification."[62] The two words "material justification" (*sachliche Rechtfertigung*) often lead to discrimination because of the range of interpretation that "material justification" allows. For example, heavy work is often valued more than intricate work that may be just as taxing. A move towards equal pay for commensurate work may be the next step towards eliminating such injustices.

The contradictions in the law and interpretations of the law could, according to legal experts, be eliminated with the enactment of anti-discriminatory legislation. Anti-discriminatory legislation would be more effective than the Equal Rights Statute or a provision such as the Equal Treatment Act because of the positive nature of the anti-discriminatory laws. Maria Berger writes:

> Anti-discrimination legislation protects in general men as well as women from sex-specific discrimination, but is enacted above all with reference to discrimination against women. There are five areas which will be addressed by existing anti-discrimination laws and future initiatives and bills: work, education, justice and penal reform, business and advertising.[63]

More far-reaching than the Equal Rights Statute, a comprehensive anti-discrimination law would protect both women and men, providing the legal basis for the elimination of sex-discrimination. For example, such legislation would allow fathers paternity leave and would forbid the present practice of sex-specific classified advertisements.

In order to work toward equal representation of women in civil service positions, the government has launched an affirmative action campaign outlined in the government's pamphlet *Mehr Tun für die Frauen im*

Bundesdienst (Do More for the Women in the Civil Service), published in 1981.[64] Because the majority of female civil servants fill lower level positions, an affirmative action program has been established:

> Through the affirmative action program a specifically targeted active promotion of female civil servants in public service will ensue. The measures foreseen in the program are not—in accordance with international agreements and recommendations—to be viewed as discrimination against other groups, specifically against males in government service.[65]

The promotion of women civil servants within the ranks is not to be viewed as discrimination against male workers, but as a necessary component of an affirmative action program determined to rectify inequalities. In addition the affirmative action program is to act as an example in the hope that private industry will set up similar programs.

Since the sweeping legal changes of the seventies, the Socialists and the People's Parties have grown very close to each other on many women's issues. This was evident at the time of the national elections in 1983 when it was often difficult to draw a clear line between the policies of the two parties. Johanna Dohnal points out the major difference:

> In general one can, however, say that the Austrian People's Party fundamentally holds onto a division of labor between women and men. From this a certain cementing of traditional role models results in different areas, but above all in the areas of the family. However, on many points—I'll mention here only the representation of women in advertising and media—total agreement exists between the women of the People's Party and the Socialist Party.[66]

The major difference, then, in the stance of the two biggest political parties on women's issues boils down to a very basic issue: women's role in the family. The People's Party continues to view women and mothers as more intimately related to the family than are men and fathers.

Political and Legal History

In Austria legislation and party policies concerning women have been connected to the political and economic situation of that country. 1918 marked the end of four years of war, the dissolution of the monarchy, and the establishment of a democratic government. Women, by being granted the right to vote and the right to be elected to public office, became potentially active members of the public arena. However, full parity for women in both public and private life was not imminent. The economic situation of the First Republic, plagued with inflation and high unemployment, set the stage for the reactionary policies that followed. To be sure, it was during the period of Austro-Fascism and National Socialism that the harshest measures restricting women were enacted. However, the end of the Third Reich was not accompanied by sudden changes in the legal status of women. Lawmakers and party leaders involved in reestablishing a free republic and concerned with rebuilding a devastated economy, found little time on their agendas for progressive women's programs.   Indeed, women's role as major caregiver can be seen as the leitmotiv in laws and party policies concerning women.   It was not until the election of a majority Socialist government that widespread reforms were carried out.   Drawing on the party platforms of the twenties, lawmakers reformed antiquated patriarchal laws.   In the eighties further legal advancement appears to be at a standstill.   At a time of economic slump, when Austria is under the leadership of a coalition government (the Socialist and Freedom Parties from 1983-1986, and the Socialist and People's Parties from 1986-present), the question remains what direction party politics and government policies will take.   One can speculate that, since this is a time of increased economic instability, it will be a period of conservative policymaking.

Women's Position in Society: A Social History

Austria, although it has had an Equal Rights Statute since 1920 and universal suffrage since 1918, continues to be a country dominated by males and traditional male-female roles.   This becomes very clear if we look at women's participation in government and the work force, and women's relationship to education, the media, and the family.

Women's Participation in Government

In the area of government women have been consistently underrepresented in positions of power both in government and within the party structure.   In 1920 there were ten female members of the National Assembly (*Nationalversammlung*), or 6% of the total membership.   In 1945 and 1949 nine women (less than 6%) were elected members of the National Council (*Nationalrat*).   The elections of years 1953, 1956, 1959, 1963, and 1966 each resulted in ten women representatives (6%).   In 1970 the number dropped to eight, then in 1973 it rose to eleven (6%), in 1979 it rose to seventeen (9%), and at the beginning of 1983 it fell to sixteen (8.79%).[67] After the elections in 1983 eighteen out of 183 members of the Lower House were women (9.8%).   The election of November 1986 resulted in the same number of women in the National Council.   The Social Democrats/Socialists have consistently sent the most women to Parliament, but considering the number of female members in the party, they continue to be underrepresented.[68]

Within the parties themselves, women comprise one-third of the membership, but the highest ranking officials are male; this results in part from the system of ranking within the parties.   In Austria voters choose parties and not individuals, the individuals being ranked by the party.   If a party puts up a list of 100 officials and it wins 40% of the vote, the first forty are elected.   Traditionally placed low on the lists, women thus have seldom been chosen.   For example, in the election of 1956, 91.8% of the People's Party's and 83.8% of the Socialist Party's female candidates were not elected because of low ranking on the lists.[69]

In addition to the internal structure of the system working against representation of women at the higher levels, the traditional patterns of women's lives often hinder full political involvement.   During the crucial years of twenty-five to thirty-five, when political careers are usually being built, women are generally involved in child-rearing activities.[70]

On the cabinet level (which includes state secretaries and ministers) women made the most inroads during the periods of one-party governments. The first female to fill a ministerial position was Grete Rehor, member of the Christian Union movement, appointed to the post of minister of social affairs in 1966 when the People's Party was in power. Since 1966 women have played a larger role in the ministerial level of government, but usually in positions that can be viewed as an extension of women's "natural" nurturing role. For example, in 1971 Federal Chancellor Kreisky appointed Dr. Hertha Firnberg to the post of minister of science and research (*Wissenschaftsminister*), Dr. Ingrid Leodolter as minister of health and the environment (*Gesundheitsminister*), and Elfriede Karl as state secretary for family affairs (*Staatssekretär für Familienangelegenheiten*) within the ministry of welfare (*Sozialministerium*).[71] In 1979 the Bureau for Women's Affairs (*Staatssekretariat für allgemeine Frauenfragen*) was introduced. From 1979 to 1983, six out of twenty-two cabinet members were female (five state secretaries and one minister). Since the national elections in 1983 when a coalition government (SPÖ-FPÖ) was formed, women's position on the ministerial level worsened. Having fewer cabinet positions to allot, the socialists reduced the number of female cabinet members from six to three. The coalition government formed after the November 1986 elections (SPÖ-ÖVP) has three women serving on the cabinet level, Hilde Hawlicek (SPÖ) as the head of the Ministry of Educaton, Culture, and Sport (*Ministerium für Unterricht, Kunst und Sport*) and Marlies Fleming (ÖVP) as head of the Ministry of the Environment, Family, and Youth (*Ministerium für Umwelt, Jugend und Familie*) and one state secretary, Johanna Dohnal (SPÖ) heading the Bureau for Women's Affairs. As Susanne Feigl points out in her report for the third UN World Women's Conference, "All government agencies headed by female state secretaries were 'newly founded' and also three of the five female ministers were put in charge of establishing new ministries."[72] Rather than being truly integrated into the government and its agencies as equal partners, women generally fill positions created for them, thus not threatening traditional male positions of power.

Women's representation within the governmental bodies and political parties remains disproportionately low for their number in the total population. The equality called for in the party platforms of the three parties represented in Parliament has been realized neither in the parties nor in the governments the parties comprise. The disparity between the policy statements espoused by the parties and the actual power configurations within the parties arises both from the shape of women's lives and the reticence of the male leadership to relinquish power to female colleagues.

Women's Participation in the Work Force

Despite the vacillation in political and social policies during the past seventy-five years, women's participation in the Austrian work force has remained fairly constant since 1910.[73] From 1910 to 1981 women have made up approximately 40% of the total work force. In 1951 the figure was 39%; in 1971, 38.7%; and in 1980, 38.2%.[74] On the other hand the percentage of women employed outside the home in relation to the total female population has dropped over the past sixty years, from 41% in 1910, to 36.7% in 1934, 31.2% in 1971, and 31% in 1981.[75] The largest drop occurred between 1961 and 1981 among the youngest and oldest groups of women, reflecting the facts that many of the younger women were extending their education and many of the older women were taking advantage of early retirement.[76] Although the overall number has remained constant, the number within different professions has fluctuated.

World War I brought about one of the greatest shifts in numbers of working women and a resulting feminization within professions. As Edith Rigler states:

> The war brought not only a quantitative increase in women's work, but by 1923 resulted also in a qualitative change: women gained ground in newly-created professions on the one hand, and in jobs up to that time considered "typically male" on the other hand. Occupations which until 1923 had been labelled "male professions" were feminized as a result; some are even today incorrectly labelled as belonging to the "traditional female domain," whereby the historical process which led to a higher percentage of women remains disregarded.[77]

Women's involvement in the work force in the war years (1914-1918) and in the early twenties led to a transformation in society's perceptions of certain professions. Many jobs thought of today as traditionally female jobs were dominated by males until this period. With the return of soldiers, the reduction in war-related industries, and the introduction of protective legislation prohibiting night work for women and children (May 14, 1919), women were forced out of the heavy industries they had entered during the war and sought work in other areas. Rigler writes of the reversal of an earlier trend:

> If the tendency up until about 1923 had been a stronger influx from the domestic professions into the newly emerging professions, then the economic situation after 1923 drove women once again into their "original" professions, i.e., back to work done out of the home, and forced them to remain from then on unqualified help who could be let go at any time.[78]

The unstable economic situation reversed the earlier trend of women's movement out of domestic professions into more non-traditional jobs. Domestic work and work women could do in their homes was emphasized. Women working outside the home faced bitter opposition as public opinion shifted against gainfully employed women.[79] The opponents contended that they were taking jobs away from men who had to support families, and that the money they brought home was for luxuries.

A study conducted in 1931 of 1320 factory workers (*Industriearbeiterinnen*) countered many of the misconceptions. 41% of the women questioned had unemployed husbands or partners they supported. One-third of the married women had to care for at least one other person in addition to herself. Of all women, married and single, 47.7% took care of from one to three persons besides themselves.[80]

Thus the period following World War I is a good example of the contradictions between social preconceptions and reality. It was clear from women's participation in the war industries that they were capable in these fields. However, after the war and with the increasing economic instability, women were to return to their "natural" roles as wives and mothers and open up more jobs for men. Yet the measures taken against working women did not take them out of the work force, but rather into lower-paying, less visible jobs.

Although women's participation in the work force has remained fairly constant, women's pay has declined in comparison to that of their male colleagues. In 1953 the male median income was 43% higher than the female median income, and by 1979 this figure had risen to 53%. In 1953 the average male income was 48% higher than the female average income, and in 1979, 58% higher.[81] In 1981 the average male income was 12,260 ÖS a month, 52% more than the average female income of 8,060 ÖS a month.[82] In 1983 40% of the male population earned more than 14,000 ÖS monthly, whereas only 10% of the female population earned more than this amount. Helga Hieden points to the following factors for the discrepancy:

> Surely one reason for these income differences lies in the educational differences between men and women—especially in the higher age groups. To a relatively lesser extent shorter work hours, part-time work, and less overtime than men are responsible for it. Further reasons are the average lower age of gainfully employed women, lack of advancement possibilities, which are often withheld from women ostensibly on account of their domestic duties, the concentration of women in female-specific educational paths with bad job prospects, and the predominance of women in professional branches and job areas within a professional branch with traditionally low pay scales. One can therefore state that the main reason still lies in the separation of the work world into one for men and another for women.[83]

Hieden finds no one single factor responsible for the disparity in wages. Although women, compared to men, work on the average shorter hours, hold more part-time jobs, and work less overtime, this has a relatively minor effect on the overall figures. Hieden places the blame for the wage discrepancies on educational differences and segregation of the working world according to sex.

Women and Education

The field of education has the potential to be a progressive force in bridging the gap between forward-looking ideas and day-to-day life by providing new role models and breaking down stereotypes. But in Austria it continues to act more as an agent of socialization rather than as one of change despite the reforms which have been initiated.

Educational opportunities have certainly improved for girls since 1945, and the number of girls continuing their education beyond the compulsory nine years has grown considerably. One indication of this is that between 1970-1980 the number of youths who did not continue their education beyond the nine years dropped sharply.

Students Not Continuing (numbers in percent)

	1970/71	1973/74	1979/80
Male	32	27	12
Female	47	41	27

Source: Brandstaller, *Frauen in Österreich*, p. 15.

Likewise, the number of female students who study beyond the compulsory nine years has risen; the following chart illustrates the increased level of education of both women and men:

Educational Standard of Residential Population, By Sex and Percentage, 1971 and 1978

Schooling Completed	1971 Male	1971 Female	1978 Male	1978 Female
Primary, secondary school	48	73	32	58
Apprenticeship	36	13	46	21
Secondary lower education	5	9	8	13
High school, grammar school	7	5	9	7
University, academy	4	1	5	2

Source: *Mid Decade 1980: Review and Evaluation of Progress* (Vienna: Bundespressedienst, c. 1981), p. 15.

The figures point to a closing of the educational gap between men and women. As women further their education, they also increase their job opportunities. But, however positive this may appear, girls' professional choices continue to funnel them into lower-paying jobs. Agnew and Fischer-Kowalski analyze the situation in their article "Werden Bildungschancen ungleicher?" (Are Educational Possibilities Becoming More Unequal?)

concluding:

1. Girls attend lower-level vocational courses with respect to duration and qualification much more frequently than boys;

2. Girls concentrate on a few school types with instructional goals closest to the traditional conception of the female role understanding (teaching, social services, health, offices, and service sector professions and so on);

3. The rising participation of girls in education involves predominantly the upper and middle classes, but not the working classes.[84]

Although the educational opportunities for girls are increasing, the choices many young women are making lead them into low paying dead-end professions. Furthermore women's increased participation in higher education is largely restricted to girls and women from the middle and upper classes.

The fair and open portrayal of girls and women in schoolbooks is vital to equal education and the development of a self-image free from stereotypes both for girls and boys. However various studies have shown that Austrian textbooks provide neither progressive alternatives nor do they reflect reality. A 1979 study came up with the following results:

"Female workers are greatly underrepresented in readers in comparison with their actual distribution in Austria. 2323 men and 212 women are depicted, that is 91.64% to 8.36%, while in reality the actual distribution is 61.28% to 38.72%. . ." The woman of the readers is in 65% of the cases housewife, farmer or farm laborer. Far behind come storekeeper, salesperson, domestic help and nurse, then teacher, hotelier, washer women, ironer, and cook. These professions make up a total of 56% of the female work force in readers. In reality 34% of gainfully employed women work in these professions in Austria.[85]

In other words the study's findings show that women are underrepresented in Austrian schoolbooks and, when portrayed, are in traditionally female roles that do not fully reflect reality. Such books serve to cement traditional sex-roles and fail to provide schoolchildren with positive egalitarian role models. Steps have been taken to change content in new texts so that they portray a more realistic picture of society, but this does not include revision of old texts. Schoolbooks published after 1977 go before a commission that carefully examines content, making sure texts conform to recommendations from international organizations and take recent legal reforms and Austrian reality into consideration.[86] These specifications only concern new texts, and therefore only a gradual change in the representation of women is to be expected.

Currently 60% of teachers employed at Austrian schools are women, but they are employed predominantly in positions of low prestige, pay, and power: most kindergarten teachers and secondary school teachers are female, whereas the majority of professors and school directors are male.[87] At the university level women have made almost no inroads; women make up 15.5% of the teaching and academic staff, and, of these, female professors comprise 2.8%. Women's position in the educational hierarchy is a reflection of their position in society as a whole.[88]

Women and the Family

Although the marriage laws promote marriage based on partnership, the reality of the situation appears to be somewhat different. Information gathered from a microcensus in 1977 shows that the assignment of jobs within the family continues along traditional lines.[89] In 82-92% of the families questioned the women take care of purchases, wash dishes, clean the apartment or house, and polish the shoes. Between 2-11% of the men questioned do the same jobs. Mothers almost exclusively take care of the children under six. This is true in 94% of the cases, whereas 70% of the women have the major responsibility for their children over six years. Most women take care of the housework without any help, because only 20.5% of the husbands help with the housework on a daily basis. Housework and childcare remain women's work despite women's participation in the work force.

Women and the Printed Media

The image of women in Austria's press portrays further contradictions in theory and practice. In 1978 a women's collective read four Austrian dailies for six months to document the portrayal of women in the printed media. The newspapers they studied were the *Neue Kronenzeitung*, with the largest circulation in Austria, the *Kurier*, with the second largest circulation, the *AZ* (*Arbeiterzeitung*), the official organ of the largest political party, the SPÖ, and the *Presse*, which is owned by the Viennese Chamber of Commerce. To varying degrees women are represented in traditional roles. The women's pages deal with cosmetics and recipes—very occasionally politics. Women's concerns may not necessarily get bad press, but feminists, "libbers" (*Emanzen*) as they are called by the press, are constantly being dismissed as witches and man-haters.[90] The classified sections are filled with sex-specific announcements. For example, in the *Kurier*, which has a relatively progressive stance on legal issues affecting women, the situation was depicted as follows: "From a total of 2264 announcements in the larger format in the April and September Saturday editions, only 443 are directed toward women. 1507 openings seek 'ambitious' men, and 314 take men as well as women."[91] Not only are many more jobs specifically offered to men, but a male-female hierarchy exists in the job offers:

The more independence and qualifications demanded, the more one exclusively needs a man. The more monotonous and poorer paid the work is, the more chance a woman has to get the job. Also, in "academic heights" professional discrimination against woman does not stop. University-educated men are sought for independent tasks, while university-educated women are offered virtually no positions.[92]

The study clearly points out that the practice of sex-specific classified advertisements lead to a systematic discrimination of women. Men are consistently offered more attractive, better-paying jobs; women, on the other hand, are paired with monotonous low-paying jobs. Even women with advanced degrees do not escape stereotyping.

Women's Movements in Austria: Mediators between Political Theory and Social Reality

Women's movements, religious, party-affiliated, and independent, have been long-time mediators between the realms of party policy, legislation, and the everyday life of women. Women's involvement in the women's question has a long tradition in Austria, reaching back to the women's movement of the nineteenth century. Before the late sixties and early seventies the women's movements in Austria have almost exclusively been affiliated with the Church or political parties.

Of the party movements, the Socialist movement has most actively sought an improvement in women's position in society and their total integration into the public sphere, as well as concerned itself with general political issues. The "Austrian Women's Movement" (*Österreichische Frauenbewegung*), the women's organization of the ÖVP, founded in 1945, began as a charity and cultural organization, only later becoming involved with political issues.[93] Women in the FPÖ are organized in a women's committee (*Frauenreferat*). Officially the women's organizations within the parties presently help form party policy on women's issues. However, the wishes of the women have often been overlooked for issues considered more pressing. Although in the past ten years women's issues have received much media coverage, leading the parties to publicize their support of women's issues, in light of the continued male domination within the parties and the lack of truly innovative legislation concerning women, this effort appears to be largely lip service to draw voters or quiet what the male leadership in the parties perceives as a potentially powerful group that can be appeased with empty policy statements.

In the seventies an independent women's movement emerged, centered around support of the legalization of abortion. Feeling that they could be freer from censorship and apply more pressure outside the party structure, the women in this movement were usually not involved with big party politics and did not want to be limited by the party structure. Since the legalization of abortion, they have not been as visible but continue to be active, as Inge Rowhani-Ennemoser writes:

> The *autonomous women's movement*, which since the attainment of abortion rights has again and again been declared dead, has *initiated* numerous *projects*, including women's research groups, a woman's press, women's art and women's counseling centers, a rape-crisis

center hotline, all forms of self-help groups, collective childcare facilities, initiatives for women parolees.   They all influence and support the life situation of at least a part of the population and point in the directions in which possibilities of change lie.[94]

The independent women's movement, then, although not as visible as it has been, continues to be a force in dealing with the conflicts and contradictions in women's lives.

Conclusion

Contradictions between laws calling for equality and the reality of women's lives continue to exist, thereby demonstrating that legislation cannot dictate consciousness.   Although women were guaranteed equal rights for the first time in the Constitution of 1920, true parity has yet to be realized in either the public or the private spheres.   The reforms of the twenties were short-lived, as the economic situation and the country moved toward fascism. The second wave of reforms in the seventies eliminated the legal basis for patriarchal marriage, liberalized divorce laws, legalized abortion during the first three months of pregnancy, and introduced an affirmative action program and the Equal Treatment Act calling for equal pay for equal work. The contradiction remains: women are not treated equally in a country that guarantees women's equality.   Women are underrepresented in government and political parties, they earn less than their male colleagues, and are usually responsible for the largest part of domestic work, regardless of whether or not they are gainfully employed.

The conflicts arising in women's lives due to these social, economic, and political contradictions are focused on and explored by the five authors of this study.   Their work articulates the anomalies in women's lives: they examine women's struggle for self-definition, the "political" structure of male-female relationships, and the form of female-female relationships in a male-centered society.

Haushofer and Bachmann's writings are particularly informed by their experiences of fascism, especially because they came of age under National Socialism.   The line between public and private disappears in their work as the major male characters display fascist behavior in their private lives.   The works of Frischmuth, Jelinek, and Schwaiger, authors of the younger generation, also do away with conventional definitions of politics.   Their literature demonstrates how women continue to be faced with a different set of problems than that of their male counterparts because of the power configurations in a male-centered society.

Notes

1.   Karl Stadler, *Austria* (London: Benn, 1971), p. 113.

2.   *Bundesverfassungsrecht*, art. 7 (1).   Quoted in Erika Weinzierl, *Emanzipation?: Österreichische Frauen im 20. Jahrhundert* (Vienna, Munich: Jugend und Volk, 1975), p. 11.

3.   Maria Berger, "Braucht Österreich ein Antidiskriminierungsgesetz?" *Frau und Recht* (Vienna: Bundespressedienst, 1981), p. 10.

4.   Karl Stadler, *Austria*, p.   115.   See also Hanna Hacker, "Staatsbürgerinnen," in Franz Kadmoska, ed., *Aufbruch und Untergang*

(Vienna, Munich, Zurich: Europa Verlag, 1981), pp. 225-245.

5.   Klaus Berchtold, ed., *Österreichische Parteiprogramme 1868-1966*, (Vienna: Verlag für Geschichte und Politik, 1967), p. 257.

6.   Berchtold, p. 257.

7.   Berchtold, p. 370.

8.   Berchtold, p. 370.

9.   Stadler, p. 115.

10.   Stadler, p. 130.

11.   Helga Hieden, *Die Frau in der Gesellschaft* (Vienna: Verlag für Geschichte und Politik, 1983), p. 19.

12.   Edith Rigler, *Frauenleitbild und Frauenarbeit in Österreich* (Vienna: Verlag für Geschichte und Politik, 1976); Alfred Hoffmann and Michael Mitterauer, eds., Sozial- und Wirtschaftshistorische Studien, Vol. 8, pp. 149-150.

13.   Rigler, p. 150.

14.   Rigler, p. 150.

15.   Rigler, p. 151.

16.   Silvia Müller, "Die Lehrpläne an Österreichs Allgemeinbildenden Höheren Schulen von 1848 bis zur Gegenwart," Diss.   Universität Salzburg 1970, p. 161.

17.   Müller, p. 57.

18.   For one of the few books that deal specifically with women in Austria from 1938-1945, see Karin Berger, *Zwischen Eintopf and Fließband* (Vienna: Verlag für Gesellschaftskritik, 1984).   For an important volume on women in Weimar and Nazi Germany, see Renate Bridenthal, Atine Grossmann, and Marion Kaplan, eds., *When Biology Became Destiny* (New York: Monthly Review Press, 1984).

19.   Herrad Schenk, *Die feministische Herausforderung: 150 Jahre Frauenbewegung in Deutschland* (Munich: Verlag C. H. Beck, 1980), p. 73. In actuality the percentage of female students was 15.8% in 1932 and dropped to 11.2% in 1939.

20.   Schenk, p. 73.

21.   Müller, p. 60.

22.   Schenk, p. 73.

23.   Hieden, p. 21.

24.   Schenk, pp. 74-76.

25.   Trautl Brandstaller, *Frauen in Österreich: Bilanz und Ausblick* (Vienna: Bundespressedienst, 1981), pp. 59-60.

26.   Dr. Gottfried Heindl of the Austrian Federal Theater Administration, during a question and answer period of a Fulbright orientation in Vienna, September 1983.

27.   Inge Rowhani-Ennemoser, "Zehn Jahre Frauenbewegung in Österreich—eine Chronologie," in Johanna Beyer, Franziska Lamott, and Birgit Meyer, eds., *Frauenlexikon*, (Munich: C. H. Beck, 1983), p. 330.

28.   Personal interview with Johanna Dohnal, October 29, 1986.

29.   Personal letter from Johanna Dohnal, 13 April 1984.

30.   Berchtold, p. 272.

31.   Berchtold, p. 272.

32.   Erika Weinzierl, *Emanzipation*, p. 27. See also Erika Weinzierl, "Die katholische Kirche," in Erika Weinzierl and Kurt Skalnik, eds., *Österreich: Die Zweite Republik*, (Graz, Vienna, Cologne: Verlag Styria, 1972),

pp. 285-296.

33. Berchtold, pp. 278 and 293.

34. Berchtold, p. 309.

35. A comparison of the minutes of the immediate postwar conferences of the Socialist women and of the official party platforms brings to light a continual overlooking of the women's demands. Compare Berthold to "Frauenkonferenz der Sozialistischen Frauenorganization" (18 & 19 October 1947). Access to the minutes was made possible by the Karl Renner Institute in Vienna, Austria.

36. Personal letter from Johanna Dohnal, 13 April 1984.

37. Johanna Dohnal, "Sozialdemokratie und Frauenbewegung (Historisch und Heute)," SPÖ, Vienna-Penzing, 15/16 October 1983.

38. Concerning the effect of the economic situation on the party's policies dealing with women, Dohnal stated, "In any case we Socialist female functionaries will have to fight more intensely for our ideas and fight against these conservative tendencies which I wouldn't deny some male functionaries find opportune." Personal interview with Johanna Dohnal, October 29, 1986.

39. The Freedom Party or FPÖ (founded in 1955 from a coalition between the *Verband der Unabhängigen* and the Freedom Party) is a liberal party in the European sense of the word with a strong nationalistic tradition.

40. Berchtold, p. 389.

41. Berchtold, p. 401.

42. Berchtold, pp. 358, 370, and 371.

43. Berchtold, p. 493.

44. Berchtold, p. 499.

45. Berchtold, p. 500.

46. Staatssekretariat für allgemeine Frauenfragen, *Frauenbericht* (Vienna: Bundespressedienst, 1975), p. 16.

47. Austrian People's Party, *Salzburger Programm* (Vienna: Vereinigung für politische Bildung, 1980), p. 37.

48. It is difficult to compare this with the situation in the United States because the laws in the United States vary from state to state for the most part. The pre-1975 legal status of women in Austria may appear to many far removed from the situation in the United States; however, as Judith Lichtman of the Women's Legal Defense Fund writes in *Women's Legal Rights in the United States* (Chicago and London: American Library Association, 1985), p. 3, "Even today, a married woman may lose the power to establish her own legal residence. The courts she may sue in, the states that tax her, the laws governing her property, her right to use public facilities and to vote—all may depend on her husband's legal domicile, regardless of the state in which she actually lives." For an introductory essay to women's status in the United States and a selective bibliography see this compact volume.

49. ABGB, § 91 (1948).

50. ABGB, § 92 (1948).

51. ABGB, § 89 (1980).

52. Brandstaller, p. 70.

53. ABGB, § 92 (1980).

54.   ABGB, § 95 (1980).

55.   ABGB, § 98 (1980).

56.   Brandstaller, p. 73.

57.   Brandstaller, p. 41.

58.   Brandstaller, p.41

59.   Brandstaller, p. 41.

60.   ABGB, § 97 (1978).

61.   Brandstaller, p. 41.

62.   Quoted in Berger, p. 11.

63.   Berger, p. 9. Here Berger offers a wide range of examples of the effects such a law would have.

64.   Staatssekretariat für allgemeine Frauenfragen, *Mehr tun für die Frauen im Bundesdienst* (Vienna: Bundespressedienst, 1981).

65.   *Mehr tun für die Frauen im Bundesdienst*, p. 8.

66.   Personal letter from Johanna Dohnal, 13 April 1984.

67.   Weinzierl, *Emanzipation*, pp. 45-46 and Hieden, p. 76.

68.   As of 1984 the United States and Austria both had between eleven to twenty women serving at the executive or cabinet levels of government.   In 1984 Austrian women fared better than women in the United States as to their number in the legislative branch, with between 11-20% in Austria, whereas the United States had 5% or below.   These figures were quoted from Joni Seager and Ann Olson's *Women in the World* (New York: Simon & Schuster, 1986), section 30, p. 71.

69.   Weinzierl, *Emanzipation*, p. 46.   Johanna Dohnal pointed out in our interview on October 29, 1986 that there were 50% more women from the Socialist Party on the ballot for the National Assembly in 1986 than in 1983.   However she did say that the placement continues to be low and she was not sure how many Socialist women would actually end up in Parliament.

70.   Susanne Feigl, *Women in Austria 1975-1985* (Vienna: Staatssekretariat für allgemeine Frauenfragen, 1985), p. 64.

71.   Weinzierl, *Emanzipation*, p. 48.

72.   Feigl, p. 65.

73.   Hieden, p. 35.

74.   Österreichisches Statistisches Zentralamt, *Ergebnisse der Volkszählungen vom 1. Juni 1951*, Vol. 12, Tabellenband I (Demographischer Teil) (Vienna: Druck und Kommissionsverlag der österreichischen Staatsdruckerei, 1953), p. 102, Brandstaller, p. 8, and Hieden, p. 35.

75.   Hieden, pp. 34-35.   According to the *Statistical Abstract of the United States* (Washington D.C.: U.S. Department of Commerce, 1986), xxi, 43.3% of the female population was gainfully employed in 1970, in 1984 53.6%, and in 1985 54.2%.

76.   Hieden, p. 35.

77.   Rigler, p. 155.

78.   Rigler, p. 135.

79.   Rigler, p. 149.

80.   Rigler, p. 138.

81.   Hieden, p. 39.

82.   Hieden, p. 38.   According to the *Statistical Abstract of the United States* (Washington, D.C.: U.S. Department of Commerce, 1986), p. 419, the

median weekly earnings of full-time wage and salary workers can be summed up as follows: in 1980 white males earned $321, white females, $203; black males, $246, and black females, $184.   In 1984 white males earned $403 a week, white females, $264; black males, $304, black females, $242.

83.   Hieden, p. 40.
84.   Quoted in Brandstaller, p. 15
85.   Quoted in Dohnal, "Weg vom Klischee," *Erziehung und Unterricht*, 132, No. 4 (April 1982), 280.
86.   Brandstaller, p. 32.
87.   Feigl p. 34.   See also Helga Hieden, "Die gesellschaftliche Stellung der Frau im Schulsystem—ein Beitrag zur geschlechtsspezifischen Erziehung?" *Erziehung und Unterricht*, 132, No. 4 (April 1982), 285.
88.   Feigl, p. 35.
89.   Brandstaller, p. 49.   See also Staatssekretariat für allgemeine Frauenfragen, *Patriarchat 1981 oder: Der Geschlechterkampf um Partnerschaft im Haushalt* (Vienna: Bundespressedienst, 1981).
90.   Arbeitsgruppe Frauenmaul, *Ich hab' Dir keinen Rosengarten versprochen   .   .   .: Das Bild der Frau in vier österreichischen Tageszeitungen—eine Dokumentation* (Vienna: Frischenfleisch und Löwenmaul, [1978]), pp. 93, 104, and 105.
91.   *Rosengarten*, p. 39.
92.   *Rosengarten*, p. 41.
93.   *Frauenbericht*, p. 16.
94.   Rowhani-Ennemoser, p. 330.

3

Beyond the Mirror

"I walked into the mirror, I disappeared in the mirror, I saw into the future, I was one with myself and I am again divided with myself."

Ingeborg Bachmann, *Malina*, *Werke*, (Malina, Works) III, p. 136.

In Austria tremendous gains in women's legal status have been made since 1945, particularly during the seventies, which theoretically should have eliminated injustices between the sexes. However, as discussed in chapter two, society remains male-centered, and traditional images and expectations prevail. As is characteristic in a society dominated by one group, the resultant values, particularly as represented in the legal restrictions that men impose on women, can be viewed as restrictive for males as well as for females. To the authors examined here, however, these values prove much more detrimental to the development of the female individual, because her interpersonal and economic options are more limited and are bound by her biological potential to have children.

Impossibility of Self

Haushofer, Bachmann, Jelinek, and Schwaiger therefore concern themselves in their fiction with the difficulty a woman has in establishing a whole sense of self in a male-centered society and in getting beyond male projections of what it means to be a woman.[1] When the "I" in Bachmann's *Malina* asks, "Am I a woman or something dimorphous? Am I not completely a woman? What am I anyway?" she expresses both her specific dilemma and that of other women found in much of the fiction of the five writers.[2] The focus of this chapter is thus the shared perceptions of the authors under discussion concerning the difficulties women face in establishing a sense of self in a male-centered society, no matter how many legal problems seem to have been resolved.

Not only are the difficulties that the authors pinpoint common to them all, but also the consequences. In the large majority of the five writers' works, the female protagonists develop either a split-self, lose a sense of self, or have not been able to develop a sense of self by the end of the work for a multiplicity of reasons which cannot be separated from one another. The authors link the identity problem to gender and the roles women play in male-centered society. Although the fragmentation of social roles and the search for identity have been much-explored motifs in literature prior to the present study, this search has always been seen in terms of the fragmentation of the male individual. It would be hard to imagine a male protagonist making the parallel statement to "I have never been woman. I have never yet existed" (*Werke*, II, 205), a familiar dilemma for the women. When the female protagonists attempt to answer the question, "What am I anyway?" the search takes on forms different from those in male literature. In every case the women fight against male definitions of womanhood. For women their loss of, or search for, self cannot be separated from women's place in society. To describe "the search for self" depicted by the female authors, then, requires us to specify their definitions of the fragmented nature of women's roles in society.

Love and Marriage Relationships

The writers pinpoint one of the major factors inhibiting the growth of a sense of self in women's love and marriage relationships. While involved with men, none of the women are able to answer the question of who they are; only if they choose to leave their partner(s) does the possibility exist.

This restriction stems from very concrete sources. Women are legally and hence socially defined by the men they attach themselves to. They bear either the name of their father (if they are "legitimate") or the name of their husband. In the literature of the five women the assumption of the husband's name becomes symbolic for the denial of their own autonomy and the expected submersion of the woman's self for her husband.

The narrator of Schwaiger's *Wie kommt das Salz ins Meer* (Why Is the Sea Salty) realizes that she does not exist as an individual in the eyes of others and is defined principally by her relationship to her husband. In marrying Rolf, she has left the custody of her father for that of her husband and has no chance to develop into an individual. As Schwaiger stated in an interview with Hilde Schmölzer, the narrator is a projection of the wishes of others, rather than an autonomous individual; furthermore "she fulfills the wishes of her father, her mother, of society. And all at once she notices that she's becoming sick."[3] She has been raised to be dependent, to seek her importance from a male individual. Feeling lost after leaving the small town where her father is a doctor, she seeks reassurance and recognition in her relationship with Rolf. After Rolf asks her to marry him, she feels she belongs. "It was so exciting. When he asked me to marry him, I thought: Life is beginning. A person who has been proposed to finally belongs."[4] Ironically, but not unexpectedly from the women's point of view, belonging to someone does not give her a better sense of self; life becomes easier because certain prescribed behavior is expected of her, but she remains a nobody. "The greengrocer bows, Frau Diplomingenieur, please, thank you, Frau Doktor, I kiss your hand, good-by. May I hold the door open for the gracious lady. I am not myself. I'm Rolf's wife" (*Wie kommt das Salz ins*

Meer, Why Is the Sea Salty, p. 45). Identified by her husband's titles (*Diplomingenieur* and *Doktor*), the deference she receives stems not from personal respect, but from the people's respect for her husband.

These notions are not isolated to Schwaiger's "Rolf's wife." Psychologists have shown that women base their self-image on their interactions with people much more than men do. Their relationships with men are particularly important, so that failed relationships with men have a profound effect on the women and their feelings toward themselves. Although it is often harmful for a woman to remain in a particular relationship, she tends to perceive herself as a failure if the relationship does not work out. Psychologist Joanna Bunker Rohrbaugh points to the seeds of this difference in childhood:

> Thus parents, teachers, and peers tend to get boys to do socially acceptable things by making use of rules, authority, physical punishment, and material rewards, while they tend to get girls to do socially acceptable things by showing approval and disapproval in an emotional way. This reinforcement leads the female child to form a sense of self-identity and self-worth that is based more on the ability to get positive emotional responses from others than it is on a sense of autonomy.[5]

Thus Schwaiger identifies a primary facet of the psychology of the modern woman. Not surprisingly, love and marriage relationships are the single most important theme in the literature of the other four writers as well. Love and marriage for women in a male-centered world thus constitute, for them, at best a negative center, from which the fragmentation of women develops.

Socialization and Roles: Housewife

As perhaps the first obstacle within the women's quest for self-realization, the authors deal with the role of women within the family and the obstacles facing them. Being a mother and housewife proves to be one of the greatest obstacles. As Evelyn Torton Beck and Biddy Martin write:

> Taken as a whole, these texts make it clear that the private sphere of the home represents a shrunken and narrowly-defined world which makes service machines out of women of whom it is demanded that they go through the same motions over and over again which in the end are not even recognized as work.[6]

A realm new to the literary work, housework, depicted as monotonous and time-consuming, proves alienating and hinders personal development.

The narrator of *Wie kommt das Salz ins Meer* (Why Is the Sea Salty) embodies this restriction and captures the monotony of her day with the following few words, "set the table, clear the table, wash the dishes, go shopping, cook, set the table, wash the dishes. What am I going to cook for dinner? Three hundred sixty-five times a year the same question: What am I going to cook for dinner?" (*Wie kommt das Salz ins Meer*, p. 44). The narrator's life revolves around the daily repetition of monotonous housework.

This view of housework as a monotonous and never-ending task is echoed in the works of all five writers, not only in my one example. In "Bleiben lassen" (Let It Be) Frischmuth's protagonist embodies the "perfect" housewife who loses herself in assuming a traditional role:

> She had *lost so much of herself* that she hardly risked expending her energy for herself alone. And what mattered to her was that it be clear to those who came by and saw her sitting in a lawn chair with her arms folded or lying in the hammock that she had washed the dishes, scrubbed the floors, dusted the books, washed the windows, and laundered the clothes: that she was now enjoying her free time after she had completed her work.[7] [Emphasis mine.]

Because she does not perceive herself as having the power to break her own expectations and those of society, the protagonist finds herself automatically limited.

The narrator shows the ambivalence between *her* acceptance of the social role and the limitations it presses up on her as not only disagreeable but leading to pathological behavior as well:

> She needed these days when she was home alone. She needed them so much, as she reassured herself again and again, that it caused her physical discomfort if one time someone, even Alex himself, stayed home during the day for some reason, not because she had more work, but because the ritualized course of her being alone was disturbed by it. It was the one single thing she could hold onto, also in times when she felt forsaken that it did not even occur to her to flee, even had she known, to whom.
>
> Her sense for external order had at the same time neurotic features about it: the exactness with which she paid attention that things be in their proper place and couldn't arbitrarily be exchanged since they fulfilled their function best at just those places where they stood; the torment she suffered when this order had been destroyed by someone and she couldn't restore it in time. ("Bleiben lassen," Let It Be, p. 95)

Margret has perfected the routine or ritual of the "housewife alone" by acting out the conditioned role to such an extent that the narrator terms her behavior neurotic. The psychological establishment confirms the narrator: "Women who fully act out the conditioned female role are clinically viewed as 'neurotic' or 'psychotic'."[8] This, then, is the specific double-bind of the housewife: when a woman actually fully accepts and acts out what she believes men want, she not only loses herself, but becomes "neurotic."

Similar to Schwaiger's narrator and Frischmuth's Margret, the narrator of Haushofer's *Die Mansarde* (The Attic) finds housework a monotonous repetition of tasks. She carefully plans the housecleaning in order not to neglect it. "Of course I work according to a strict plan. If I didn't do that I could never get my work done, or I would gradually stop cleaning completely because in truth I loathe this work. I only pretend it is fun—that also belongs to my system."[9]   Thus once again, the female protagonist revolves her day around work that she admittedly despises.

Not only are the negative consequences of housework for women pointed out in this novel, but also how the work of women is invaluable for and at the same time unappreciated by men:

> What does a man do who doesn't have a wife and no cleaning woman, but a big library? I can't imagine. Anyway, where do men think the dirt goes which collects around them? I think they don't think about it at all, or only in the abstract. Approximately so: Frau Maier has to come here again and tidy up. And while such a man sits in his clean office, clean because another Frau Maier has just cleaned it, his Frau Maier rages around the house and leads the fight against dust and dirt. And when the man then comes home everything is clean again. It doesn't surprise the man in the least because he doesn't know how it all takes place behind his back. He lies down in a freshly-made bed, and the next morning he puts on a white shirt, which a third Frau Maier has washed and ironed for him, and leaves the house suffering from the delusion that the world is a clean and orderly place. The single bit of waste that he has to clear away himself is his own beard, and he groans about it in front of the mirror, leaving the bathroom in a condition that also draws a moan from his Frau Maier. And when he comes home, he is not surprised in the least that everything is once again orderly. The unlucky ones who have no Mrs. Maier raise untidiness to a virtue, even growing beards only so they won't have to lift a finger. (*Die Mansarde*, p. 52)

Haushofer exposes the injustice done to an army of silent women workers who make life easier for unappreciative males. The work may be done in exchange for love or money, but in either case an inordinate amount of energy goes into work which is not viewed by the greater society as work.

In her novel *Die Liebhaberinnen* (Women in Love) Elfriede Jelinek uses a different approach to critique the institution of marriage. It is this very life of the "housewife alone" that her two working-class protagonists seek. For Brigitte, a factory worker, and Paula, a dressmaker's apprentice, the possibility of working only in the home is a dream and a possible escape from the drudgery of their present lives. For Brigitte marriage to the "right" (financially well-situated) man means escape from the factory as well as material gain. However positively she views this life, the narrator makes clear the costs when she describes Brigitte after her successful marriage: "hate has already eaten her up inside. but the joy of possession has remained. she hangs on to that with an iron fist."[10] She has made material gain and is better off than she would be had she continued working in the bra factory. However, the narrator does not find her new state gratifying. The other major protagonist, Paula, marries an alcoholic and is never able to realize her vision of paradise, a home of her own:

> erich drinks, which paula will also put a stop to, hardly having crossed the threshold of the new home which they can't afford because erich drinks. together with squabbling and fighting, alcohol

will remain outside. (*Die Liebhaberinnen*, p. 113)

Thus, for some, marriage may bring with it the desired life of housewife and mother, preferable to work in a factory, but the women still remain precariously dependent on men.

Jelinek also points to the emptiness of the family for women in her play *Was geschah, nachdem Nora ihren Mann verlassen hatte?* (What Happened after Nora Left her Husband?), her sequel to Ibsen's *Nora: A Doll's House*.[11] Here again Jelinek portrays the plight of working-class women who are alienated by their work outside the home. She thereby criticizes the bourgeois women's movement as self-indulgent and as having failed to understand the position of working-class women. She accomplishes this by juxtaposing Nora, a middle-class uneducated divorcée, with her fellow female workers, who are all working-class. In the second scene of *Was geschah, nachdem Nora ihren Mann verlassen hatte?* (What Happened after Nora Left her Husband?) Nora Helmar, recently divorced from her husband Torwald, desires to "find" herself and become a "person," but because of her lack of education is forced to work in a factory. In her first conversation with the other women workers, conflicts in the interests of working- and middle-class women become clear. For the workers marriage provides an escape from their alienating work, whereas for Nora it is a place of confinement.

For her, work outside the home provides a means to escape the dependency associated with traditional marriage. She therefore finds the working-class women's desire to escape into marriage incomprehensible (*Was geschah, nachdem Nora ihren Mann verlassen hatte?*, pp. 171-173). Despite the differences between middle- and working-class women, it becomes clear in the drama that self-realization is denied women from both classes through the traditional bond of women to the family.

Schwaiger, Haushofer, and Frischmuth depict the role of housewife as non-conducive to women's search for self. The protagonists either place the routine as housewife at the center of their lives or spend a large part of their time carrying out such work, and are prevented from developing other outlets for self-expression. Jelinek, too, considers the narrow world of the housewife restrictive. However she points out that class is an added factor to a person's position in society. For women faced with factory work and housework, the latter is definitely more attractive.

Socialization and Roles: Mother

Within the family and society as a whole, all five authors agree that women are still defined by their biological role. The authors question the naturalness of perceiving women as the major caregivers and discuss the far-reaching ramifications for mother and child of the structure of the traditional family and traditional role fixation. The role of mother in a male-centered society is for them destructive for the woman's image of self. More severely, these restrictions turn women into negative role models for their children, especially for their female children, who in turn internalize a restrictive image of self.

Elfriede Jelinek depicts the most brutal relationship between mother and daughter in her novel *Die Klavierspielerin* (The Piano Player). As a typical housewife cut off from an active role in society, Erika's mother tries to live through her daughter. She forces her to study the piano in hopes that she will become a concert pianist. Yet while pushing her to become an artist, she still does everything in her power to control Erika's life and make Erika her puppet. She sacrifices everything for Erika, but exercises complete control over her daughter, exhibiting the characteristics of de Beauvoir's archetypical mother:

> Another common attitude, and one not less ruinous to the child, is masochistic devotion, in which the mother makes herself the slave of her offspring to compensate for the emptiness of her heart and to punish herself for her unavowed hostility. Such a mother is morbidly anxious, not allowing her child out of her sight; she gives up all diversion, all personal life, thus assuming the role of victim; and she derives from these sacrifices the right to deny her child all independence. This renunciation on the mother's part is easily reconciled with a tyrannical will to domination; the *mater dolorosa* forges from her sufferings a weapon that she uses sadistically; her displays of resignation give rise to guilt feelings in the child which often last a lifetime: they are still more harmful than her displays of aggression. Tossed this way and that, baffled, the child can find no defensive position: now blows, now tears, make him out a criminal.[12]

Erika's mother, like the mother de Beauvoir describes, displays the traits of masochistic devotion that can only be harmful for mother and child. Frau Kohut wishes to live her lost life through Erika, thus denying her child any autonomy. Erika, so controlled by the mother, cannot develop a healthy independent sense of self.

In an interview Jelinek answered a question concerning the extent to which the behavior of Erika's mother is a result of a society that forces mothers to sacrifice themselves and to live through their children, replying:

> I would also say that, but of course to a large extent a society which perhaps doesn't exactly deny women self-realisation but complicates it unbelievably. A woman who hasn't lived will naturally want her daughter to live in her place, but at the same time also hinder her from doing so. On the one hand she would like to live through her daughter, on the other hand she wishes that her daughter will be destroyed exactly as she herself.[13]

Echoing de Beauvoir's words, Jelinek connects women's denigrated position in society with harmful mother-daughter relationships.

Only in Frischmuth's *Kai und die Liebe zu den Modellen* (Kai and the Love of Models), in which the relationship between Amy and her son Kai is central to the narrative, does a writer depict a positive relationship between mother and child. Moreover, only in *Kai* does the protagonist think of possible alternatives to the traditional nuclear family and traditional role of mother. Amy chooses not to marry her son's father, but to live apart from him in order to maintain her independence. She refuses to take financial support from him for fear of the consequences:

> Not because Klemens would behave like a pascha, but because he

couldn't afford to do otherwise than have me take upon myself all that for which he now uses a restaurant, laundry, and a cleaning woman. I ask myself, how many hours a day could I *just write* because then Kai would surely also stay at home.[14]

If she were to accept the traditional role of housewife and mother, she believes she would be forced to sacrifice her independence and her role as writer.

Socialization and Roles: Male Definition and Projections of the Female

Aside from their programmed need for the male, the fictional women are constantly confronted with male projections and definitions of womanhood. In a male-centered world, "humanity is male and man defines woman not in herself but as relative to him; she is not regarded as an autonomous being."[15] Even her search for identity must be conducted in terms which equate activity with male characters.

Still, it becomes clear in the works of the five women that as long as women measure themselves against the male projections and definitions, it will not be possible for them to develop a healthy sense of self. Indeed when a woman fits the description of what is generally considered to be female, the same traits exclude her from being considered a psychologically healthy human being:

> The major research to date has examined the definitions of mental health that are used by practicing clinicians. The classic study was done by Broverman and her colleagues (1970) with seventy-nine clinically trained psychologists, psychiatrists, and social workers twenty-three to fifty-five years old, forty-six of them male and thirty-three female. These clinicians were given a 122-item questionnaire containing thirty-eight sex-role-stereotypic items such as "aggressive," "independent," "hides emotions," "competitive," "acts as leader," "talkative," "tactful," "gentle," "religious," and "expresses tender feelings." Each item had two poles, such as "not at all aggressive" and "very aggressive." The instructions asked the respondents to indicate which pole would be closer for a "mature, healthy, socially competent" adult. One-third of the clinicians filled out the questionnaire for any adult (sex unspecified), one-third for a man, and one-third for a woman.
> Broverman found that both male and female clinicians gave the same descriptions for healthy adults and healthy men but described healthy women as differing from healthy men "by being more submissive, less independent, less adventurous, more easily influenced, less aggressive, less competitive, more excitable in minor crises, having their feelings more easily hurt, being more emotional, more conceited about their appearance, less objective, and disliking math and science."[16]

Women find themselves in a no-win situation. If they possess the qualities expected of a woman, then they do not possess qualities valued as part of a psychologically healthy individual.   But if a woman deviates from expected behavior, she also meets with reproach.   In a society in which human characteristics are delineated along the lines of human = male, female = other, traditional sex-roles continue to play an important part of its dynamic, and a dichotomy results.   The world is divided into male and female realms, with the male being valued more than the female:

> In actuality the relation of the two sides is not quite like that of two electrical poles, for man represents both the positive and the neutral, as is indicated by the common use of *man* to designate human beings in general; whereas woman represents only the negative, defined by limiting criteria, without reciprocity.[17]

Because a man is not totally reduced to his biological function, he can be both human and male, whereas a woman is a woman.   The five authors under consideration reflect this reality in their literary work.

The impact on female children of the arbitrary division of the world into female and male realms is central to the works of Marlen Haushofer; this manifests itself in an "external" split among the main characters that the author views as unnatural and facilitated by socialization.   The children in Haushofer's works begin as a *tabula rasa*, but are shaped and molded, told what they may and may not do as a girl or boy.   "Haushofer illustrates this opinion through her powerful images of children, images not characteristic of either sex as adults, but which still appear undetermined, equipped with qualities which only later will be guided into specific sex roles."[18]   In the short story "Die Kinder" (The Children) Haushofer depicts children who have not yet gone through the socialization process that will direct them toward prescribed roles.[19]   Meta, the young protagonist of the novella *Himmel, der nirgendwo endet* (Never-Ending Sky), grows up unaware of sex-roles until she realizes she is treated differently from her brother and that she has less worth in the eyes of her parents.[20]

Because of the programming of children, then, a dichotomy arises between Haushofer's adult female and male characters.[21]   The most obvious contrasts manifest themselves in the female protagonist and her partner: passive versus active, weak versus strong, protective of life versus destructive, and contemplative versus non-contemplative, with the first of each pair typifying the female protagonists and the latter their partners.[22]   With the exception of the quality of wanting to protect life, the qualities are not biologically, but socially determined, according to Haushofer, and the children's native potential must be lost.

In *Eine Handvoll Leben* (A Handful of Life), *Die Tapetentür* (The Wallpapered Door), *Wir töten Stella* (We're Killing Stella), and *Die Mansarde* (The Attic), each major female protagonist is typical of this socialization.   As Tauschinski writes, "Elisabeth (*Eine Handvoll Leben*, A Handful of Life) is only one of many variations of a type of woman to whom Haushofer turns her psychological interest and whom she never tires of depicting."[23]   They are consistently passive, weak, and contemplative, while the primary male characters display the opposing qualities.   For example, Richard, Anna's husband in *Wir töten Stella*, Gregor, Annette's second husband in *Die Tapetentür*, and Lenart, Elisabeth's lover in *Eine Handvoll Leben*, can be characterized as healthy, non-contemplative, destructive, active, and sexually desirable.   The males also suffer from a split self, captured in their "two faces," as Haushofer puts it.   Toni Pfluger, Elisabeth's first husband in *Eine Handvoll Leben*, Gregor in *Die Tapetentür*, Richard in *Wir töten Stella*, and Elisabeth's father develop two "faces" which reflect the irreconcilability of the role of family man and public person.   Elisabeth's husband possesses both the face of Anton Pfluger, the stern factory owner, and Toni, her husband.   In Annette's description of Gregor *Die Tapetentür*, she captures the essence of the male split as Haushofer sees it.   "But when I look at his face, I see behind it the face of the good-natured child overflowing with vitality, a face slowly changing into the mask of a professional liar and cold speculator, and I can't separate the two faces from another."[24] The male characters are then also victims of the socialization process.

An implicit characteristic associated with men is senseless destruction. Originally the active impulse in the male child, this impulse has been perverted into a destructive one in the women's view.   From the perspective of the female protagonist, men are oblivious to their faults.   Annette writes of this characteristic in her diary:

> I was always touched by the blindness and clumsiness of men, but now I am slowly becoming afraid of it.   Hidden in this apparently so lovable awkwardness is something horrible and inhuman—a lack of interest for organic life.   Little boys and men of all ages in the newsreel, in front of the pictures of the latest missiles, in front of countless parking lots.   Cold chills run up and down my spine at the sight of this.   And the enemy is hiding in them whom we must love.   I can't live without love, and I can't love the inhuman. (*Die Tapetentür*, The Wallpapered Door, p. 104)

Annette feels alienated from men, as do Haushofer's other female protagonists, particularly concerning what they view as male disregard for human life (*Wir töten Stella*, pp. 19-20 and 23, and *Die Wand*, pp. 63-64, 155-156, and 264).

Haushofer's female protagonists, sensing an incompleteness caused by the imposed split in the self, view neither men nor women as being able to develop to their full potential.   Only the major female protagonists notice the "lack" or split.   In Haushofer's novels *Die Tapetentür* and *Die Wand* love is viewed as a potential means of eliminating this split and of joining two opposite halves to make a whole being.   However, because of male blindness and unwillingness to view themselves as lacking certain qualities, love fails.   In *Die Tapetentür* Annette writes in her diary, "He [Gregor] gives me the one thing which I really need, and I have nothing to give him for it because that which perhaps only I could give him is incomprehensible and worthless to him" (*Die Tapetentür*, p. 151).   Within the bounds of society the split remains irreconcilable.   Only in the novel *Die Wand* does the dichotomy disappear, enabling the female "I" to synthesize the qualities which had been divided according to the sex of the individual.   Only at some point outside of society, the woman author finds that her protagonist has the opportunity to develop into a "human being."

The "I" in Bachmann's *Malina*, too, finds herself caught between her own desires and male definitions of womanhood, which leads to a split.

Here the "I" realizes that her sense of self has been formed and affected by her relationship with Ivan and by the male projection of what a woman is. After buying a dress, for example, she wishes to try it on without Malina or Ivan around. Searching for a self buried under or already destroyed and perverted by male projections, she looks in the mirror and asks herself if it is herself she sees or a "composition" and concludes that the image in the mirror is not herself:

> A composition emerges, a woman is to be created for a housedress. Completely in secret a woman is once again defined; it is thus something from the very outset, with an aura for no one. The hair has to be brushed twenty times, the feet rubbed with ointment and the toe nails polished. Hair has to be removed from the legs and underarms. The shower is turned on and off, a cloud of body powder fills the bathroom. One looks in the mirror, it is always Sunday; one poses a question to the mirror on the wall, it could already be Sunday. (*Werke*, III, 136)

Because she has internalized male expectations and projections of "woman," the image in the mirror offers the "I" no insight into herself but rather captures her fragmentation into a male image.

Bachmann's choice of language, "one poses a question to the mirror on the wall," reminds the reader of the dilemma of the wicked stepmother in "Snow White and the Seven Dwarves," who needs the reassurance of the mirror's voice to establish her identity. In her essay "The Self-reflecting Woman," Elisabeth Lenk uses the metaphor of the mirror to exemplify woman's dilemma in the search for self:

> The relationship of woman to herself can be explained by the mirror—that is, the gaze of others, the anticipated gaze of others. Ever since ancient times woman has asked the anxious question of her fairy-tale stepmother. "Mirror, mirror on the wall, who is the fairest of us all?' And even then, when the gaze of others is replaced by the gaze of one other, of the husband or the lover, the anxious question is still asked. There are still the terrible moments when woman searches for herself in the mirror and cannot find herself. The mirror-image has got lost somewhere, the gaze of men does not reflect it back to woman.[25]

Bachmann thus uses the mirror metaphor to capture a basic problem in a woman's search for self: the image and voice emerging from the mirror is neither a "true" reflection of the "I" nor the voice of the queen, but "the patriarchal voice of judgement that rules the Queen's—and every woman's—self-evaluation."[26] Women internalize the patriarchal voice assuming the reflections they see are their own, although they may not be comfortable with them. John Berger argues:

> To be born a woman has been to be born, within an allotted and confined space, into the keeping of men. The social presence of women has developed as a result of their ingenuity in living under

such tutelage within such a limited space. But this has been at the cost of a woman's self being split into two. A woman must continually watch herself. She is almost continually accompanied by her own image of herself. Whilst she is walking across a room or whilst she is weeping at the death of her father, she can scarcely avoid envisaging herself walking or weeping. From earliest childhood she has been taught and persuaded to survey herself continually.

And so she comes to consider the *surveyor* and the *surveyed* within her as the two constituent yet always distinct elements of her identity as a woman.[27]

Being "surveyor" and "surveyed" necessitates the split of the "I" exemplified so well in the mirror scene.

Having internalized the male projections and definitions, *Malina*'s "I" develops an irreconcilable internal split or fragmentation. Ellen Summerfield, the first critic to investigate the fragmentation of the main character in detail, writes, "The characters are simultaneously extensions and projections of the narrator and separate, independent persons."[28] However the major extension of the female "I" is Malina, her male alter-ego; Bachmann, thus, describes an internal split defined by sex. There is no possibility for coexistence between the two halves, but, as an astrologer explains to the "I," the split signals a deadly internal conflict:

> . . . she showed me my horoscope which appeared uncommonly strange to her. I have to see it for myself, how sharply it's drawn, she said. An uncanny tension can be read from it on the first glance. It is actually not the picture of one person, but of two who stand in the utmost opposition to one another. It must be a constant ordeal for me. I asked politely: the torn man, the torn woman, isn't it true? Separate, Frau Novak thought, would be livable, but as it is, hardly. In addition, the masculine and the feminine, intellect and emotion, productivity and self-destruction appear in such a remarkable way. (*Werke*, III, 248)

The "I" realizes that her self is divided into a male and female side, which are irreconcilable and therefore self-destructive. But, as Sandra Frieden writes, the split is unavoidable in contemporary society:

> The female in contemporary society—educated to whatever degree—must nevertheless create a separation in herself between emotion and rationality; between the way in which she was brought up and taught to respond to life, and the way in which the world expects her as an "intellectual" to respond.[29]

In response to the demands of society, the typical female has to separate intellect and emotion.

However, Bachmann's "I" hopes that love will alleviate her fragmentation caused by women's position in society, only to be destroyed by her love. Because the split in the "I" existed before the narrator met Ivan, he does not assume a positive role in restoring the split-self to a whole, as the "I" had hoped.   Their relationship actually exacerbates the split: the manner in which the "I" loves, drives her male ego further from her.   Only interested in the narrator's feminine wiles, Ivan fails to recognize the Malina side of her, while the "I" makes no effort to integrate this side of herself into their relationship.[30]   Ultimately, the "I" dies an unconventional death, and she disappears into the wall, signaling Bachmann's pessimistic view of the possibility of a reconciliation of the split.

In a vein different from Bachmann, in her play *Clara S.*, Elfriede Jelinek deals with women's dilemma of fragmentation exemplified in the main female character, Clara.   At times using Robert Schumann's own words from his letters to his wife, Jelinek unmasks Clara's "fragmentation because of the prescribed woman's role."[31]   Clara's fragmentation or split is rooted in the conflict between Clara's reality, her wishes to be a creative artist, and her husband's projection of womanhood.   Clara, modelled after the pianist Clara Schumann, is so involved with the roles of wife and mother that she finds it impossible to devote any time to her art.   In addition her composer husband has forbidden her to practice piano because it disturbs him.   For Robert she must be both caretaker, protecting him from life's unpleasantries, and muse, providing him with inspiration.   A creative woman—for him a contradiction in terms—has no place in his world.   In a conversation with her husband's patron, poet Gabriele d'Annunzio, Clara speaks of her dilemma:

> The destruction of my person followed quickly once I was made into a saint, an ideal figure.   Into the passive present, distant and harmless.   I have consequently not lived the entire time.   But in order to be certain of my total demise, Robert killed me with his genius.[32]

Defined by her father and husband, Clara is not allowed to develop an autonomous self, but rather is forced into the passive role of an ideal, thereby being rendered harmless.   She then embodies the conflict of a creative and intelligent woman married to a creative artist in a male-centered world.   Because she is a woman, her creative side is to be killed, if not through the tasks she has, then through the definitions.

This is not Jelinek's only statement of this conflict.   In *Die Klavierspielerin* (The Piano Player) Jelinek makes obvious the negative effects of male definition of the female by carrying them to an extreme.   Erika Kohut, piano teacher at the Vienna City Conservatory, embodies Freud's characterization of "woman."   She is passive, masochistic, and narcissistic.   Erika becomes a subject and active only when she turns her body into the object of her aggression:

> When no one is at home she deliberately cuts her own flesh. . . . This razor is meant for HER flesh . . . SHE sits down with legs spread in front of the magnifying side of the shaving mirror and executes a cut which should enlarge the door leading into her body. She knows through experience that such a cut with a razor doesn't hurt because her arms, hands, legs often had to submit to such tests.   Her hobby is cutting her own body.[33]

She separates her mind from her body, and uses her body as a means of being a subject.

This split becomes clear when Erika looks in the mirror and is confronted by the image of a body foreign to her. She attempts to find her lost or alienated self in the bodies of the women at a peep show, as in her other voyeuristic ventures:

> Erika pays close attention. Not in order to learn. In her nothing stirs or moves anymore. But she must look anyway. For her own enjoyment. Whenever she would like to go away, something from above presses her well-coiffed head energetically against the pane, and she must continue to look. The turntable where the beautiful woman is sitting goes around in a circle. Erika can't do anything about it. She has to look over and over again. She is tabu for herself. (*Klavierspielerin*, The Piano Player, p. 70)

Erika, alienated from her own body, seeks the lost part of herself in others. Denied the role of subject in society, Erika becomes a passive observer or voyeur; Jelinek describes the situation as follows:

> It is a seemingly private story. It is, however, also about the destruction of a woman through the predetermined model of female upbringing. Just as she [Erika] is a voyeur of life, she is also a voyeur out of perversion, who doesn't take part actively in life, rather participates only passively. . . . That is the sanctioned role of woman and the extension of this role in deviant behavior. (September 19, 1983)

Erika is thus forced into the role of voyeur, a logical extension of women's assigned role in society. Through the exaggeration of this passive trait, Jelinek points out the perversion of socialized roles.

In none of her works, with the exception of *Die Bienenkönige* (The Bee Kings—odd because of the difference), does Jelinek portray a positive female figure who has not been fragmented in some manner by male definition.[34] Although Jelinek believes the step necessary to get beyond male definitions is for women to define themselves, she does not yet see this as a possibility for her fiction. "I have no single book, no single work where I could elucidate a positive figure of femaleness. I can also only define it negatively as its been defined by men" (September 19, 1983). Jelinek thus uses male definitions of the "female" in her writing; however, she does not agree with the definitions. By taking them to an extreme and exaggerating them, she negates the negativity.

Another variant of the female-male split can be found in Frischmuth's *Bindungen* (Bonds), that deals in part with an arbitrary split imposed on a woman working in a profession that has been viewed as a male's terrain.[35] Fanny finds herself in the awkward position of being a capable female archaeologist in a man's world. As a participant in the "male" world, Fanny is "renamed" Max by her professor Maurice. Her sexuality is neutralized with the name change, and it no longer poses a threat. This is not the only way in which sexual tension is reduced. In addition to the name change, Frischmuth makes Maurice a safe number of years older than

Fanny. The intellectual exchange remains on one level between "Max" and
Maurice and is prevented from becoming a sexual exchange.   Maurice
continues to view Fanny as a "man" when he suggests that she needs
someone like his wife Olga to take care of her daily needs.   He affirms a
system where one person submerges herself for the benefit of the other.   He
fails to recognize that for Fanny, a woman, there is no Olga.

When Bachmann's "I," Haushofer's female protagonists, and Jelinek's
Clara S. and Erika Kohut attempt to discover "what am I anyway," they
find themselves trapped between male projections of the "female" and their
own desire for self-expression.   The projections inhibit the process of
self-expression and lead not only to a male and female world, but to the
fragmentation within the fictional characters themselves.   Frischmuth's
Fanny, on the other hand, is faced with a different problem.   Her male
professor imposes a split on her, symbolized by his renaming her Max.   He
thereby demonstrates his uneasiness with a female intellectual.   In both
cases, whether the female characters suffer from the split or it is imposed,
the projections leading to the split are implicitly viewed as harmful.   This is
not the only place where women are forced to react to male imagination.

Socialization and Roles: Male Definitions and Projections of Female Sexuality

The area that all five writers view as being controlled and defined by
men to women's greatest detriment is women's sexuality.   The writers
address the problem from different angles and to varying degrees, but they
represent women's sexuality as an integral part of the personality that has
been controlled by men or by male representation.   As female reactions to
the male's projections of themselves, all five authors view men as either
totally unreceptive to their partners' sexual needs, or they depict a situation
in which women's fantasies have been perverted so by male projections of
female sexuality as to prove harmful to the women.

Relationships: The Unreceptive Partner

In Haushofer's *Die Tapetentür* (The Wallpapered Door), Bachmann's
Malina, and Frischmuth's "Baum des vergessenen Hundes" (Tree of the
Forgotten Dog), the female protagonists bemoan the fact that their male
partners are totally unreceptive to their sexual needs, while they themselves
must be aware of their partners' desires.

In Haushofer's *Die Tapetentür* and Bachmann's *Malina*, Gregor and
Ivan, the partners of the protagonists, are interested in the women largely
because of sex. Both are concerned with their own sexual needs and ignore
those of the women, erroneously assuming the women have no desires outside
of their own.   Haushofer portrays the sexual needs of men and women as
being worlds apart, with no hope of reconciliation:

She never tried to move Gregor to tenderness because she clearly
felt that it meant nothing more to him then the preparations which
a woman needed to get in the mood or the unavoidable
consideration which one owes her after having possessed her.   And

it gave her an ugly feeling and made her uneasy. Even Gregor, as experienced as he was in matters of love, couldn't stifle this quiet uneasiness in her. It wasn't his fault that he was a man, just as little as it was her fault that she felt as a woman. It was only a little disturbing, and sad and she couldn't do anything but accept it just as she accepted everything that came from Gregor. (*Die Tapetentür*, The Wallpapered Door, pp. 107-108)

Because intercourse is the ultimate expression of his sexuality, the tenderness Gregor exhibits is only a prelude to the sex act to follow. Thus Gregor's projection of female sexuality revolves ultimately around his own desire, and he is not receptive to Annette's needs.

Whereas Annette places the blame on no one specifically for the male's lack of receptiveness, Bachmann's narrator bluntly points to men and their "sick" attitude toward woman. The men treat every woman the same, and sex becomes merely an endless repetition of the same motions.

If he likes to kiss feet, he'll kiss the feet of another fifty women. Why should he occupy his thoughts with a creature who at this time gladly lets him kiss her feet, that's what he thinks in any case. A woman has to deal with the fact that now it's her feet he's interested in. She has to invent incredible feelings and for the entire day conceal her true feelings in the invented ones, first so that she can stand it, then above all, so that she can stand what is even beyond that, namely the fact that anyone who is so attached to feet neglects a lot of other things. (*Werke*, III, 270-271)

It never occurs to the men to consider their partners' desires. The women, on the other hand, suppress their desires and put up with the eccentricities of each lover. The situation is hopeless, with Annette and women in general the great losers because they fear the loss of their lovers if they do not comply with their desires.

As a third and most drastic variant, Schwaiger's narrator in *Wie kommt das Salz ins Meer* (Why Is the Sea Salty) and Jelinek's Brigitte in *Die Liebhaberinnen* (Women in Love) suppress their sexuality in order to put up with their husbands' desires. Schwaiger's narrator becomes frigid out of protest and compares her husband to a necrophiliac in no uncertain terms: "What he's doing is desecration of a corpse" (p. 80). Sexually she has become a corpse and a part of her self is dead—the ultimate victim of sexual tension.

Jelinek provides a material rationale for this situation in her novel *Die Liebhaberinnen*. Although unaware of it, Brigitte is sexually dead, like Schwaiger's narrator, and does not respond to any sexual desire when she goes to bed with Heinz. She, however, hopes only to get pregnant and secure herself a husband with a promising financial future:

heinz is happy finally to have found a person for screwing. hardly has heinz caught sight of the person brigitte does he unbutton and go into start position. while brigitte is still explaining to him that she loves him and feels at the same time something like respect for his professional success, while brigitte lets her thoughts wander from love and respect to wedding and house renovation, before she's aware of it she already has heinz the screwer hanging on her body like a leech. (*Die Liebhaberinnen*, p. 43)

Jelinek's portrayal of sex between Brigitte and Heinz as brutal and painful for Brigitte thus explicitly criticizes the source of women's acceptance of projection: the male-centered society that defines Brigitte totally by the man to whom she is attached. In order to secure herself a better life, she must deny herself completely. The denial becomes so automatic as to be accepted as a natural response by the participants. The author's purpose is to make the readers question this by means of such narrative techniques as *Verfremdung*, through the juxtaposition of clichés about love with Heinz' sexual brutality.

The Intrusion of Male Fantasy

Although they depict men as unreceptive to their partners' sexual needs, Frischmuth and Jelinek stress much more the infiltration of male desire into women's fantasies and the negative effects this has on them. In Frischmuth's "Baum des vergessenen Hundes" (Tree of the Forgotten Dog) Sybill and Theo's sexual relationship reveals the sad state of their marriage. Sybill derives no pleasure from sex with her husband, although he is unaware of it. To stomach the ritual which has evolved in their three years of marriage, she fantasizes obscene pictures and scenes among people with over-dimensional genitalia ("Baum des vergessenen Hundes," p. 117).

Sybill's situation is typical for many women, as psychologist Natalie Shainess points out:

Men usually employ fantasy in order to *engage* in sex despite problems; women use it to help themselves to *submit* to sex where it seems unavoidable. . . . They need the assistance of an often elaborately constructed story to enable them either to tolerate something that is intolerable or to perform something that without the fantasy would be impossible.[36]

In this literary case, to go to bed with her husband, Sybill conjures up gigantic sex organs, but she becomes sexually excited without the aid of such fantasies when she happens upon a man sleeping during an outing. Her vision of sexual gratification involves her as conqueror and rapist:

She asked herself what would happen if she really were on top of him, and through her mental image flickered the picture of the knife thrower at the circus, only that this man should be nailed down to the floor by the knives, like Christ, his hands and feet would be pierced, he, however, should not be nailed to a cross, but to the ground, and exactly as helpless and exposed, with arms spread apart and legs pressed over one another out of lust. ("Baum des vergessenen Hundes," p. 113)

The poverty of Sybill's imagination and the influence of male power structures is captured in this fantasy. Sybill merely reverses the power structure of the male-centered world, eschewing the role of victim as she assumes the role of conqueror.

As with Frischmuth, the intrusion of male fantasy on women's fantasy and the control of them through the media appears repeatedly in Jelinek's work. Erika Kohut, the protagonist of *Die Klavierspielerin* (The Piano Player), participates in sex and life almost entirely as an observer. Her passivity becomes a metaphor for the objectification of the female subject and representative of women's dilemma in a world where women's sexuality is so often shaped by male projections. Erika's mother has tried to kill any sexual feelings Erika might develop, wanting Erika to devote all her time and energy to the piano. Finding no models at home, Erika seeks them elsewhere by becoming a voyeur and a masochist. She spies on couples making love in the park (*Prater*), goes to peep shows and pornographic movies, and cuts herself up with razors. In this Erika experiences her body as strange and separate from herself. Thus when she goes to the peep show where she watches women behind glass who have been turned into total objects by the male customers, she is looking at herself vicariously, trying to observe the model for the self she does not have. She puts herself even more in the role of sexual object during her visits to the pornographic films in which women are portrayed as deriving pleasure from being beaten and raped. "Pain is itself only a consequence of the will for lust, for ruination, for destruction and in its highest form, a type of pleasure. Erika would gladly cross over the border to her own murder" (*Die Klavierspielerin*, p. 135).

As Natalie Shainess writes about the societal role of pornography:

> Pornography is a growing cultural force that continues to reinforce women's belief that the sexually masochistic role is rightly and properly theirs. Pornographic films and photographs generally show the woman serving the man, by definition a display of unequal power: The woman follows the man's dictates, does things that please him.[37]

Following this typical description of the derivation of pleasure through pain at the hands of a man, Erika is taken in by the illusion of pleasure projected in the pornographic films. Her letter to her student Klemmer, with whom she has a brief and brutal affair, prescribes how he should sadistically treat her. Yet her hopes for a fairy-tale ending make it clear that she does not want the blows which follow, but that she has not found the language to express an alternative. "Please don't hurt me stands illegibly between the lines" (*Die Klavierspielerin*, p. 283). Erika hopes for the happy ending she is used to seeing on television and the pleasure she is used to seeing on the faces of the women in the films. She gets neither. Jelinek thus demonstrates the grip which male projections of female sexuality have on one individual and points to the harm and brutality of the rape-porno ideology. The novel, *Die Klavierspielerin* destroys any idea that rape can be pleasurable or sexually satisfying, even if the pervasive ideology suggests it as an alternative. Unable to discover herself sexually, Erika adapts to the projections. Just as there are no models, there is also no language for her to express herself.

This dilemma with language, which Jelinek's work has suggested, is dealt with more precisely in Haushofer's *Eine Handvoll Leben* (A Handful of Life) and Bachmann's "Ein Schritt nach Gomorrha" ("A Step towards Gomorrah"). In both works the protagonists discuss the existence of two language registers, one for women and one for men. Elisabeth/Betty in Haushofer's *Eine Handvoll Leben*, upon realizing there is a register for masters and one for slaves, uses this to her advantage:

> At that time she didn't know that a slave has to understand and speak the language of his master if he wants to hold his own to some degree in this world. Only much later did she comprehend and begin to learn everything about which one could talk with men. Her knowledge was, it is true, only superficial, but it was enough to understand the jargon of businessmen, politicians, and artists. She had the reputation of being a woman with whom one could talk like a man and from this time on her endeavors were crowned with some success.[38]

Yet, no matter how well she "masters" the language, it will never truly be her own; by the very virtue of her sex, she will remain a talented "slave," who can converse with the "master."

In similar fashion, Charlotte in Bachmann's "Ein Schritt nach Gomorrha" finds both the language of men and women repulsive:

> The language of men, insofar as it was applied to women, had been bad enough already and doubtful; but the language of women was even worse, more undignified—she had been shocked by it ever since she had seen through her mother, later through her sisters, girlfriends and the wives of her men friends and had discovered that absolutely nothing, no insight, no observation corresponded to this language, to the frivolous or pious maxims, the jumble of judgments and opinions or the sighed lament.
>
> Charlotte liked looking at women; they frequently moved her or they pleased her visually, but so far as possible she avoided talking to them. She felt separated from them, from their language, their suffering, their heart.[39]

Charlotte, alienated by men's language and horrified by women's, finds herself alone and unable to identify with either group. Women feel isolated in a world without the words to express their situation in terms that a woman would identify with. Then, just as the protagonists lack the language to express themselves, so, too, do they find themselves without fantasies of their own.

Denial of Women's History

Not to be separated from male projections and definitions of the female, the denial or misrepresentation of women's history/experiences is also a factor in a male-centered culture. Each author agrees that the ways in which the past is perceived, particularly in regard to the roles women have played, shapes the perceptions of all women, either perpetuating or shattering conceptions.

Women have been left out of the chronicles of history. Their absence from standard accounts has in turn been taken as proof that women have had no part in history, which is both a misrepresentation and a manipulation of women's experiences. This is generally replicated in the literature in question. Leo Jordan in Bachmann's *Der Fall Franza* (The Case Franza) attempts to "erase" his wife, and thus essentially a part of her history, by denying her contributions to a research project:

> He wanted to obliterate me, make my name disappear, so that I really could be done away with after that. And then it hit me once again more deeply, because although every name was superfluous and didn't mean anything more than a signature, so that it could be verified and everyone could be held responsible, it had been everything which I had ever done except for the work I had done for him. My work had kept me going some years and allowed me to survive, my zeal, my convictions. (*Werke*, III, 410-411)

By forgetting her name, Jordan destroys the only bit of life Franza considers her own. He wipes out her accomplishment, and with it her life, her identity. The effect of Jordan's treatment proves devastating, and is an example of the effect that the exclusion of women from the chronicles of history has been for women as a group.

Her name erased from the report, Franza symbolically attempts to regain herself by obtaining a visa in her birth name. After she leaves her husband, physically and mentally devastated by the experience, she has a passport issued in her birth name for her trip to Egypt with her brother. When she crosses over the border with her "falsified" passport, she acts as if she has always travelled with false documents. "She seemed almost absentminded and acted as if they had crossed the border their whole lives with false papers" (*Werke*, III, 398). She adapts consciously quite early to that to which she has always had to adapt unconsciously since her marriage. Franza has travelled with a "false" identity during her adult life; she had denied herself when she married Jordan and assumed his name. Jordan, who had systematically destroyed her and her contribution to his work, denies her entire past, as he has with his previous wives.

A second variant of "disappearing from history" is demanded of the female protagonists themselves when they write. In Bachmann's *Malina* men attempt to prevent the "I" from telling her "story." Ivan calls upon her to write stories with a happy ending:

> He takes another one in the hand and reads amused: TYPES OF DEATH. And from another piece of paper he reads: The Egyptian Darkness. Isn't that your handwriting, did you write that down? Since I don't respond, he says: I don't like that, I already suspected something similar. All these books standing around in your crypt—no one wants them. Why are there only such books? There must be others, there must be, like EXSULTATE JUBILATE, so that you can jump out of your skin for joy. You often jump out of

your skin for joy, too, why don't you write like that?   (*Werke*, III, 54)

Ivan refuses to accept the "I"'s perceptions of reality as legitimate and, in effect, rejects them.   This constitutes a demand that she trivialize her writing, in accordance with the view of women as trivial supported by men.

In one of the dream sequences in the second chapter the "I"'s need to write and her father's fear of her words is expressed as a metaphor for the patriarchy's fear of an authentic women's history:

> My father is looking through a magnifying glass; only his clouded eyes can be seen.   He would like to read my sentences and take them from me.   But with the greatest thirst after the last hallucinations, I still know that he sees me die without words.   I have concealed my words in a statement of reason which is always safe and secret from my father, so strongly do I hold my breath. (*Werke*, III, 229-230)

Her need to express herself becomes essential to her very existence. However, her father, who can be interpreted as a representative of patriarchy, carefully monitors her words, denying her the expression of her experience.

Conclusion: Search for Self

As indicated at the start of the chapter, very few of the protagonists are able to answer the question "what am I anyway?"   The few protagonists who do attempt to answer the question for themselves—an indication in itself of a certain consciousness—have an uphill struggle.   Each search takes on a different form, but in every case the women fight against male definitions of womanhood.   In this the five authors mirror a very present reality described by writer/critic Elisabeth Lenk.   She fights against various literary and cultural reflections that face her just as they face the protagonists in the works of the five writers:

> I'm tired, although I was fresh just a while ago and the day is only just beginning.   Is it writing that tires me so much?   Perhaps it is all the false gods in me which I'm accusing as I write.   I am also accusing myself because I have educated myself and gained strength from living up to them.   I have believed in culture, education, art.   I have felt a great sense of achievement when I've managed to live up to my idols, and devalued when I did not.   At times I have sensed that I stand outside society, that as a woman I am excluded; that all women are excluded.[40]

She, like the five authors, writes against the projections of "woman" in society, questioning the culture, education, and art she has grown up with, finding that women are excluded from them.

All five authors evaluate the chance of a woman's successful search for self.   For example, *Malina*'s "I," in the face of her "false gods," walks into the mirror beyond the projections to be united with herself and be

independent of the demands and desires of the men in her life.   "I walked
into the mirror, I disappeared in the mirror, I saw into the future.   I was
one with myself and I am again divided with myself" (*Werke*, III, 136).   By
doing the impossible and walking into the mirror, she finds a momentary
utopia.   At the point the "I" walks into the mirror, the text is interrupted
with the two text fragments that appear in italics intermittently in the first
chapter:

> *Someday all women will have golden eyes, they will wear golden
> shoes and golden dresses.   She combed her golden hair, she messed it
> up, no!   In the wind her golden hair blew when she went up the
> Danube on her stallion and arrived in Raetia . . .*
> *A day will come when women will have red-golden eyes and red-
> golden hair, and the poetry of their sex will be recreated . . .*
> (*Werke*, III, 136)

This vision of the future, which has interrupted the text throughout chapter
one, converges here with a section of the tale of the Princess of Kagrain,
signaled by both the switch from the future tense (utopia) to the past tense
(tale), and from the plural *sie* (they—women) to the singular *sie* (she—the
princess).   Only in a utopian moment, when a real woman can live a fairy
tale, can her fairy-tale representation of her relationship with Ivan be
reconciled with her vision of the future.[41]

This vision of the future is also glimpsed by Charlotte in "Ein Schritt
nach Gomorrha" ("A Step towards Gomorrah").   Here she too desires to
destroy old definitions and projections of "woman."   In both instances,
Bachmann presents the reader with a paradoxical situation: the necessity and
impossibility of eluding old definitions or of defying definition in an attempt
to break down the split demanded by society.

Even when the search is successful the typical author shows it as
temporary.   The narrator in *Malina* escapes the male projections and   her
subsequent fragmentation, if only for a moment, to be swallowed up later by
a wall.   "It is a very old, a very strong wall out of which no one can fall,
which no one can break open, out of which nothing can ever be heard"
(*Werke*, III, 337).   In this, Bachmann summarizes the problem of search for
self and transforms an innocent-looking wall into a metaphor for a male
projection of reality which, with its prescribed definitions of what it means
to be a woman, has hindered the development of an autonomous self and
then denied women's experiences.[42]

In Bachmann's "Ein Schritt nach Gomorrha" ("A Step towards
Gomorrah"), Charlotte finds herself faced with a similar situation.   She, too,
desires to destroy the images of women that have been held up as models
for female behavior.   She wishes to wake up in a world that does not divide
people according to their sex:

> I wasn't born into any picture, thought Charlotte.   That is why I
> feel like breaking off.   That is why I want a counter-picture, and I
> want to construct it myself. . . .To hope for the kingdom.   Not the
> kingdom of men and not that of women. (*The Thirtieth Year*, p.
> 136)

Just like *Malina*'s "I," Charlotte wishes to break out of the images she has been trapped in and find one of her own. She finds neither the realm of men nor the realm of women as holding the potential for the new image she seeks, thereby lamenting the split in society. The images she finds now, although false, continue to be more potent than reality because they manipulate the perception of society by its members. Moreover they still come from a male-dominated world:

> It was time for the change of shifts, and now she could take over the world, name her companions, establish rights and duties, invalidate the old pictures, and design the first new ones. For it was the world of pictures that remained when everything had been swept away that had been condemned by the sexes and said of the sexes. (*The Thirtieth Year*, p. 136)

Charlotte kills the past, but she is not able to build alternatives. As Karen Achberger writes, "She sees the past clearly and rules it out, rejects it, declares it dead. However, the life of the present and future, which is to be changed, her life with Mara, she can't imagine. She does not possess any clear counter images, no alternatives."[43] This is typical for the majority of the literature, with one exception.

The only protagonist who escapes the projections and the "mirror" is the narrator in Haushofer's *Die Wand* (The Wall). She does so in a situation she does not seek out, but one imposed upon her through what she takes to be the work of one of the super-powers, i.e., that of a male rather than one of her own doing or of other women. On vacation in the mountains, she awakens one day to find herself cut off from the world through an invisible wall. On the other side of the wall, all life has been killed without the landscape being destroyed. The wall separates her from her past, from society and its expectations. It is only in this situation, totally removed from any society, totally alone, that she can define herself.

When freed from this old position, Haushofer's narrator reflects on her life before the wall and sharply critiques women's position in society. The narrator views her self of the past as a totally different person—a woman in a world that has little understanding for women:

> Today, when I think about the woman I once was, the woman with the small double chin who tried very hard to look younger than she was, I feel little sympathy for her. However, I wouldn't want to judge her too harshly. She never had the opportunity consciously to form her life. . . . She knew a little about many things, of many others, absolutely nothing; seen as a whole, a horrible confusion ruled in her head. It exactly suited the society in which she lived, which was just as unknowing and hurried as she herself. But one thing I'd like to give her credit for: she always felt a dull uneasiness and knew that it was all much too little.[44]

Although the narrator never quite felt at ease in her past life, she did not undertake action to change her situation. In that society the possibility to actively form her life did not exist.

The narrator, when referring to her past, repeats her uneasiness and her feeling of being out of place as an example of the only articulation of her problem that she could have while still in society. The feeling grows when she loses her function as mother. "I was a good mother for small children. As soon as they got older and went to school I failed. . . . Later I was never happy. Everything became bleak, and I stopped really living" (*Die Wand*, p. 195). As a woman in society her major function had been that of nurturer. Thus as the role gradually diminished, so did the content of her life.

During the two-and-a-half years since the wall closed out the narrator, the reader shares with the narrator her gradual shedding of the layers of projected personality acquired through socialization. Thus the reader shares the realization that it is only after the wall comes into her life that she can near the state of innocence of a child before the socialization process:

> Since my childhood I had unlearned to see things with my own eyes, and I had forgotten that the world had at one time been young, untouched, very beautiful and terrifying. I couldn't find my way back to it, I wasn't a child anymore and no longer capable of experiencing as a child, but solitude brought to me moments of seeing, without memory or consciousness, life's grand brilliance. (*Die Wand*, p. 203)

Children, not having gone through the socialization process, possess an innocence and naiveté lost on adults. The narrator, removed from the confines of society, cannot totally lose her cynicism; however she is able to experience brief moments of innocence.

Another progressive change happens to the narrator: she is no longer tormented with the passivity and indecisiveness of the other protagonists. Her consciousness of herself as a woman fades, and she sees herself in many roles:

> Strangely enough I looked younger at that time than at the time I still had led a comfortable life. The womanliness of a forty year old had fallen from me along with the curls, the small double chin and the rounded hips. At the same time I lost consciousness of being a woman. . . . I could easily forget that I was a woman. Sometimes I was a child looking for strawberries, then again a young man sawing wood or, when I sat on the bench holding Perle [the cat] on my skinny knees and following the sinking sun with my eyes, a very old sexless being. (*Die Wand*, p. 79)

In her old world she was confined to one role, but here she finds it necessary to be flexible in order to survive, and discovers that her previous limitation was artificial.

Only two human qualities remain constant before and after the wall: woman's role as protector of life and man's as destroyer. The narrator speaks of the need to protect life not only as a burden she has carried all her life (*Die Wand*, p. 69), but also as "instilled" (*eingepflanzt*) and a "drive" (*Trieb*) (*Die Wand*, p. 72). She contrasts this urge with the destructive "male" urge:

> If all people had been like me, there would never have been a
> wall, and the old man wouldn't have to lie petrified in front of his
> well.   But I understand why the others always had superior
> strength.   To love and take care of another being is always a very
> arduous task and much more difficult than to kill and destroy.   To
> raise a child takes twenty years, to kill it ten seconds. (*Die Wand*,
> p. 155)

The narrator's words contain an ominous warning for the world; the
destructive urge is responsible for the state of the world, for the repression
of individuals, and for the near destruction of her new world.   Her world is
invaded by a man who for no explained reason kills her dog Luchs and her
bull Stier.   The narrator does not stand by and allow the destruction of her
world she has so carefully built, but kills the intruder.

As nearly the only one of the five who states what the other four only
intimate, Haushofer paints a grim picture of a humankind that would
continue to stay in the hands of men.   Like the other authors in question,
her hope lies with women and love:

> There is no more sensible impulse than love.   It makes life more
> bearable for the lover and beloved.   But, we should have recognized
> in time that this was our only possibility, our only hope for a
> better life.   For a never-ending army of dead humankind's one
> possibility is forever squandered. (*Die Wand*, p. 229)

In the world Haushofer portrays, which captures the essence of that world
depicted by the other four authors, women only have the opportunity to get
beyond the projections when they are in an isolated world.   The society the
narrator leaves behind, like that seen by all authors, is closed, and the
"society" she creates for herself, although open, will die with her.   What is
more, not even outside the confines of society does the chance for a
successful female-male relationship exist.   When the narrator speculates what
life would have been like had she not been alone, she can draw only
negative conclusions about the possibility of men losing their socialization:

> Who knows what captivity would have done to this ordinary man.
> In any case, he would have been physically stronger than I, and I
> would have been dependent on him.   Perhaps he would lie around
> today lazily in the hut and send me out working.   The opportunity
> to get out of work must be a great temptation for every man.   And
> why should a man, who doesn't have to fear criticism, continue to
> work at all?   No, it's really better that I'm alone. (*Die Wand*, pp.
> 63-64)

The narrator is disenchanted with the idea of sharing her new life with a
male.   She suspects that any male would assume a position of power and
resist setting up an egalitarian "society."   This most negative message of all
five writers, but one tacitly agreed to, doubts the ability or desire of males
to change and relinquish the power inherent in a male-centered system.

One of these authors does, however, point to a way of overcoming the
negativity of the present position.   In her trilogy Frischmuth portrays

(re)discovering and (re)defining women's past as an essential part of finding a female self.   Both the form and content of these novels become a metaphor for women's search and discovery of self.   The two major female protagonists, Sophie Silber and Amaryllis Sternwieser/Amy Stern, are examples of the utopian vision become real.

In *Die Mystifikation der Sophie Silber* (The Mystification of Sophie Silber) Sophie Silber rediscovers her past and renews herself when she returns to her childhood home in Altaussee upon the invitation of a group of fairies.   Through the aid of the fairies, she confronts and accepts the past she has long tried to bury.   The novel ends with her decision to accept an engagement at a Viennese theater and live with her son, whom she barely knows.   Her confrontation and acceptance of her past aids her in her decision, but the reader does not find out how this helps her in her further life.

Yet, through the portrayal of another character, Frischmuth delves more deeply into the importance of (re)discovery and (re)defining women's past for the search for self.   The main focus in the exposition of a search for self is Amy Stern, the reincarnation of the fairy Amaryllis Sternwieser of the first book.   In Book Two, *Amy oder die Metamorphose* (Amy or the Metamorphosis), the reader witnesses more than Amy's change from fairy to human, but also an attempt to recover both past and self.   She is in the archetypical situation of women agreed on by all five writers: women, as the product of the male imagination, transformed into beings without a history, and male-centered chronicling of history leading to the denial of women's experience.   As a fairy she was the creation of the author's imagination and has been transformed into a woman with no apparent past.   Amy's question "Who am I and what are my problems?"   becomes a leitmotiv of her search for her forgotten self, and this question is clearly echoed by all five authors.[45]   As the story progresses she becomes more involved in her search for self, and has more of a chance of becoming a subject and not just a repository for male imagination: "Who am I and what are my problems? . . . Am I ceasing to be just a vessel?" (*Amy oder die Metamorphose*, p. 94) The result of this question, Amy's decision to be a writer, is an act of asserting herself and a step in breaking down male projections by using her imagination to oppose the system.   It is an act of asserting herself and her perspective and accepting the legitimacy of her own experience/perspective. Parallel to the requirements that other authors place on their characters (and implicitly on their readers), her interest in the lives of other women and her desire to find new models maintain the legitimacy of the existence of a wide variety of women's experiences in a male-centered society.[46]

Frischmuth's fairy tale come true thus brings full circle the theme of the difficulty of establishing a healthy sense of self in the works of the five writers.   The question "what am I anyway" plagues the protagonists of the five writers.   The struggle involved in seeking the answer points to the more limited opportunities and limiting attitudes facing women.   The fictional characters discover that they are defined by their relationship to men or to a role, rather than by their qualities as human beings.   For example, Schwaiger's narrator of *Wie kommt das Salz ins Meer* (Why Is the Sea Salty) finds that, upon marrying, she is defined by her relationship to her husband and not as an autonomous person.   Margret of Frischmuth's "Bleiben lassen" (Let It Be) is trapped in the role of housewife and does not have the strength to break out of her monotonous, albeit secure routine. Jelinek demonstrates, however, that the elimination of a class structure must coincide with the decentering of male power to eliminate injustices. Society's socialization process, intrinsically interconnected with male definitions and projections of the "female," necessitates a split in the fictional women who have any desire to reach beyond such narrow confines. Haushofer's adult protagonists, both male and female, and Bachmann's narrator of *Malina* present the most extreme examples of the imposed fragmentation. However, Haushofer, Bachmann, and Frischmuth stress the immediate necessity incumbent upon women to go beyond the mirror and think beyond that which has been thought in order to break down old categories. New dogmas are not required, but rather new pictures of the world, which can accommodate the strengths of the female vision.

Notes

1. The most research on women's search for self has been done on the works of Bachmann and Frischmuth. The major studies include:

TEXT + KRITIK: Sigrid Weigel, ed., *Ingeborg Bachmann* (Munich: edition text + kritik, 1984). See especially Irmela von der Lühe's article "Erinnerung und Identität in Ingeborg Bachmanns Roman *Malina*," pp. 132-149.

Sandra Frieden, "Bachmann's *Malina* and *Todesarten*: Subliminal Crimes," *The German Quarterly*, 56, No. 1 (January 1983), 61-73. This work deals with the split of the female individual.

Ellen Summerfield, *Ingeborg Bachmann: Die Auflösung der Figur in ihrem Roman* Malina (Bonn: Bouvier Verlag Herbert Grundmann, 1976). Based on her dissertation, this first in-depth study of *Malina* provides a close reading of the text and discusses the fragmentation of the "I."

Inta Ezergailis, *Women Writers—The Divided Self: Analysis of Novels by Christa Wolf, Ingeborg Bachmann, Doris Lessing, and Others* (Bonn: Bouvier Verlag Herbert Grundmann, 1982). *Malina* and several other works by women writers are viewed as testament to the female individual's struggle to return to a lost naive state.

Sara Lennox, "In the Cemetery of the Murdered Daughters: Ingeborg Bachmann's *Malina*," in *Studies in Twentieth Century Literature*, 5, No. 1 (Fall 1980), 75-105. *Malina* is interpreted as a statement of the absence of a female voice in male discourse and the impossibility of finding one.

Bernd Witte, "Schmerzton—Ingeborg Bachmann: Perspektiven einer feministischen Literatur," *die horen*, 28, No. 132 (Fall 1983), 76-82. The author points to a correlation between the destruction of female subjectivity and the destruction of the world as depicted in Bachmann's work.

Gabriele Bail, *Weibliche Identität: Ingeborg Bachmanns >>Malina<<* (Göttingen: edition herodot, 1984). Erikson's and Krappmann's theories of the individual are used to investigate the split of the "I" in *Malina*.

Karen Achberger, "Bachmann und die Bibel: 'Ein Schritt nach Gomorrha' als weibliche Schöpfungsgeschichte," in Hans Höller, ed., *Der dunkle Schatten, dem ich schon seit Anfang folge* (Vienna, Munich: Löcker, 1982), 97-110. Achberger provides an in-depth analysis of Bachmann's short story and discusses it as a female creation story.

Christa Gürtler, *Schreiben Frauen Anders?: Untersuchungen zu Ingeborg Bachmann und Barbara Frischmuth* (Stuttgart: Akademischer Verlag Hans-

Dieter Heinz, 1983). This study deals in part with the search for identity of the female protagonists in the works of Bachmann and Frischmuth.

    2.   Christine Koschel, Inge von Weidenbaum, and Clemens Münster, eds., Ingeborg Bachmann, *Werke*, 4 vols.   (Munich, Zurich: Piper Verlag, 1982), III, p. 278.   Further references to Bachmann's work in this chapter appear in the text.

    3.   Hilde Schmölzer, *Frau sein und Schreiben: Österreichische Schriftstellerinnen definieren sich selbst* (Vienna: Österreichisher Bundesverlag, 1982), p. 142.

    4.   Brigitte Schwaiger, *Wie kommt das Salz ins Meer* (Vienna, Hamburg: Paul Zsolnay Verlag, 1977), p. 158.   All further references appear in the text.

    5.   Joanna Bunker Rohrbaugh, *Women: Psychology's Puzzle* (New York: Basic Books, 1979) p. 398.

    6.   Evelyn Torton Beck and Biddy Martin, "Westdeutsche Frauenliteratur der siebziger Jahre," in Paul Michael Lützeler and Egon Schwarz, eds., *Deutsche Literatur in der Bundesrepublik seit 1965* (Königstein/Ts.: Athenäum, 1980), p. 137.

    7.   Barbara Frischmuth, *Rückkehr zum Vorläufigen Ausgangspunkt / Haschen nach Wind* (Munich: Deutscher Taschenbuch Verlag, 1978), pp. 85-86.   (*Haschen nach Wind*, a collection of four stories, was first published by Residenz Verlag in 1974.)   All further references to this short story and "Baum des vergessenen Hundes," also in the collection, appear in the text.

    8.   Phyllis Chesler, *Women and Madness* (Garden City, New York: Doubleday and Company, Inc., 1972), p. 56.

    9.   Marlen Haushofer, *Die Mansarde* (Hamburg, Dusseldorf: Claassen Verlag, 1969), pp. 107-108.   All further references appear in the text.

    10.   Elfriede Jelinek, *Die Liebhaberinnen* (Reinbek bei Hamburg: Rowohlt, 1975), p. 111.   All further references appear in the text.

    11.   Elfriede Jelinek, "Was geschah, nachdem Nora ihren Mann verlassen hatte?" in Helga Geyer-Ryan, ed., *Was geschah, nachdem Nora ihren Mann verlassen hatte?* (Munich: Deutscher Taschenbuch Verlag, 1982), pp. 170-205.   All further references appear in the text.

    12.   Simone de Beauvoir, *The Second Sex*, trans. and ed. H. M. Parshley (New York: Vintage-Random House, 1974), p. 574.   Reprint of the 1953 edition published by Knopf, New York.

    13.   Jacqueline Vansant, "Gespräch mit Elfriede Jelinek," *Deutsche Bücher*, 15, No. 1 (1985), 7.

    14.   Barbara Frischmuth, *Kai und die Liebe zu den Modellen* (Salzburg, Vienna: Residenz Verlag, 1979), p. 197.   All further references appear in the text.

    15.   de Beauvoir, p. xviii.

    16.   Rohrbaugh, pp. 423-424.

    17.   de Beauvoir, p. xviii.

    18.   Dagmar Lorenz, "Biographie und Chiffre: Entwicklungsmöglichkeiten in der österreichischen Prosa nach 1945, dargestellt an den Beispielen Marlen Haushofer und Ilse Aichinger," Diss. University of Cincinnati 1974, p. 84.   See also Dagmar Lorenz, "Marlen Haushofer—eine Feministin aus Österreich," *Modern Austrian Literature*, 12, No. 3/4 (1979), 177.   She notes here: "Both writers [Haushofer and de Beauvoir] stress that the mental and intellectual difference between man and woman is brought

about by the traditional Christian-oriented education of children."

19.   Lorenz, *Modern Austrian Literature*, p. 177.

20.   Lorenz, *Modern Austrian Literature*, p. 178.

21.   Oskar Jan Tauschinski, in his introduction to Haushofer's collection of short stories *Lebenslänglich* (Graz: Stiasny, 1966), pp. 5-28, discusses the sexual polarity in Haushofer's works.

22.   Secondary characters do not follow this division as closely. Haushofer's Käthe (*Eine Handvoll Leben*), Meta (*Die Tapetentür*), Anna's daughter (*Wir töten Stella*), and the narrator's daughter in *Die Mansarde* do not suffer the same split as the main figures, but are rather healthy and non-contemplative.   The men deviating from the schema include Alexander (*Die Tapetentür*), to some extent Toni (*Eine Handvoll Leben*), Anna's son Wolfgang (*Wir töten Stella*), and Hubert (*Die Mansarde*).   They suffer, however, from the lack of socialization, and tend to be intellectual, passive, weak, and sexually undesirable.   Although Haushofer differentiates between her characters and does not have the women strictly one way and the men strictly another, the fact that the main female and male protagonists fit into a scheme correlating with socialization points to her belief in its ultimate negative effect.

23.   Tauschinski, p. 10.

24.   Marlen Haushofer, *Die Tapetentür* (Vienna: Paul Zsolnay Verlag, 1957), p. 153.   All further references appear in the text.

25.   Elisabeth Lenk, "The Self-reflecting Woman," in Gisela Ecker, ed., *Feminist Aesthetics*, trans. Harriet Anderson (Boston: Beacon Press, 1986), p. 57.   The original essay "Die sich selbst verdoppelnde Frau," appeared in *Ästhetik und Kommunikation*, 7, No. 25 (September 1976), 84-87.

26.   Sandra M. Gilbert and Susan Gubar, *The Madwoman in the Attic* (New Haven, London: Yale University Press, 1980), p. 38.   For a discussion of the importance of the mirror see also Bail's study, p. 66, and Lennox's article, p. 94, and Sigrid Bortenschlager's article "Spiegelszenen bei Bachmann: Ansätze einer psychoanalytischen Interpretation," *Modern Austrian Literature*, 18, No. 3/4 (1985), 39-52.

27.   John Berger, *Ways of Seeing* (London, Middlesex: British Broadcasting Corporation and Penguin Books, 1972), p. 46.

28.   Ellen Summerfield, "Die Auflösung der Figur in Ingeborg Bachmann," Diss. University of Connecticut, 1975, p. 2.   The quotation is taken from Summerfield's abstract.   Any other Summerfield citations refer to her book based on her dissertation.

29.   Frieden, p. 68.

30.   Summerfield, *Ingeborg Bachmann*, pp. 49-50.

31.   Personal interview with Elfriede Jelinek, 19 September 1983.   All further references to the interview appear in the text.

32.   Elfriede Jelinek, "Clara S.: musikalische Tragödie," *manuskripte*, 21, No. 72 (1981), 10.   All further references appear in the text.

33.   Elfriede Jelinek, *Die Klavierspielerin* (Reinbek bei Hamburg: Rowohlt, 1983), pp. 109-110.   All further references appear in the text.

34.   Elfriede Jelinek, "Die Bienenkönige" in *Was geschah, nachdem Nora ihren Mann verlassen hatte?*, pp. 7-47.

35.   Barbara Frischmuth, *Bindungen* (Salzburg, Vienna: Residenz Verlag, 1980).

36.   Natalie Shainess, *Sweet Suffering* (Indianapolis, New York: The

Bobbs-Merrill Company, Inc., 1984), p. 93.

37.   Shainess, p. 87.

38.   Marlen Haushofer, *Eine Handvoll Leben* (Vienna: Paul Zsolnay Verlag, 1955), p. 132.

39.   Ingeborg Bachmann, *The Thirtieth Year*, trans. Michael Bullock (New York: Alfred A. Knopf, 1964), p. 133.

40.   Lenk, p. 54.

41.   For an article on Bachmann's use of the fairy-tale motif in relationship to women as subjects, see Karen Achberger's "Beyond Patriarchy: Ingeborg Bachmann and Fairytales," *Modern Austrian Literature* 18, No. 3/4 (1985), 211-222.

42.   Lennox, p. 95, draws a correlation between the wall in *Malina* and the wall in Charlotte Perkins Gilman's story "The Yellow Wallpaper," in *The Charlotte Perkins Gilman Reader*, edited by Ann J. Lane (New York: Pantheon Books, 1980), pp. 3-20.   "The Yellow Wallpaper" appeared originally in the January 1892 issue of *The New England Magazine*.

43.   Achberger, pp. 108-109.

44.   Marlen Haushofer, *Die Wand* (Gütersloh: Mohn, 1963), p. 80. All further references appear in the text.

45.   Barbara Frischmuth, *Amy oder die Metamorphose* (Salzburg, Vienna: Residenz Verlag, 1978), pp. 75, 93, and 94. See also Dina Mansour, who in her "Die Frauengestalten im Erzählwerk von Barbara Frischmuth," M.A. University of Cairo 1983, p. 20, writes, "A fairy becomes a mortal woman, most importantly, a woman becomes a person, searches for and finds her identity."

46.   Frischmuth's technique also supports the assertion of the female individual.   The trilogy moves from being totally in the third person narrative in the first book to a gradual shift in the second book that combines both the third and first person.   The focus of the third person is on Amy and her experiences, and it is her "I" that gradually asserts itself and takes over the narration.   In the third book, the narrative alternates between Amy's observations and the experiences of her young son and his friends.   The "I" asserts itself slowly until it takes over completely in the third book.

4

War, Violence, and Struggle
in Love and Marriage

Reflecting upon relationships between the sexes, the female narrator in Bachmann's *Malina* concludes, "There is always war./ Here, there is always violence./ Here, there is always struggle./ It is eternal war."[1] War (*Krieg*), violence (*Gewalt*), and struggle (*Kampf*) typify the love and marriage relationships depicted in the works of the five writers under discussion. As the terms suggest, the writers imply that there is a political configuration to heterosexual relationships in their fiction that extends beyond legislative bodies, political parties, or governments. This is sexual politics, typically revealed in "power-structured relationships, arrangements whereby one group of persons is controlled by another."[2] In the literature of Haushofer, Bachmann, Frischmuth, Jelinek, and Schwaiger, the concepts of *war* and *violence* are consistently characterized as negative, but *struggle* comes to be regarded positively as the fictional women's struggles become outwardly directed. The gradual transformation of struggle from a self-destructive to a positive value coincides with the advancement of women's legal rights in Austria during the seventies. Although the shift in options after 1975 allowed women more control over their lives, the portrayals of unsatisfactory relationships, present not only in the works of the older writers but persisting in the later works of the younger generation, indicate that male-female relationships continue to be problematic. This chapter reveals an ambivalence in the literature that shows that legal and perceived reality do not always coincide. Thus, instead of progress, problems to be overcome still serve as major material for the writers; limiting expectations in love and marriage, suffering, male dominance and questions of female dependence remain. Consciousness has been raised and laws changed, but have the expectations of the individuals as well?

The five authors discussed here address the problems women encounter when involved in a heterosexual relationship. As discussed in chapter three, the writers demonstrate that, in placing men at the center of their lives, the female protagonists relinquish a part of themselves; their development into autonomous individuals is unwittingly inhibited. Only the women who elect to remain unattached or who choose to leave a relationship have a sense of self or the chance of developing one. Their split, loss of self, or inability to develop a sense of self, then, result directly from relationships with men, and reveal experiences radically different from the expectations one normally has of love relationships. Yet all five authors show that this loss is a factor not only of woman's existence, but also of her role as partner in love or marriage, as part of a social interaction. Ideally partners in marriage and love should complement one another, without one partner being forced to submerge her/his individuality for the other. This has been a recurring theme since the eighteenth century in literature by men, showing how man has sought his complement in one or several relationships with women.[3] Typically in this literature, the male is depicted as a dynamic, growing individual, whereas the female is viewed as the embodiment of the naive or "natural." The natural element lost to the male as a result of industrialization in the eighteenth century is only to be regained through the union with the naive female.[4]

In contrast to this traditional position, the works by the five female writers under consideration show that a union with a man does not represent the recovery of a lost unity for a woman, but it either precipitates or furthers a split. Margret Eifler's analysis of the thematization of love in Bachmann characterizes the position of all five writers:

> The thematization of love here deals by no means any more with that static femininity, which had to serve for years as the ideal of perfection and thus as the catalyst for the self-realization process of the male; as soon as the woman had made herself superfluous in her function as emotional and sexual stimulus, the male, in his belief in progress paid tribute to the next thing, if not that, then to himself.[5]

Thus in the literature of the late twentieth century, the misused "beautiful souls" (schöne Seelen) of the eighteenth and nineteenth centuries have gained many voices to tell of the varied forms of abuse they suffer in all types of love and marriage.

Expectations in Love and Marriage: Medicine, Mysticism, and Religion

The majority of the female protagonists in the writings of the five authors consider love an essential part of their relationships to their partners. The women's expectations, however, fall into two distinct categories. They either expect love to transform them and the world with its mystical-curative power and to develop a "religion" of love, or they hold a more realistic view of love. Those who maintain the former view find themselves destroyed by the relationship or trapped in an unhappy one; those with a more realistic view are able to break off unsatisfactory relationships. A very small group of women [Margret in "Bleiben lassen" (Let It Be) and Sybill in "Baum des vergessenen Hundes" (Tree of the Forgotten Dog)] do not mention love as a factor in their marriages at all.

Both Haushofer's Annette (Die Tapetentür, The Wallpapered Door) and Bachmann's "I" (Malina) are convinced of the healing power of love. Annette writes of love's curative qualities in her diary, "The world is dying of coldness and apathy. The tragic mistake—to consider love a matter of secondary importance."[6] If only given priority, Annette believes love could rid the world of coldness and apathy. Bachmann's "I" refers to love as a "healthy force" (*gesunde Kraft*) (*Werke*, III, 37), which also has the potential for healing the world:

> But very much more has occurred since this possession, and it appears very strange to me that medical science, which regards itself as a rapidly progressing science, knows nothing of this incident; that here, in my neighborhood, pain is waning; that between 6 and 9 Ungargasse accidents are becoming fewer, that cancer and tumor, asthmas and heart attacks, infections and breakdowns, even headaches and weather sensitivity are reduced, and I ask myself if it is not my duty to inform the scientists of this simple method, so that research, which thinks all evils can be fought with more and more sophisticated medicines and treatments, could make a great jump forward. (*Werke*, III, 30-31)

The medicine of love is definitely expected to produce a new world for the woman. In typical words, Bachmann pinpoints the importance that Ivan holds for the narrator and she for him. "This woman loves so extraordinarily that nothing can match her love. For him, she's an episode in his life; for her, he is the transformer which changes the world and makes it beautiful."[7] The experience of transformation for the "I" and Annette precipitates a loss of protective reserves built up over the years; the transformation proves only temporary and ultimately fatal. The female expects that the rules and games that lead to the coldness and games of the world outside the relationship will be inoperative in the love relationship, whereas actually the male acts no differently in the personal relationship than he does in others. For this reason, the female is particularly vulnerable and subject to injury. Bachmann and Haushofer refute women's assumptions about the healing power of love through the death of Bachmann's "I" and the extreme emotional injury of Haushofer's Annette. The relationships' magic creates expectations, but does not change society's realities.

Bachmann best captures the tenuousness of the curative power of love when, in verse form, the "I" expresses Ivan's importance in her life and her fears concerning her love:

> I think about Ivan.
> I think about love.
> About the injections of reality.
> About the length of their effect, so few hours only.
> About the next, the stronger injections.
> I think in the stillness.
> I think that it's late.
> But I survive and think.
> And I think, it will not be Ivan.
> Whatever happens, it will be something else.
> I live in Ivan.
> I will not survive Ivan. (*Werke*, III, 45)

The concept of the miraculous power of love mentioned in the earlier passages takes on very different connotations through the use of the drug metaphor. Ivan continues to be the "I"'s connection to life, but just like a heroin addict, she has developed a dangerous dependence.   In a rare realization of the "I," she understands that Ivan has become her reality—her present and her future—both of which are very limited.

In addition to the curative power Haushofer's Annette and Bachmann's "I" bestow on love are the religious qualities they also attribute to love. Annette, like Bachmann's "I," views her husband as her lifeline.   "Gregor is the bread which keeps me alive.   Only he succeeds in making the world alive and aglow for me" (*Die Tapetentür*, The Wallpapered Door, p. 151). Gregor's meaning for Annette has assumed mystical-religious proportions, expressed in the metaphor of Gregor as the bread of life.   Unlike Bachmann's "I," Annette is better able to survive her lover's withdrawal, but not without the expense of emotional scars.

In Bachmann's *Malina*, the "I," believing in the mystical-curative power of love, takes the logical step and   builds her love for Ivan into a religion for which she later becomes the sacrificial lamb.[8]   The depiction of the protagonist's love as the creation of a religion and her death as analogous to Christ's Passion makes clear the more critical stance of the author.   For the duration of her affair with Ivan, the narrator transforms her room into a sanctuary for love; objects, such as the telephone, a vital connection to her lover, take on religious value for her.   Yet Ivan does not play this game or worship such idols.   Ironically Ivan is more familiar with her phone number than her body, or of any other object with an intimate connection to her:

My Mecca and my Jerusalem!   And so chosen am I before all other telephone subscribers and so am I being called, my 72 31 44, because Ivan already knows how to find me by heart on each and every telephone dial, and more certainly does he find my number than my hair and my mouth and my hand. (*Werke*, III, 43)

The telephone remains a holy object only as long as their relationship is going well.   It turns against her when Ivan has no time for her:

So, Ivan has no time, and the receiver feels ice cold, not out of plastic, out of metal, and slips up to my temple.   I hear when he hangs up, and I would like this noise to be a shot, short, quick, so that it would be over.   I don't want Ivan to be like this today and it always to be like this.   I would like an end. (*Werke*, III, 44)

Thus in a typical letdown after overly unrealistic expectations, her attempts to build up a sacred atmosphere around objects   associated with Ivan fail because of the one-sidedness of the relationship.

This "religion," with its accompanying false expectations about relationships, has rituals to accompany its talismans.   Bachmann's narrator mystifies gesture and language to cover up the void created by the empty relationship and the lack of communication.   The "I" and Ivan spend much of their time constructing sentence groups, such as "teaching sentences," "example sentences," "head sentences," "chess sentences," "fatigue sentences," and even "insult sentences," a game that arises by chance.   There are, however, no "emotion sentences."   The "emotion sentences" she so desperately needs and which her mystical expectations would lead her to expect are not forthcoming.   Ivan shows no interest in constructing new sentences to express feelings he does not possess:

> . . . we stop talking and awaken each other despite our great
> drowsiness. Until the wake-up service calls, I don't stop looking at
> Ivan, who may sleep another quarter of an hour, hoping, praying
> and believing I heard a sentence which came not from fatigue and
> would insure me in the world. But around my eyes something
> draws together; the secretion from the glands is so insignificant that
> it's not even enough for a tear in each corner of the eye. (*Werke*,
> III, 74)

Throughout this passage the reader feels the desperate hope of the narrator
and anticipates her future pain. Because of her conditioning about the
expectations of love, the narrator fills the void created by Ivan's refusal to
love by attaching a religious ritual-like quality to gestures, and in the
excerpt to sex.

The few words and gestures they do share remain to the narrator a
tenuous mystical connection holding the relationship together. The narrator
goes so far as to transform a phrase of Ivan's into an incantation to scare
away the demise of the relationship. Not sure whether she and Ivan
communicate and converse as others do, she takes Ivan's phrase to heart. "I
don't even know if you could say that we talk with one another and
converse like other people. But we're not in a hurry. We still have *our
whole lives*, says Ivan" (*Werke*, III, 37-39 [emphasis mine]). Ivan uses the
phrase lightly, but the "I" loads it with meaning, interpreting it as a means
of reassurance that betrays her insecurity and the sense that she has
unrealistic expectations. "He will find out what's wrong with me in the end
because we do have our whole lives. Perhaps not ahead of us, perhaps only
today, but we do have life, there can be no doubt about that" (*Werke*, III,
48-49). She is not repeating words exactly, but exposing a doubt about her
faith. By deleting the "ahead of us" after "life," uncertainty is expressed
about the duration of the narrator's life with Ivan. They certainly have
their whole lives, but will it last longer than today? In order to excuse
Ivan's lack of attention, she reassures herself again with Ivan's hollow phrase:

> Today, however, Ivan doesn't want to drive into town; he lets the
> chess figures stand, empties his glass in one gulp, goes particularly
> quickly to the door, as always without saying good-by, perhaps
> because we still have our whole life ahead of us. (*Werke*, III, 50)

Again, the word "perhaps" underscores the narrator's doubts about Ivan's
sincerity. The author, then, exposes the mystification in an empty
relationship by rendering the narrator's use of the "incantation" almost ironic
and by juxtaposing Ivan's casual use of language with the narrator's desire
to put meaning and magic back into language.

Jelinek's Brigitte and Paula (*Die Liebhaberinnen*, Women in Love)
similarly view their partners as a connection to life, but in less a religious
sense than a material one, which nonetheless leads to a dramatic
transformation. Brigitte sees her financial security in her love for Heinz: "i
love you just because you are a man who has learned a profession, i am a
woman who hasn't learned a profession. your profession has to suffice for

the both of us."[9] Paula, after she falls in love, experiences a transformation in finding another:

> then: before this life had been only work, the house, housework, girlfriends, work, work at home, and the work at the dressmakers (only recently!), therefore a false or incomplete life. this, however, is now going to be over, and love is here, and finally it has arrived. and finally paula is now a person. (*Die Liebhaberinnen*, p. 30)

Upon falling in love Paula no longer feels she is subhuman—the result of her position in her family and society. Through the attentions of a male individual, she views herself a human being.

Annette, temporarily transformed by her love, Bachmann's "I," waiting like an addict for her next injection, Brigitte, hoping for financial security, and Paula, feeling worthy for the first time, resemble de Beauvoir's archetypal woman in love:

> She chooses to desire her enslavement so ardently that it will seem to her the expression of her liberty; she will try to rise above her situation as inessential object by fully accepting it; through her flesh, her feelings, her behavior, she will enthrone him as supreme value and reality: she will humble herself to nothingness before him. Love becomes for her a religion.[10]

This is the ideology of love that the writers disavow and that their protagonists have internalized. The results reveal a chasm between the protagonists' visions of love and the reality of the love affair. Haushofer in *Die Tapetentür*, Bachmann in *Malina*, and Jelinek in *Die Liebhaberinnen* delve behind the purported curative power and religious-mystical quality in the protagonists' vision of love, exposing the manipulation and political configurations of an ideology. The authors believe that love does not transform one's life; nor is it mystical or curative. However their protagonists try to maintain that it does and is.

Expectations in Relationships: Money, Position, Sex

Of all the writers Jelinek most consciously analyzes the gulf between the reality and the ideology of love. According to Jelinek love is perverted by capitalism and patriarchy.[11] To gain status, attain financial security, and find an alternative to unpleasant work outside the home, the unskilled women in Jelinek's works must attach themselves to men using the only capital they have, their bodies. This unfair exchange becomes more palatable to the average woman because it occurs under the guise of love. Jelinek as narrator strips away the layers veiling the manipulative nature of love by juxtaposing cliché and reality in her character's pain:

> love hurts brigitte. she is waiting for a call from heinz. why doesn't it come? it hurts so much to wait. it hurts because brigitte longs for heinz. brigitte says that heinz is her entire world. brigitte's world is for that reason small. life appears meaningless to her without him. life doesn't appear very meaningful with him, it

only seems more meaningful, in any case more meaningful than her work in the bra factory. (*Die Liebhaberinnen*, p. 20)

In actuality, Brigitte needs Heinz as an escape from the bra factory and as a ticket to a materially better life, although she has bought the illusion of love and a relationship as a meaning for her life.

These private illusions are not the creation of the individual. Jelinek is critical of the media, which help perpetuate the myth of romantic love.[12] She not only states a connection between the "picture magazines" Paula reads and Paula's conception of love, but also uses the media's language to expose its message:

> love in itself is something special, to be sure, but how special does it have to be if the circumstances seek out paula and erich for love. erich and paula are one in a thousand, perhaps one in a million! (*Die Liebhaberinnen*, p. 31)

The illusion of the total uniqueness of love and the element of chance involved in two lovers meeting is satirized, shown to be a creation not of Paula's making, but rather reinforced by society.

If women hold love to be an essential part of a relationship, love plays little role in the men's relationships with the fictional women. With few exceptions, the men either hate the women, view the relationships as business arrangements, or carry on relationships purely for sexual reasons. Franza in Bachmann's *Der Fall Franza* (The Case Franza) believes that hate, not love, forms the basis for her husband's relationships with women. "He didn't like women and he always had to have a woman in order to provide himself with the object of his hate" (*Werke*, III, 409-410). Similarly, love plays no part for Toni Marek in Bachmann's novel fragment *Requiem für Fanny Goldmann* (Requiem for Fanny Goldmann) in his affair with Fanny Goldmann (*Werke*, III, 483-524). Their relationship serves as a means for career advancement through her professional connections and nothing else. As another alternative, Haushofer's Richard (*Wir töten Stella*, We're Killing Stella) sees love as possession. "As a very young woman I asked him once: 'Why do you love me?' His response came swift and certain: 'Because you belong to me.' "[13] Anna correctly assesses the situation and realizes that it is not her uniqueness as a human being that attracts Richard to her. "Not because of my looks, then, or because of my lovable qualities did he love me, but only as his possession" (*Wir töten Stella*, p. 28). For him she is interchangeable: "He would have loved any person in my place just as much, and in this manner he loves his children, his house, in short, everything which belongs to him" (*Wir töten Stella*, p. 28). Theo, in Frischmuth's short story "Baum des vergessenen Hundes" (Tree of the Forgotten Dog), like Richard, views his wife as his property and considers his marriage a business deal. He finds it unjust of Sybill to want to leave him. He has provided her with an apartment and vacations; he has carried out his part of the deal and feels that Sybill should keep her side of the bargain. " 'Sybill,' he said over and over again, 'you can't do that, that's unfair, that's really unfair, you can't abandon me, I'm doing everything, you know it, the apartment and trips, oh, Sybill. . . . ' "[14] These male feelings of lovelessness in relationships occur in all the authors' works. Ivan, in *Malina*, makes it clear that love is not a factor in his liaisons with women. "That you will have certainly already figured out. I love no one. The children, of course, but otherwise no one" (*Werke*, III, 58). With this renunciation of love, he justifies his lack of commitment and refuses to accept any responsibility for the narrator's feelings. For Haushofer's Gregor Xanthier, love is connected with a transitory physical attraction. Annette writes in her diary, "Whenever Gregor says to a woman, 'I love you,' it is the pure truth of the moment, and thus Gregor's truths continuously cancel each other out and are perceived as lies" (*Die Tapetentür*, p. 93). Thus Xanthier compartmentalizes his love according to the roles in which he places the women. When Annette can no longer fulfill his sexual needs, she passes in his view from lover to the mother of his child, and he seeks sexual fulfillment elsewhere. He is not attracted by a woman's individuality. Jelinek's Erich in *Die Liebhaberinnen*, who has never experienced love, is able to respond with such feelings only for his children.

The men in these stories are thus not, in all five authors' opinions, subject to the mystical expectations to which the women are prone. A few of the men do love their partners, but even then they often love them more for the roles they fill as wife and mother. Haushofer's Toni (*Eine Handvoll Leben*, A Handful of Life) and Schwaiger's Rolf (*Wie kommt das Salz ins Meer*, Why Is the Sea Salty) accept the traditional role of women in marriage and neither question their own behavior nor society's value systems. Herbert in Haushofer's *Die Mansarde* (The Attic) succumbs to pressure to conform, and of all the couples portrayed in Haushofer's works, the narrator and Herbert are by far the "happiest." If the relationship breaks up (as in Schwaiger's *Wie kommt das Salz ins Meer* and Frischmuth's *Kai und die Liebe zu den Modellen*, Kai and the Love of Models) or loses its initial "magic" (as in Haushofer's *Die Mansarde*), it is because of the failure of the men to break away from these established roles, combined with the unrealistic roles imposed on them by the women's mysticism. Society has thus placed restrictive role expectations on both male and female and caused their estrangement. Frischmuth's Klemens loves Amy (*Amy oder die Metamorphose*; and *Kai und die Liebe zu den Modellen*) but is unwilling to sacrifice anything in society's terms for the relationship. Love and the relationship to their partners is not the first priority in the men's lives—their first priority is usually their work.

All the authors agree that the women are forced into a position of weakness in the male-female relationships. They are not allowed the chance to love "in strength" but only as partners who surrender to the image of the other. De Beauvoir writes of women's dilemma:

> On the day when it will be possible for woman to love not in her weakness but in her strength, not to escape herself but to find herself, not to abase herself but to assert herself—on that day love will become for her, as for man, a source of life and not of mortal danger.[15]

Society's expectations, internalized by both men and women, do not allow this possibility, according to the five authors we have here: the women look to love for strength, and destroy themselves in their relationships; the men look to their prescribed roles in society. Moreover, the fictional women who demand more autonomy and rights in their relationship do not have more successful relationships, merely less injurious ones.

Suffering in Relationships

Considering the radical difference in expectations of love between female and male characters and the personal sacrifices the women make for the relationship, it is not surprising that the women characters and authors alike experience suffering as a central part of love and marriage. The types of suffering the fictional women endure range from death, extreme emotional injury, and mental and physical disorders, to injuries caused by physical violence.

In Bachmann's unfinished trilogy *Todesarten* (Types of Death) and her fragment "Gier" (Greed), women are murdered   literally and figuratively by their partners.[16]   Their "murders" are preceded by a period of drawn-out suffering. The "I" in *Malina*, hoping to be restored to a whole person by Ivan, is actually driven to her death as a result of the affair.   In an interview Bachmann comments on the death of the "I": "She has already been murdered or come to this outermost border so often.   Only she hasn't yet taken the last step, namely to cause the 'I' to disappear, the 'I' being no longer useful because it is too destroyed."[17]   That is, the affair renders the final blow which destroys, or murders the "I." Her death, or murder, as the last three words of the novel ("It was murder") indicate, is not conventional. As Ellen Summerfield writes, "It has to do with treating a person in such a way that it ultimately means his end.   Murder and suicide are both contained within it."[18] The "I" lived through Ivan; she made herself into what she thought he wanted. Therefore this side of her cannot go on living, as the "I" ascertains, "I have lived in Ivan and I am dying in Malina" (*Werke*, III, 335).   Just as she predicted earlier when she said, "I will not survive Ivan" (*Werke*, III, 45), after her affair with Ivan is over, so is her life.   Bachmann criticizes the social expectations that have programmed the narrator to turn herself into her own sacrifice.

Women dying as a result of love relationships is a theme Bachmann takes up again and again.   In writing a book about his relationship with Fanny, Toni Marek in her *Requiem für Fanny Goldmann* (Requiem for Fanny Goldmann) butchers Fanny through literature.   She later dies as a result of the affair.   In *Der Fall Franza* (The Case Franza), yet another woman dies as the result of a love relationship.   Jordan's brutal mental torture makes Franza unable to fight her aggressors.   After her rape in the desert, which is symbolic for all that has happened in her relationship in Vienna, Franza dies of self-inflicted head wounds.   Elisabeth Mihailovics in the short story fragment "Gier" (Greed) dies most brutally at the hands of her husband, who subsequently kills himself.[19]

Haushofer's protagonists Anna (*Wir töten Stella*, We're Killing Stella), Annette (*Die Tapetentür*, The Wallpapered Door), and the narrator of *Die Mansarde* (The Attic) have also suffered so much in their marriages that they are incapable of taking any action to change their lot.   Anna captures the feeling of hopelessness when she writes, "Life with Richard has corrupted me and made me useless" (*Wir töten Stella*, p. 33).   Similarly Annette in *Die Tapetentür* becomes "corrupted" through her marriage to Gregor, a less ruthless version of Anna's husband, Richard.

This type of suffering in male-female relationships is often portrayed through the metaphor of respiratory illness. Bachmann's juxtaposition of Franza's breathing attacks in Vienna with her narrow escape from almost being buried alive in the desert echoes an assumption that Franza was literally buried in her marriage.[20]   Air, so vital to speech, has been squeezed out of her. Moreover, her ability to articulate her problems is impaired at the time of her "escape" from Vienna: Jordan attempts to make her "disappear" not only by leaving her name off a publication, but by taking away her ability to articulate her feelings and problems. She ultimately attempts to communicate with Jordan through letters, but this fails, too—again a loss of breath or life. Once away from Jordan, she gradually finds the words to condemn him. "I wasn't sick, I didn't come to him as a patient, that would have justified his actions. I went to him, I confided in him; what else could a marriage be other than confiding, putting oneself into someone's hands no matter how small it is" (*Werke*, III, 407). Her suffering is translated by him into an illness to be used against her.

In a similar case Margret in Frischmuth's "Bleiben lassen" (Let It Be) is plagued by asthma attacks; her body reacts to an unbearable situation:

> Once she had made the mistake—she was more and more convinced that it had been a mistake—of telling her childhood friend about the choking attacks which tormented her especially after "unfounded" crying and which were, in her opinion, the reason that she had the feeling from time to time that she couldn't stand it any longer, that it was getting worse and worse instead of better, and that "putting up with it" no longer made any sense. ("Bleiben lassen," p. 88)

Respiratory problems are therefore not only a metaphor for the suffocating aspects of a relationship, but also for words stolen from women. Marek, in writing Fanny's story in Bachmann's *Requiem für Fanny Goldmann* (Requiem for Fanny Goldmann) steals her words and causes her to die of an inflamed lung.

Despite their preoccupation with suffering and illness, none of the writers delve into physical violence suffered by women at the hands of their husbands except for Elfriede Jelinek. The interpersonal dynamics in Jelinek's works are characterized by physical violence and brutality in sexual relations. Alienated by their work, Jelinek's men exercise power in the one realm where they are stronger. "the article paula is controlled by erich whose physical strength is controlled by yet others, until his organs degenerate into an early death, for which alcohol does its part as well. erich controls the life of paula and the life of his daughter susanne" (*Die Liebhaberinnen*, Women in Love, p. 101). He beats Paula and experiences his physical power over her as the only area in which he can exercise power over anyone.

Because the centralness of men to women's lives creates a vacuum for women after the affair is over, the men continue to exert a telling effect on the lives of many of the fictional women, extending the suffering beyond the existence of the relationship. Even before the relationship is formally over, Bachmann's "I," Haushofer's Annette, and Schwaiger's "I" begin to suffer from the thought of the end as soon as it appears inevitable. In a typical statement, Bachmann's "I" expresses the fear of the impending end of her affair with Ivan in her very remembering of its beginning:

> One day we'll have less and less time, and one day it will have
> been yesterday and the day before yesterday and a year ago and
> two years ago. Besides yesterday there will also be tomorrow, a
> tomorrow that I don't want, and yesterday . . . Oh, this yesterday,
> it now also occurs to me how I met Ivan and that always from the
> very beginning I . . ., and I'm frightened because never did I want
> to think how it was in the beginning, never, . . . But one day I
> will want to know and from that day on I will remain behind and
> fall back into yesterday. (*Werke*, III, 150)

That is, she in her societal weakness cannot conceive of a life without a
relationship and assume a strong role.

In another example Annette seeks contact with Gregor through objects
with which he has had contact. She drinks out of his coffee cup after he
leaves and slides into his bed to reestablish contact, instead of questioning
her submission to a vanished man. After she leaves Gregor she savors her
pain as a means of reliving what she will probably never experience again.
"It [the pain] was everything that remained to her, and she dare not lose
this last thing" (*Die Tapetentür*, p. 229). Bachmann's Fanny and Franza
continue to suffer after their relationship dissolves. They attempt to deal
with the lost love, but their love is perverted to hate, both for their partner
and for themselves.

The women who do leave a relationship without incurring incurable
injury still suffer in their lovers' absence. In yet another variation, the
narrator of Schwaiger's *Wie kommt das Salz ins Meer* (Why Is the Sea
Salty) realizes before she ends her marriage that her suffering will not
necessarily end as well:

> When he sleeps, because he must, I cuddle up to him, because
> I'm so afraid of the nights I will lie alone. I'll sew a doll out of
> material for myself with very long arms in which I can wrap myself.
> Why do I want to leave him when even I admit that I need him,
> he would ask. Because I have to. Who said that? I did.[21]

Despite the inevitable suffering Schwaiger's "I" realizes she must leave and
assert herself. Frischmuth's Amy too expresses her ambivalence to
separation when she associates her separation with physical pain filled with
emptiness. "I tried to imagine being alone from the most interesting angles,
but under all these new or perhaps not so new musings it raged like a
toothache."[22] In an extreme objectification of this sense of loss after a
relationship, Amy's apartment has spaces in it left by Klemens's absence:

> Although Klemens never lived with us, it seems to me now as if
> he left behind empty places in the apartment. Now, when the
> possibility no longer exists of unexpectedly finding him at home if
> he could have for once made himself free, I have the feeling, the
> unpleasant feeling, of returning to an empty apartment. (*Kai und
> die Liebe zu den Modellen*, Kai and the Love of Models, p. 168)

This "unpleasant feeling," however, does not in this case bring terminal suffering.   Amy, unlike Bachmann's "I," is not consumed by the spaces but proceeds with her life; she has her work, her friends, and her son.   As such women become more autonomous, suffering still remains a part of their experience in love and marriage, but it does not destroy them.

Because women suffer so much in love and marriage a logical question might be: Do the women enjoy the pain or are they not to blame for the situation?   Although a modification of behavior could change the situation, the women cannot be blamed for a behavior that they have been taught. As Susan Brownmiller writes in her book on rape, "Force, or the threat of force, is the method used against her, and a show of force is the prime requisite of masculine behavior that she, as a woman, has been trained from childhood to abjure.   She is unfit for the contest.   Femininity has trained her to lose."[23] Each of the writers under question stresses that literary women, just like their real-life counterparts, have been raised to be victims. Haushofer, Bachmann, Jelinek, and Schwaiger relate the protagonists' present behavior as victims to the role of their fathers.   The manner in which the women interact(ed) with their fathers influences the interaction with the authority replacements, and predisposes them to accept, at least initially, society's definitions of male-female relationships.

Sexual Politics: Male Control in Relationships

The political configuration of the fictional relationships represented in the works of all five authors points to and condemns male control in love and marriage relationships, and, when taken to a logical conclusion, implies that the program of each author is a radical critique of society.

Psychological Terror

The first facet of these critiques is the question of control as psychological terror. Haushofer and Bachmann, the only two writers to have lived through Austro-Fascism and National Socialism, depict male characters who exert such extreme control over their partners that the female protagonists view them as criminals, both capable and guilty of murder in a metaphorical sense.   In Haushofer's *Wir töten Stella* "Richard is a born traitor. . . . Richard is a monster; solicitous father, respected lawyer, passionate lover, traitor, liar, and murderer" (*Wir töten Stella*, p.   19). Franza in Bachmann's *Der Fall Franza* claims that her husband, respected psychiatrist Leo Jordan, is her murderer.   "My husband, please excuse this ridiculous, meaningless expression, is murdering me" (*Werke*, III, 406).   The narrator in Bachmann's *Requiem für Fanny Goldmann* views writer Toni Marek as a murderer, too: ". . . he had butchered her, she had been butchered on 386 pages in a book" (*Werke*, III, 515).   With these metaphors for male power over female lives, Haushofer and Bachmann juxtapose socially valued qualities with criminal qualities in order to force the reader to look behind the facade of respectability in the relationships and question society's value systems.   In this the writers break down the divisions between the public and the private; the readers ask themselves if it is possible to be upstanding citizens and "murderers" at the same time.   The authors stress that these men have accomplished their status at the extreme sacrifice of others: their wives. Society's system of values has been so perverted that the Richards, Jordans, and Tonis are respected, whereas the wives are victims of the assumed power of the partners' positions.

Such a fusion of public and private questions is not uncommon for each writer. Bachmann, for example, describes male-female relationships in radically political terms. She states:

> It [fascism] doesn't begin with the first bombs which are thrown; it doesn't begin with the terror about which one can write in every newspaper. It begins in relationships between people. Fascism is the first thing in the relationship between a man and woman.[24]

In the present context fascism does not refer specifically to a political or economic system; it goes beyond the political and manifests itself in personal relationships—in its crassest form in male-female relationships. Patriarchal in nature, fascism is anti-female, destructive of life, hierarchical in nature, and intolerant of the other.[25] Thus in the characters of Richard (Haushofer's *Wir töten Stella*), Leo Jordan (Bachmann's *Der Fall Franza*), and Toni Marek (Bachmann's *Requiem für Fanny Goldmann*), fascist traits in the personal sense reveal themselves in their behavior toward women. Metaphorically, however, fascism in personal relationships is most vividly represented in the protagonist's dreams of being murdered in a gas chamber of a death camp. Using this imagery Bachmann suggests that fascism and National Socialism were and remain much greater problems than people care to admit: the ideology of power and dominance continues, having gone underground, erupting in the violence of male-female relationships.[26] In similar fashion Bachmann's Franza (*Der Fall Franza*) also likens her plight to that of colonized peoples. Like Bachmann, Jelinek also defines interpersonal relationships in political terms in that she views fascism as an element of male-female relationships. In *Die Liebhaberinnen*, this critique is in less explicit terms than in Bachmann's *Todesarten* (Types of Death). The men are less diabolical than they are in Bachmann, but the fascist tendencies have become a way of life in the authoritarian structure of the family and marriage. Jelinek comments on her use of fascism:

> It is not the political phenomenon which is to be analyzed, but the connection between fascism and capital, the petty bourgeoisie as the class which produces fascism—fascism, which as Bachmann says begins in the family, in the relationship between woman and man. However, she already said that in the fifties when it wasn't said out loud, and it's still true—fascism is a general state of mind. It can be seen in the horribly authoritarian raising of children which is still used here, in the beating down of deviant opinions, intolerance and authoritarian behavior pure and simple.[27]

Jelinek echoes Bachmann's sentiments and connects a term usually thought of on a purely political level with personal relationships, thus repudiating a separation of private and public spheres.

The Battle of Male-Female Relationships

A second facet of the political nature of love and marriage is further exemplified by the fact that the five writers do not depict any love/marriage relationship as a partnership. In all cases the women are forced into a defensive position in a battle for which they are usually ill-equipped. Relationships based on mutual respect and an atmosphere in which both individuals can grow do not exist in this fiction. Bachmann in *Der Fall Franza* offers the extreme example of a protagonist who is likened to a hunted animal:

> I was trapped in this labyrinth, in the entire house, in the apartment I mean, . . . I was suddenly no longer co-worker, no longer married. I was *separated from society*, with a man, *in a jungle*, in the middle of civilization, and I saw that *he was well-armed* and that *I had no weapons*. (*Werke*, III, 404-405 [emphasis mine])

Franza is forced into the position of a hunted creature, a situation that she neither expected nor is prepared to face in a world she assumes civilized.

Similarly, in Frischmuth's "Bleiben lassen," Margret views her husband not as a partner, but as an unbeatable opponent. He has not taken her seriously as a partner; she at least wants him to take her seriously as an opponent:

> And then it all occurred to her, everything she had wanted to tell him, to toss in his face—her entire desolation and her unhappiness—how she had wanted to climb out of her shadow into the light of fury, which should have broken over him so that he would finally once again perceive her correctly, bargain with her as an opponent. And she thought about her inability, about her boundless failure, that she again and again couldn't make herself understood, at least injure him so that he had to think about her day and night. ("Bleiben lassen," p. 105)

Only in her mind is she able to express her pain, and it is in part her inability to articulate that prevents Alex from taking her seriously as a partner. When she finally confronts Alex, he quickly counters by throwing the guilt for the affair on her ("Bleiben lassen," p. 104). In placing the guilt for his affair on Margret, Alex fails to take Margret or her attempt to protest seriously.

Game- and Role-Playing in Love and Marriage

Aside from the question of power and control, the images of game and play that are often found in the works indicate relationships of opposition and competition. Bachmann's and Haushofer's protagonists are coerced into playing games in which chance is superseded by male control; a partnership cannot exist. Chess, a war game, becomes emblematic for the relationship between Bachmann's "I" and Ivan—at best they have a draw, and this only when Ivan coaches. When Ivan does not cooperate, play is broken off:

> We begin playing a game of chess and don't have to talk
> anymore. It becomes a tedious, troublesome, halting game; we make
> no progress: Ivan attacks, I am on the defensive. Ivan's attack
> comes to a halt; it is the longest, silentest game that we have ever
> played. Ivan doesn't help me one single time, and we don't finish
> the game. (*Werke*, III, 125)

The narrator is always on the defensive in a game/relationship at which she is not skilled. As their relationship deteriorates, so does their chess game.

Similarly the relationship between Richard and Anna of Haushofer's *Wir töten Stella* (We're Killing Stella) deteriorates into a game. "Without having spoken about it there were two camps in our home: Richard and Annette—Wolfgang and myself, and we played strictly according to the rules of the game" (*Wir töten Stella*, pp. 15-16). The rules of this game consist in avoiding certain topics in order to avoid arguments. This game of playing family is easily upset by the intrusion of an outsider; the facade of happy family does not hold up when an inexperienced player happens along. Stella, the daughter of a school colleague of Anna's who comes to live with them and has an affair with Richard, is the catalyst that forces Anna to reassess her relationship. Anna foresees anarchy as the only alternative to game-playing if everyone does not hold to the rules. Although Anna's love for Richard has been misused and the basis for a healthy relationship does not exist, the facade of a happy family must be kept if society's game is to be upheld from the point of view of male control:

> He hates nothing more than conditions which he calls sloppy and
> loose, perhaps because he himself constantly exists in this condition.
> It's crazy and not respectable in his opinion to use separate
> bedrooms, not to spend the vacation with one's wife, and not to go
> to the zoo or movies with the children on Sunday. He would never
> leave me. I am the guardian of his home and children, and as a
> person who secretly lives in the deepest anarchy, he treasures
> nothing more than superficial order and exactness. (*Wir töten
> Stella*, p. 28)

The facade of decency serves Richard's purposes but allows Anna little freedom.

In a commensurate situation in Bachmann's *Malina*, Ivan demands that the narrator play hard-to-get, forcing her to become the unwilling player in a game for which she has no skill. "He demands that I continue to play the game because he doesn't know that it's not a game for me anymore,

that the game's over" (*Werke*, III, 84).   For the narrator, love means
rejecting the usual game-playing, but without game-playing she fears she will
not be able to hold Ivan.   "One can only trap conditionally, with little
retreats, with tactics, with that which Ivan calls the game" (*Werke*, III, 84).
In this case the power in the relationship becomes unbalanced; Ivan wants
the "I" to play rather than to have an honest relationship.   He makes up
the rules for a game with himself as the dubious prize.   It is generally
recognized that love under these circumstances can only be destructive for
women.   Shulamith Firestone's analysis of love corrupted aptly describes the
typical situation depicted in the women's fiction we see here.   Love in our
society "becomes complicated, corrupted, or obstructed by *an unequal balance
of power*. . . . love demands a mutual vulnerability or it turns destructive:
the destructive effects of love occur only in a context of inequality."[28]   The
authors under consideration here argue with Firestone's assertion that women
are ill-prepared for the lack of "mutual vulnerability" and the war and
violence facing them in love and marriage, because they have been socialized
to react in ways basically harmful to themselves.   Men, on the other hand,
do not relinquish the power that is generally afforded them in society in
their personal relationships.

This absolute underdog situation is not the only one depicted in the
literature in question.   Even as women gain more autonomy and refuse to be
put at such a great disadvantage, an oppositional relationship continues.
While playing with her son's train, for example, Frischmuth's Amy Stern
likens her relationship to her lover and the father of her child to two trains
on a collision course.   "Klemens is travelling in a freight train, pulling many
cars in the opposite direction, but since my passenger train is quicker and
the tracks form a circle, a collision is unavoidable" (*Kai und die Liebe zu
den Modellen*, Kai and the Love of Models, p. 28).   Klemens, carrying with
him society's game rules, cannot help but collide with Amy, who is
interested in a non-traditional personal relationship.

Thus even at the best of times the writers do not portray male-female
relationships as partnerships.   As a group they see that there can be no
relationship based on "mutual vulnerability" as long as women continue to
be economically dependent on men.   However the writers do not see the
answer to better relationships in merely the relief of such dependence because
of the socialization on both sides.

The reason that economics is not the only constraint on women is that
not only game-playing, but also acting out a role becomes an integral part of
the power politics of marriage and love.   Historically women have had a
much narrower choice of socially accepted roles, the primary one being that
of nurturer, of wife and mother.   Often, in assuming a socially accepted and
expected role, either consciously or as a result of socialization, women do not
directly communicate their personal needs or desires.   In exchange for
security and/or being attached to a man, women take on the role of
housekeeper, mother, and lover.   The examination and critique of these roles
is an essential element of a feminist critique, as typified by two feminist
scholars of the eighties:

The exposure of the heterosexual nuclear family—the institution of
modern industrial society in which individual freedom and privacy
are supposedly at home—as the realm of male control and extreme

female alienation is an essential element of a feminist analysis.[29]

The roles women typically find themselves playing extend beyond the roles of wife, mother, and lover to include the prostitute and martyr. With the exception of the role of the mother, and that for only a limited time, the roles are those of outsiders, of the powerless.

The writers in question are generally unable to show women who have transcended this position of powerlessness. Having power over nothing else besides their own bodies, many of the protagonists martyr themselves—they either die or endure "great suffering on behalf of any belief, principle, or cause," usually the relationship with a man.[30] The female protagonists in Bachmann's *Todesarten* (Types of Death), Haushofer's *Die Tapetentür* (The Wallpapered Door), and Frischmuth's "Bleiben lassen" (Let It Be) either die or suffer greatly because of their "belief" in the liaison, and because they have been socialized into the female half of the power hierarchy. Only in "Bleiben lassen" does the protagonist "savor" playing the martyr:

> And whenever circumstances were particularly favorable, this condition didn't last just until morning when they sat sleepily across from each other at breakfast, but several days, on which she could, however, forget none of her fundamental reproaches. It appeared to give her tremendous pleasure to accept everything, to take it on and devote herself to it without consideration of justice, which normally was so important to her, but more with a preference of suffering. As if all the agonizing up to now had been the price and that from now on it would be better. ("Bleiben lassen," p. 99)

Yet even in this situation, where Margret assumes the guilt for a relationship that does not work, her sacrificial posture underscores her powerlessness. Rather than confront the problem, she assumes the guilt and experiences masochistic gratification. As Simone de Beauvoir writes, "Martyrdom remains open to the oppressed," while action is reserved for the powerful.[31] Women are portrayed as sacrificing personal desires for the good of their relationships and to their own detriment.

Frischmuth, Schwaiger, and Jelinek draw further and more overt comparisons between prostitution and women's position in marriage. Their women prostitute themselves for financial or emotional security. Frischmuth's Margret ("Bleiben lassen") for example, "enjoys" her prostitution just as she does her martyrdom:

> And it had the aftertaste of prostitution to her whenever she showed him how much it meant to her to be offered tenderness without regard that anyone else could see her. But she also savored this taste, she enjoyed standing, while he sat in a wicker chair, embracing him from behind, and pressing her face to his while her long hair fell over his shoulders. ("Bleiben lassen," p. 99)

Begging for affection, exposing her need of warmth to others, she prostitutes herself for the affection that is "supposed" to be an integral part of marriage.

In a second case, Jelinek's *Die Liebhaberinnen* (Women in Love) describes prostitution both within and outside marriage as a normal part of women's experience. Paula, unskilled and uneducated, prostitutes herself because her husband literally drinks his salary away. Brigitte uses her body to catch her husband and improve her social status. Jelinek points out that these unskilled women, more than other women, are forced to use their bodies as their only resource to gain economic security and/or status.

Schwaiger's narrator in *Wie kommt das Salz ins Meer* (Why Is the Sea Salty) also realizes during her coming to consciousness that she has become no more than a housekeeper and a prostitute. "Why doesn't he hire a housekeeper? Why doesn't this machine indulge himself with a whore?" (*Wie kommt das Salz ins Meer*, p. 132) Describing her husband as a "machine," the narrator no longer sees a personal element in their marriage.

Haushofer's Annette in *Die Tapetentür* (The Wallpapered Door) goes beyond a consciousness of prostitution by describing her behavior explicitly in terms of a role in the theatrical sense. "It already costs me enough effort as it is just to continue playing my role satisfactorily" (*Die Tapetentür*, p. 157). She consciously models her personality according to what she presumes Gregor desires, expressing another version of the powerless role. "You see, I have to be careful and observe exactly in order to find out how Gregor imagines his wife" (*Die Tapetentür*, p. 87). She acts out her role so skillfully that it is exactly the quality that she acts out that Gregor admires the most. Building her relationship on a lie, Annette recognizes that one false move could bring it tumbling down. "It was ridiculous and stupid of her, but since she had built her entire life with Gregor on a lie, pretending she could stand his way of life, she couldn't move even the smallest stone of this structure" (*Die Tapetentür*, p. 136). Again, as in *Wir töten Stella*, Haushofer demonstrates the fragility and emptiness of the traditional marriage relationship when the women assume such a role. Haushofer, like all other writers, thus equates marriage with prostitution and martyrdom to make a critique of the institution on the grounds of the inherent power hierarchy.

Politics of Social Pressures

Social pressures inherited for generations tend to reinforce modes of powerlessness. Expectations derived from male advantage often lead women to change their lifestyles when involved with a man, whereas men do not substantially change their lives. The changes range from women quitting work outside the home, changing residence, to shaping their lives entirely around the idiosyncrasies of their partners. In a typical situation portrayed in Haushofer's *Eine Handvoll Leben* (A Handful of Life), Elisabeth/Betty discontinues work as her husband's secretary after their marriage; she is not allowed even to do the gardening, for her husband, Toni, fears people would think him miserly. Similarly Bachmann's Franza discontinues her medical studies and throws herself into her husband's research. Frischmuth's Margret ("Bleiben lassen") and Sybill ("Baum des vergessenen Hundes," Tree of the Forgotten Dog) either reduce their outside work, doing it at home along with the housework, or channel their talents totally into domestic life. In Jelinek's *Die Liebhaberinnen* (Women in Love), Brigitte quits her work at the bra factory in order to work in her husband's shop. She makes the change gladly, wanting to escape factory work, despite the fact that her new job exposes her much more directly to her husband's power base. These examples show that the authors still see women as much more likely to give up their work outside the home. The husbands often expect it of their wives because of their social or professional status. Another reason offered by Jelinek is that work inside the home seems preferable to low-paying jobs outside the house.

The authors identify a further cause for the powerlessness inherent in a male-female relationship: In Frischmuth's "Bleiben lassen," Haushofer's *Die Tapetentür*, and Bachmann's *Der Fall Franza*, the women move from familiar surroundings into a territory known well to their husbands but alien to them. Alex in "Bleiben lassen" works outside the home, comes home to an immaculate house, feels at ease with his family (parents, brother) and friends; he is an insider in the community. Margret, as a newcomer to both the family and community, feels isolated in her outsider role. In a similar relinquishment of power, Annette in Haushofer's *Die Tapetentür* lives with her in-laws in her first marriage; then in her second marriage she vacates her old apartment to move in with her husband. She furnishes only one room with her own possessions. "I have furnished my own room with my own furniture—an island in this large, strange apartment" (*Die Tapetentür*, p. 88). Her room serves as an island of refuge, a familiar landmark in unfamiliar terrain. Gregor, unlike Annette, has kept the same apartment in both marriages. Moreover, he has erased all traces of his first wife from the apartment, a power move which will probably recur after Annette leaves him. Bachmann's Franza moves into her husband's apartment, in a parallel situation, unaware of the "jungle" that awaits her; her husband, Jordan, has stayed stationary, merely exchanging one wife for the next. The women's powerlessness is magnified by their loss of familiar turf, and they find themselves ill-equipped for the "game" of marriage. Their psychological disorientation is exploited both consciously and unconsciously by their partners' desire to exert control over them.

Not only houses, but also lifestyles are surrendered in the struggle, again setting up games which the women have to lose. Haushofer's Annette; Bachmann's "I," Franza, and Fanny; and Jelinek's Paula and Brigitte gladly, at least initially, take on their husbands'/lovers' interests in the name of love. They seek total identification with their partners' work as an expression of love. Annette, for example, drastically changes her schedule and undertakes activities to please Gregor:

> If I had earlier spent Sunday at home dillydallying, reading and sleeping—a cup of tea and a roll with butter often sufficed as a meal—now on Sundays I have to get up particularly early and spend the entire day in the car. That is quite strenuous for me, particularly since I'm not even allowed to show it. Gregor is convinced that I'm happy to have something from life in this manner. Of course, it's not a lack of consideration on his part: he can't put himself in my position, and his back doesn't hurt him after long hours of sitting, while I simply can't move. (*Die Tapetentür*, pp. 147-148)

Instead of offering suggestions, Annette remains silent, hoping to please Gregor.   This is a no-win game with rules set up by the man, and reinforced by society's picture of the happy family, no matter what the individuals say.

Similarly Fanny and Franza both throw themselves into their lovers'/husbands' careers, identifying totally with their husbands' work.   The "I," too, adopts similar interests; she wants to learn how to sail when she discovers Ivan sails; her enthusiasm wanes with the disintegration of the relationship.   Jelinek's Paula and Brigitte also modify their behavior after they fall in love.   Seeing Heinz as a means of improving her status, Brigitte consciously sets out to catch him.   Blinded by love and having internalized the ideology of romantic love, Paula attempts to figure out Erich's wishes. Since both Paula and Brigitte will be defined in society by the man to whom they attach themselves, it is incumbent upon them to be flexible, ready at any moment to serve and assume the follower role in the game, as players, not initiators.

It is not surprising that these games of surrender-of-self demanded of the women by social expectations degenerate into an immobility arising from the protagonists' restrictive lifestyles, expressed by the writers in both form and content.   In Haushofer's novels, for example, the major exposition unfolds in an enclosed area, either in one room or in a house, with very little taking place outside this small area.   Haushofer's choice of the very private diary form further increases the sense of confinement found in all the works of all five women writers.

The chess games between "I" and Ivan (*Malina*) become a metaphor for the "I"'s feeling of confinement in Bachmann's novel.   "Ivan says, you play without a plan, you don't bring your pieces into the game, your queen is already immobile again./ I have to laugh, then I brood again about the problem of my immobility" (*Werke*, III, 46).   The immobility of her chess piece is intended to be seen by the reader as applying to her behavior as well as to the limiting aspects of the relationship.   She and her queen are in precarious positions: no matter what move they make, they are surrounded by danger—the "I" in her relationship with Ivan, the queen through the remaining chess pieces.

Another literary technique to stress the protagonists' confinement or powerlessness is repetition.   In Jelinek's *Die Liebhaberinnen* the parallelism of the narrative underscores the similarities between the women because of their sex and their limited mobility.   The beginning and ending passages are almost identical, and thus hermetically seal the characters into a world of brutality and limited possibilities.

The essence of the powerlessness of all the women in these works of fiction, then, is the game that society prescribes.   For love, the women shift their center of gravity, either from themselves to their mate, or from óne authority (father) to another (the mate).   They desire, like the archetypical woman de Beauvoir describes, "total identification with the loved one":

> The measure of values, the truth of the world, are in his consciousness; hence it is not enough to serve him.   The woman in love tries to see with his eyes; she reads the books he reads, prefers the pictures and the music he prefers; she is interested only in the landscapes she sees with him, in the ideas that come from him; she

adopts his friendships, his enmities, his opinions; when she questions herself, it is his reply she tries to hear; she wants to have in her lungs the air he has already breathed; the fruits and flowers that do not come from his hands have no taste and no fragrance. Her idea of location in space, even, is upset: the center of the world is no longer the place where she is, but that occupied by her lover; all roads lead to his home, and from it.[32]

The decentering of women's lives, as described by de Beauvoir and experienced by the fictional female protagonists, underscores the political nature of heterosexual relationships.   The psychological and physical decentering experienced by women in love and marriage sets the stage for the ensuing battles and/or games.   The game and role-playing demanded of the women in a male-centered society sets up a situation in which women are inherently disadvantaged: they play games to which they did not make up the rules, and thus are relegated to passive powerless roles.

The Politics and Violence of Economic Dependence

Because of societal programming, game-playing is not the only way in which marriage relationships victimize women.   In those works in which women are economically dependent on men, the writers depict this as a further source of violence against women. The women in all these works are forced into compromising positions with few alternatives, as seen in society's terms. For example, the thought of leaving their comfortable homes acts as mental violence for some of the fictional women, keeping them non-mobile, unable to seek options to traditional marriage to the detriment of their personalities.   For those women subjected to physical abuse in marriage, the violence of economic dependence is much more immediately felt.

Haushofer's Anna (*Wir töten Stella*, We're Killing Stella), though she contemplates leaving, confirms typically, "The thought occurred to me to pack my bags and go away with Wolfgang. I could rent two rooms for me and the children in another city, and begin over again.   But, of course, I knew that it was impossible" (*Wir töten Stella*, p. 51).   In 1958, when the book was published, Anna would have been faced with many problems.   At that time, in order to obtain a divorce, a guilty party had to be named. Although Richard had had many affairs, it would have been hard at that time to prove that he had had them, in light of his conniving. Anna would not only have been faced with the difficulty of obtaining a divorce, but it would have been difficult for her to maintain herself and her family on alimony payments.

In Frischmuth's short story "Baum des vergessenen Hundes" (1974, Tree of the Forgotten Dog), also published before the reforms in the divorce laws, when Sybill comtemplates leaving Theo, it is the loss of material security that occupies her thoughts. Sybill realizes that it would be harder to leave a child with him, and, in any case, it would be hard to give up the apartment. "Later perhaps, but when she imagined that it would be even harder for her to leave Theo, to give up the spacious apartment and all the conveniences of downtown, then she always had less desire to do it" ("Baum des vergessenen Hundes," p. 118).   Although Sybill has no child and does have the ability to support herself, her material comfort acts as an important discouraging factor when she considers divorce.

Bachmann's Franza in "Das Gebell" (1972, "The Barking") (and also *Der Fall Franza*, The Case Franza) is kept in check because of her dependence on her husband's financial generosity (*Werke*, II, 373-393). Unlike many fictional women, Franza does have a rainy-day fund to use in emergencies, but uses it instead to make Jordan's mother more comfortable, a socially approved action.   Not only does she depend on Jordan as her major source of income, but she is also faced with his arbitrariness and feels that she must account for money spent.   She is forced into the role of child asking her father for money—a further act of violence against her adulthood.

Jelinek most explicitly equates women's economic dependence with an act of violence against women.   Paula, untrained, pregnant, or "spoiled goods," to use Jelinek's market-value term, has to grovel to get Erich to marry her.   Paula, unskilled and a mother, sees no alternative to her economic dependence.   In addition she is subjected to physical violence, but, because of her dependent situation and her dreams of material comfort in marriage, she does not see an alternative.   When her husband, an alcoholic, drinks away his earnings, she chooses to prostitute herself secretly, having no other capital than her body.   After she is found out, she is forced to give up her children.   With shattered dreams, the emotionally bankrupt Paula finds a job as an unskilled worker in a bra factory.   Marriage does not bring the world of bliss she expected.   Her precarious financial situation makes obvious her essential powerlessness in the relationship and society and the violence she is subjected to because of it.   Brigitte, hoping to escape the factory, seeks out Heinz.   This arrangement brings a material improvement, but in this case, Brigitte experiences the accompanying sex as brutal (*Die Liebhaberinnen*, Women in Love, p. 43); Jelinek is again portraying physical violence accompanied by psychological violence.   Yet like Margret in Frischmuth's "Baum des vergessenen Hundes," Brigitte fantasizes a reversal of society's hierarchy, finding her only escape in brutal fantasy:

in one of numerous passionate situations which heinz brought about without considering how repulsive this could be for brigitte, if brigitte could only, for example, hold out a sack instead of her cunt, in which on the inside there are a whole lot of long thorns, and heinz hops like a rabbit into it, heave ho, working his way in with his prick drawn, and there's nothing like going in! go, into the thorns or nails! that would certainly be no pleasure, how helplessly heinz's legs would then poke about in the air! (*Die Liebhaberinnen*, Women in Love, p. 44)

Brigitte counters the physical and psychological violence resulting from her dependent situation with ineffective fantasies.   These women are typical of modern women, because they can realize themselves neither at home nor at the work place.   Jelinek depicts women as being exploited on two levels, at the work place as cheap labor, and at home, as free labor, subject to the moods of the husband.   But whether it is physical or psychological violence that the women experience, all writers agree that the women's economic dependence on their partners places them at a severe disadvantage in their relationship and in society.   Women are placed in the position of a child, faced with the moods and generosity of the surrogate father.   The resulting violence against women is seen as legitimate for the financial security they receive.

The Trap of Marriage for Women

The authors' works thus all point out a reverse in society's expectations, when seen from the woman's point of view. For women locked into unhappy marriages, the condition they find themselves in becomes primary and the relationship secondary. Even after the basis for the relationship has dissolved, the women find themselves trapped. Thus contrary to the accepted belief that women find their fulfillment in marriage and the family, they are confronted with confinement and violence. "Love" and "marriage" as defined by society precipitate the situation; the women try to retreat into a shell from the ever-present war or power game—a violent situation.

Both Haushofer's Anna (*Wir töten Stella*) and Elisabeth/Betty (*Eine Handvoll Leben*, A Handful of Life) describe their states as prison-like and find little fulfillment in the societal expectations of the roles of wife and mother. Because of Stella's death, Anna becomes more aware of just how she has been trapped in her marriage:

> Whenever I'm in the house alone, I'm always conscious of the fact that the house is not mine. I sometimes feel like an overnight guest in it. Only the view into the garden belongs to me, otherwise nothing. Earlier I sometimes believed that I at least had a home, but since Stella has been dead, the gilded cage has turned into a prison. (*Wir töten Stella*, p. 22)

She makes a double analogy; before her new state of awareness her home was a gilded cage, now it is a prison. She is "out of circulation," subject to her husband's rules, and has lost the illusion of love she held earlier to discover the reality of the war game.

Betty uses similar words to describe her life with her first husband. Elisabeth plots a fake death and leaves behind a life of comfortable captivity with a well-to-do factory owner for freedom. "She had at one time chosen freedom, coldness, and independence and had her life long despairingly desired tenderness, warmth, and security. Only the knowledge of her nature had kept her from pursuing this longing."[33] Betty weighs the positive and negative aspects of her decision and realizes that she does not have the personality for a traditional marriage, which she equates with captivity.

In a series of impressionistic thoughts with a similar emphasis on marriage, the narrator of Schwaiger's *Wie kommt das Salz ins Meer* (Why Is the Sea Salty) compares an apartment to a top-security prison: "A beautiful apartment is a maximum security prison" (*Wie kommt das Salz ins Meer*, p. 20). Jelinek's Paula and Brigitte transfer from one prison to another. They, as nonreflective characters, do not view themselves as "in prison." Jelinek, however, uses the metaphor of death to show how little freedom of movement there is for men or women, but particularly for women, because they build their world around their relationships with men:

> awful, this slow death. and men and women die away together;
> the man has some diversion with it, he guards his wife like a

> watchdog outside, he guards her dying. . . . thus, they die on each
> other. and the daughter can hardly wait any more to be allowed to
> die, and the parents already make purchases for their daughter's
> death: linens and washcloths and dish towels and a used
> refrigerator. that way at least she stays dead but fresh. (*Die
> Liebhaberinnen*, Women in Love, p. 15)

In Jelinek's grim picture of interpersonal relationships, marriage is seen as
the beginning of death. The fairy-tale image of living happily ever after is
turned on its head and exposed as unrealistic in a capitalistic and
patriarchal society in which women achieve financial security through
relationships with men.

There are mitigating circumstances possible that loosen the entire focus
from the relationship. For example Amy's home never becomes the prison
the homes of Elisabeth, Anna, and Schwaiger's "I" become for them, because
she and Klemens never live together, and she is thus able to maintain a
greater amount of independence. She realizes that if she were to live with
Klemens or have him support her financially, she would find herself in a
prison of sorts:

> If I were clever, Maya told me, clever in the sense of art and in
> the sense of many artists, I would get Klemens to take care of Kai
> and me. Then I wouldn't even need to work for the broadcasting
> network and could just write. But that's an illusion. Not because
> Klemens would behave like a pascha, but because he couldn't afford
> to do otherwise than have me take upon myself all that for which
> he now uses a restaurant, laundry, and cleaning woman. I ask
> myself, how many hours a day could I *just write* because then Kai
> would surely also stay at home. And the next impossibility consists
> simply in the fact that I couldn't manage to adapt to circumstances
> which don't have to be my circumstances at all. (*Kai und die Liebe
> zu den Modellen*, Kai and the Love of Models, pp. 196-197)

Amy here sees no alternatives to either the trap of the relationship or herself
alone, because society has given her no options.

Similarly unable to imagine alternatives, Haushofer's Anna and
Frischmuth's Margret (and Sybill) act out their frustrations in personally
nonproductive ways, which are nonetheless considered acceptable behavior by
women in society. For example both Anna and Margret seek solace in the
garden. However Anna does not really enjoy venturing out into the garden,
because she always finds this disappointing. "Earlier I sometimes gave in to
the temptation and went down into the garden, but it was always a
disappointment for me. Here, from the window it is just at the right
distance for me" (*Wir töten Stella*, p. 36). From afar she sees only the
beautiful and is not confronted with the ugly. Getting too close destroys the
magic, just as getting too close to Richard has destroyed her as an
individual personality and submerged her in the field of the relationship.
Being in the garden leads to a loss of its magical function, which is similar
to that of the acacia tree in Haushofer's *Die Mansarde* (The Attic). The
protagonist of this work describes its function as follows:

The most wonderful thing about the tree, however, is that it can suck out wishes and extinguish them. Not that I still have especially burning wishes, but there are anxieties, vexations, and annoyances. The tree pulls all that out of me, lays it to rest in the forks of its boughs and covers it with white clouds until it disappears into the damp cold. Then I can turn my head, empty and light, and sleep another half hour.[34]

The garden, like the tree, extracts pain and memory from Anna, allowing her to continue to function, although as an alien within the real world. When looking at the garden from afar, it sucks out all her dreams and desires. In both instances, the tree and garden make life more bearable for the women in facilitating a "loss" of memory.

In the garden of Frischmuth's "Bleiben lassen" (Let It Be) Margret fills her life with fantasies; the fantasies fulfill needs and desires lacking in her relationship with Alex. The only time love is ever mentioned is in connection with the garden. "She truly loved the garden" ("Bleiben lassen," p. 90). Her attachment is so great that when she considers leaving Alex, the garden holds her back. "The garden played an important role whenever she thought about leaving. She couldn't imagine ever finding a garden again which so suited her and her life. Even then she wouldn't have known how to gain entrance to it, with what she should acquire it" ("Bleiben lassen," p. 101). Margret fears the loss of the one part of her life that is hers alone. She views the garden as her only success, a success she is unable to transfer to other realms.

The significance of the garden for Margret is underlined in that the only time Margret's name is ever mentioned is in connection with the garden. "And whenever the children or anyone else who just happened to be visiting got into anything in the garden, then immediately it was said: Margret's going to be mad! or: tidy that up before Margret sees it!" ("Bleiben lassen," p. 101). Otherwise, Margret is just a "she," whose identity is not strong enough to impress itself on others. In her duties as housewife she is an interchangeable cog. The garden becomes her small area of power—the only turf allotted her, her battleground after accepting Alex's terms.

It is in the garden that the system allots Margret an identity that suits her better than the one she presents to family and friends. Through her fantasies she creates her world as she would have it. Here she finds power and both sexual and emotional fulfillment, albeit temporarily. However the garden becomes both a place of escape and a prison for Margret; she can realize her desires in her daydreams, but because of her intimate relationship with the garden and the "power" she has gained there, she would find it hard to leave Alex. The garden is therefore ersatz, the best she can do. She is also trapped into inactivity by her dreams. The women, seeing no alternatives, direct their energies into socially acceptable, but personally nonproductive alternatives, locking themselves further in their prison by accepting what their husbands provide and not making changes. They hold on to the false hope of winning a place within their partners' game.

Struggle Becomes Positive

Struggle has a negative meaning in works in which the *fight* or *battle* of the relationship is directed toward the female protagonist. In works in which the women do not assert themselves in love and marriage relationships, assume a victim stance and, moreover, identify more with the male-victor than with the female-victim, the negative struggle is inherent to the relationship. In such works the women direct any feelings of dissatisfaction inward and fail to take any positive steps to change their relationship. Conversely, the writers view struggle in relationships as positive when it becomes outwardly directed, i.e., when the women assert themselves, articulate their needs, and confront their partners, refusing to back down on their demands.

In Haushofer's *Eine Handvoll Leben* (A Handful of Life), Frischmuth's Books Two and Three of her trilogy (*Amy oder die Metamorphose*, Amy or the Metamorphosis; and *Kai und die Liebe zu den Modellen*, Kai and the Love of Models), and in Schwaiger's *Wie kommt das Salz ins Meer* (Why Is the Sea Salty), the female protagonists escape or terminate unhappy marriages or love relationships. In these works, therefore, the concept of struggle is depicted positively as it changes from a fight/struggle against women to an outwardly directed struggle urged by the women.

Haushofer's Elisabeth/Betty, Frischmuth's Amy, and Schwaiger's "I" assert themselves and terminate their relationships, actions predicated on critical assessment of their own behavior and that of their partners, the authors underscore these actions by using the narrative technique. In *Eine Handvoll Leben* Haushofer builds the narrative around the protagonist's confrontation with and acceptance of her past. Elisabeth Pfluger fakes her own death in 1932 to escape an unsatisfactory marriage, but later returns to her first husband's home as Mrs. Betty Russel in 1951. Toni Pfluger's sudden death and the family's financial problems have finally provided her with the opportunity to return as buyer of the Pfluger property. Betty relives the past she rejected as she leafs through old postcards and photographs she discovers in the guest room.

Thus Haushofer has structured two levels of distance and confrontation within the same person, Elisabeth examining her actions before leaving her first husband, and Betty reviewing her past years later. In the narrative Betty's view of the past is not colored by her experiences after she left. Not the first person, but rather the third person is used to relate Elisabeth's life, creating more distance and a sense of objectivity. Young Elisabeth intuitively feels uneasy in her traditional marriage, so she makes an important step and reflects on her situation. The distance she places between her acting and conscious self leads her to her drastic solution.

When considering her situation Elisabeth realizes that a difference exists between the world she finds herself in and the one she desires. Her attachments to husband Toni and lover Lenart, as contrary as they may have seemed, do not provide Elisabeth the opportunity to grow or experience the world:

> She thought about everything she would never know: the desert, the great ocean, jungle and steppes, the Northern Lights, the stone canyons of great, distant cities, England's parks. . . . She thought

about the embraces of strangers she would never know.   (*Eine Handvoll Leben*, pp. 140-141)

Relationships with both men are static, with no possibility of travel or experiencing the exotic countries she wishes to visit.   In such a situation Haushofer sees no reconciliation between the static private sphere and the dynamic world.   Elisabeth's emigration to an English-speaking country after she "escapes" her marriage suggests that Haushofer does not view a European country such as Austria as part of the dynamic world.   Elisabeth rejects a life where her behavior would be determined by her environment. Haushofer, however, does not find a suitable solution, nor does she depict Elisabeth's life after she leaves Austria.   Twenty years later, Betty Russel intellectually reviews her behavior as a young woman and accepts her earlier emotional decision.

Reflection leading to a productive confrontation with a woman's role does not always have to happen retrospectively.   In Schwaiger's *Wie kommt das Salz ins Meer* (Why Is the Sea Salty), which begins with the narrator's marriage and ends shortly after her divorce when she returns to her parents, the narrator's constant reflection and growing critical stance lead her to leave her unhappy marriage.   The narrator views what is going on around her, seeing herself as a person outside herself.   In the opening scene, her family is preparing to go to her wedding.   As if watching a home movie of the wedding preparations, the narrator describes what is going on around her without initially bringing herself into the picture in the "I" form.   The narrator then changes her focus from describing the hectic scene (where the major concern of the mother, father, and grandmother is appearance), to entering her thoughts through a statement of the father: "Come on now, father is saying, or have you reconsidered?" (*Wie kommt das Salz ins Meer*, p. 9).   Here, the narrator switches the focus to herself and thinks:

> And what if I've reconsidered?   If we call and leave the message that we're not coming.   Perhaps sometime later, but not today. I've thought about it, I don't want to because I actually never wanted it, because you tricked me.   Because you said: Only a formality.   And now you're all up in arms, taking it completely seriously, are all against me.   Don't be afraid, my child, you said, it's only tradition. (*Wie kommt das Salz ins Meer*, pp. 9-10)

In her thoughts she confronts her own behavior and treats herself as a partner in a dialogue, and thus turns to a productive war against her stereotypes.

From the outset of the novel she is inclined to eschew a role without meaning for her, and her reflections gradually lead her to the point where she takes herself seriously.   "Ok, what's wrong with you?   I think I'm missing a meaning to life.   Surprised looks from Rolf and Blitz: Aren't we any?   Responsibility, an interest, that's what I need" (*Wie kommt das Salz ins Meer*, Why Is the Sea Salty, p. 131).   The contrast between past and present tense in this statement illustrates that her development is an ongoing process, in which she describes past actions in the context of her more critical consciousness.   By examining her own behavior and juxtaposing people's statements next to their behavior, she gains distance from herself and learns to trust her own perceptions and question the monolithic view of the world as presented to her by her immediate surroundings:

> But I sometimes ask myself if we don't have different brains, if we don't just imagine that we see the same colors, for example, how does one think who's colorblind? Do we all smell the same smell? I also asked myself that earlier, says Rolf, and I decided to assume that we all see and smell the same and so on and so forth and good-night. But I often assume, Rolf, that there isn't a universe and no people either—that I only imagine it all. (*Wie kommt das Salz ins Meer*, p. 156)

Her critical, questioning posture is a step toward emancipation—a productive step in a war against stereotypes.

Because she rejects the view of the world presented to her, she also begins to accept her own perceptions as valid:

> Since we've been married he always says: I must. And another thing Rolf, yesterday I made an important face while drying dishes. I pretended as if I were doing something very important, and all at once I did indeed appear important to myself, and drying dishes appeared to me the most important thing in the world! (*Wie kommt das Salz ins Meer*, pp. 156-157)

Even though this is still within the sphere of house and home, she has caught the essence of psychological liberation: *her* ideas become a world for her. After this, she both accepts her perceptions and questions former ones. "Rolf, I think that I have always admired the wrong thing" (*Wie kommt das Salz ins Meer*, p. 159). This is a model for the newer, more productive struggle. She gradually modifies her behavior from an inwardly directed struggle to her confrontation with Rolf and her past behavior.[35]

Written later than either *Eine Handvoll Leben* (A Handful of Life) or *Wie kommt das Salz ins Meer*—and perhaps reflecting the legal changes outlined in chapter two—Frischmuth's *Amy oder die Metamorphose* (1978, Amy or the Metamorphosis) and *Kai und die Liebe zu den Modellen* (1979, Kai and the Love of Models) concerns Amy, who is much more self-assured and willing to disagree with Klemens from the outset of the relationship. Productive conflict is obviously becoming desirable. Unlike many of the other fictional women, Amy is at no point prepared to place herself behind Klemens: her relationship with Klemens is characterized by positive struggle from its outset. In the early days of their relationship, after Klemens discovers her diary, they discuss the effect her writing could have on their relationship. Klemens, afraid of the consequences, asks her to consider giving up writing before she even starts:

> You can still decide, decide differently. You can still leave it at concocting comedies for me, whose single, but highly considerate audience I will be. Wouldn't that be something for you? Klemens took her chin and forced her to look at him. Couldn't you be content with that at all?[36]

He wants the traditional battle, with woman in the position of powerlessness. Amy, however, demands a partnership, not a relationship where she would be the woman behind the man.   Moreover, because of her unwillingness to place herself behind Klemens, her desire for independence and partnership, and Klemens's reluctance to sacrifice his time (which becomes crucial once they have a child), conflict cannot be avoided or suppressed at his request. Klemens, unlike Toni (*Eine Handvoll Leben*) or Rolf (*Wie kommt das Salz ins Meer*) does manage to explain his behavior and the conflict he has been going through in a letter to Amy Stern, but only after he has left Vienna for professional reasons without consulting Amy first (*Kai und die Liebe zu den Modellen*, pp. 165-167).   Thus, despite Amy's sense of an optional, constructive battle, Klemens puts his career before personal considerations and equates professional success with personal worth, thereby assuming a traditionally male position and battle stance.   This conservatism is brought to light even more when he asks Amy to give up her work in Vienna to follow him.   Amy, realizing that such a life would not be enough for her, continues to fight for her rights.   "I don't understand why I should leave here.   The reason would be solely Klemens.   My, our love for him.   And there where he now is we'd have only him" (*Kai und die Liebe zu den Modellen*, p. 196).   She demands a rethinking of the same rules, but because of society, cannot get her way.

Haushofer's Elisabeth/Betty, Schwaiger's "I," and Frischmuth's Amy, after confronting either themselves or partners, refuse to place themselves behind the men, "winning" at least one aspect of the war in relationships. However the men fail to question their behavior or traditional sex roles. The women have either gained or maintained their independence, but society has not been educated, and further relationships will still be doomed to failure.   Despite legal reform, alternatives in battle remain at the individual level.

Relations to Men, Relations to Women

Concomitant with the critical process of women vis-à-vis men, the authors portray an ongoing problem of women's identification with other women.   As women become more critical of their partners' and their own behavior, they grow more aware of the commonality of women's experience. Haushofer's Anna, and the women in Frischmuth's collection of short stories *Haschen nach Wind*, (Chasing the Wind) do not make connections between themselves and other women.   In this literature a problem long ignored is finally articulated, even if obliquely.   In writing a collection of four short stories with women as the protagonists in male-female relationships, for example, Frischmuth suggests a connection between the single isolated woman and women in general.   In Jelinek's *Die Liebhaberinnen* (Women in Love), Brigitte and Paula do not reflect on their situation, nor do they make connections between themselves and other women.   The author, however, structures the entire book with the goal of exposing persistent patterns that cross class lines to keep women apart.   Solidarity is impossible in the world Jelinek depicts, as the plot shows; but the narrative technique points to the commonality of women in their parallel situations.

In similar situations, which draw attention not only to men, but to women, Haushofer's Annette and Elisabeth/Betty, and Bachmann's Franza, Fanny, and the "I" originally view themselves as unique but draw larger

connections between themselves and other women.   Exemplary is Annette's
and Franza's behavior: both compare themselves to their husbands' former
wives.   Annette even becomes disturbed by the ghost of Gregor's first wife
in their relationship.   It is not jealousy that upsets her, but Gregor's
dismissal of his former wife as hysterical:

> Yesterday at the theater.   In the intermission Gregor met his ex-
> wife, who was with some other people in the lobby. . . . On the
> drive home I asked Gregor why he divorced.   He looked at me
> surprised and explained then that his wife had always been
> hysterical and one day she maintained she couldn't live with him
> any longer. . . . Suddenly, I was cold.   His clear, smooth face and
> the face of that woman, her hungry look.   I should never have met
> her, everything suddenly appeared so hopeless and muddled to me.
> (*Die Tapetentür*, The Wallpapered Door, p. 146)

Annette sees this woman as a projection of her future self.   Like the woman
before her, she will leave no traces in Gregor's life.   She realizes too late
that to struggle successfully in the marriage war, she must be conscious not
only of the man's world, but also of women's positions.
    In a parallel situation Franza (*Der Fall Franza*, The Case Franza),
wanting to be unique among Jordan's wives, initially fails to see similarities
between herself and Jordan's former wives.   At first she is incapable of
viewing Jordan as the cause for the disintegration of his former marriages,
thereby overlooking the position of her predecessors:

> Only now have I asked myself about the other women and why
> they all disappeared without a sound, why the one never leaves her
> house anymore and why the other turned on the gas, and now I'm
> the third with this name, I was the third, she corrected herself, was.
> It's as if a spotlight went on over the entire time which laid in
> darkness—everything is lying there, naked, awful, indescribable,
> evidence not to be overlooked, and how willingly I believed they
> were dumb, umcomprehending, defective, unworthy creatures, who
> punished themselves with a descent into silence for their failure in a
> higher morality, an authority, a standard, which I wanted to make
> my own. (*Werke*, III, 400)

Franza originally believed she had some special quality which attracted
Jordan.   She had set herself apart from the other women, whom she
originally perceived as rivals.   She realizes too late that women are
interchangeable for Jordan, and she and his former wives are his victims.
As de Beauvoir summarizes about the psychology of such an isolated woman,
"In a state of uncertainty, every woman is a rival, a danger.   Love destroys
the possibility of friendship with other women because the woman in love is
shut off in her lover's universe; jealousy increases her isolation and thereby
narrows her dependence."[37] Traditional marriage isolates the women; they see
their situation as unique and perceive other women as rivals, cementing
themselves further in their isolation.   Franza is thus typical in ignoring until
too late the possibility of a woman's group truth.
    The very fact that Haushofer's Elisabeth/Betty, Schwaiger's "I," and

Frischmuth's Amy make the connection between their situation and that of other women reveals that this critical analysis is necessary for changing their situation.   The women must compare themselves to women and view their problems as typical.   No matter to what degree this happens, however, only Amy Stern seeks the friendship and support of other women.   In contrast to this positive view of women's commonality, Haushofer's Betty can conjure up only a picture of a broken woman who ceases to exist as an individual when she speculates what her life would have looked like had she stayed with Toni:

> Betty imagined what her life would have been like without the brutal interruption from outside.   Perhaps she would have once and for all resigned herself to it and become with the years a friendly, slightly absent-minded woman, who walks with her child, reads novels, receives guests, arranges flowers in vases and feels life slipping away peacefully and without regrets.   One of the many women whose will has been broken and who doesn't really exist anymore. (*Eine Handvoll Leben*, A Handful of Life, p. 143)

Her drastic measure has saved her from what she sees as the bad, isolated fate of many women.   Although she does eventually make a connection, she continues to see herself as different from most women, indicating continued ambivalence in her feelings toward her sex and her incapability of finding community with women.

The narrator of *Wie kommt das Salz ins Meer* (Why Is the Sea Salty), frustrated and unhappy in her marriage with Rolf but not yet able to assert herself, also envisions lonely balconies full of women, all caught in men's relationship games:

> Whenever I desert the marriage bed at night, quietly, in order not to wake Rolf, Blitz comes quietly, in order not to wake Rolf, trotting toward me out of the guest bathroom.   He protects me on my wanderings through the dark rooms.   We feel our way through the kitchen to the kitchen balcony.   Cement wall.   One can't see the other women who, perhaps, are also standing on their balconies and would like to jump or fly. (*Wie kommt das Salz ins Meer*, p. 85)

Even with this realization, the narrator's possible ally, Hilde, becomes her rival once she becomes involved with Hilde's husband.   The narrator makes connections between her life and that of other women, but the connections remain only mental reflections, not to be translated into reality.

In both *Amy oder die Metamorphose* and *Kai und die Liebe zu den Modellen*, Frischmuth portrays a community of women who share their diverse and common experiences.   In these cases, the experiences of women are not seen as monolithic, but as sharing certain traits due to the structure of society.   Frischmuth thus not only portrays strong independent women, but also women who have not reached a critical level of consciousness and continue to be dissatisfied in their relationships.   They have community as refuge, not as a possibility of changing the structure of relationship games. In Amy's conversations with her women friends, a common basis of understanding and frustration in their relationships is depicted. Pola, the young actress who lives in a commune with midgets and circus freaks, explains how even a group outside the normal constraints of society holds onto traditional values:

> And since I've moved in with him into this trailer society with all the fire-eaters, stiltwalkers, and freaks, I have to justify myself for the time I'm not there. And we don't even have children. But when Madeleine, the dwarf with the hypnotic look, and Edwin the Strongman are invited for tea at five o'clock, the entire group takes offence if I'm not there; a woman belongs in the wagon during the day. (*Kai und die Liebe zu den Modellen*, p. 102)

An alternative lifestyle does not mean a consciousness of the politics in relationships. Amy and her friend Maya discuss their love relationships with men, while Helene, Amy's editor, encourages her to talk about her relationship with Klemens. Their experiences may not be the same, but they are similar, and the ability to articulate the problem predicates change and breaks down isolation between women.

Amy, in thinking about her relationship with Klemens, draws a vague connection between herself and other women, "I compare my life to Klemens' and I ask myself in what way do the scales have to be tipped that the world would accept this comparison as possible and play it out in endless variations" (*Kai und die Liebe zu den Modellen*, p. 95). Her life, seen in this light, is one of many lives whose scales are tipped in the male's favor and accepted as the norm.

This ability to view oneself as a part of a greater whole is concomitant with the development and discussion surrounding women's rights in the seventies, with two exceptions. In Haushofer's *Eine Handvoll Leben* (1955, A Handful of Life) Elisabeth/Betty makes the connection between her life and those of other women, but the realization does not ultimately lead her out of her isolation. She chooses a solution which really cannot be viewed as a solution, because in faking her death and leaving Austria, she chooses a course of action that is not viable for readers. In contrast, in Jelinek's *Die Liebhaberinnen* (Women in Love), the characters do not make connections between themselves and other members of their sex, but the structure of the book and the narrative technique indicate similarities in women's lives. Despite the reforms of the seventies, Jelinek feels that there are still fewer options in society for women—particularly for working class women—than for men. Capitalist and patriarchal society is based on competition and the violence of the competition, no matter how many laws have been changed. These women are still trapped in the roles of powerlessness because of their own consciousness and isolation.

War, Violence, and Struggle in Language

One further level of the battle between the sexes is confronted in the works of the writers discussed here. In this women's fiction male control extends to control of women's language. Moreover, women's relationship to language is directly correlated with their ability or inability to terminate unhappy relationships, perhaps as a corollary to their inability to conceive of optional games. The writers' concern with the power of language thus acknowledges that language is not divorced from social reality and can be used as a means of either oppression or liberation.

Haushofer points to the male's power to name and demonstrates that the consequences are devastating for women. For example, Gregor does not hesitate to call his first wife hysterical, and Annette is frightened by his quick judgement because she realizes she may find herself in the same position. Even before she meets her husband's first wife, she dreads the thought of being labelled hysterical, a word defined by him with no consideration of the common reality of women's experience. Because of her fear, she avoids asking Gregor to turn down the radio. "Of course he would have turned it down or even off if she had wished, but she simply didn't dare ask him. The thought that he could consider her nervous or hysterical was unbearable for her" (*Die Tapetentür*, The Wallpapered Door, p. 136). After their son's death, she pictures Gregor telling his "next" wife that his second wife had been hysterical. "For a moment she had the vision of a big healthy man looking up from the steering wheel and saying to his wife: 'I don't know, my dear, she was probably hysterical'" (*Die Tapetentür*, p. 228). She thus realizes that Gregor's language portrays his opinions and insights as truth, and so it is perceived by the world—the community of men.

Margret's ("Bleiben lassen," Let It Be) similar inability to articulate her desires both contributes to and results from her powerlessness and lack of independently controlled language in her relationship with Alex. Unable to find the words for her feelings, she is prevented from venting her anger, although her inner censorship is not without external reasons. Still, the narrator cannot quite put her finger on the cause of Margret's feeling ill-at-ease:

> It seldom happened that she really took these words in her mouth, like the most of her attempts to defend herself remained silent. As if a particular sort of shame prevented her from saying out loud whatever was bothering her again, or perhaps it was the fear of being misunderstood and exposing herself once and for all. ("Bleiben lassen," p. 88)

As a woman Margret's feelings are not legitimate in a male-dominated society, which leads to a sense of embarrassment or fear. The power of language is suggested here in the idea of "protecting herself." The author suggests the impossibility of Margret's ability to use language in her favor: "And it happened that she sought to master her resentment with sentences in talking to herself" ("Bleiben lassen," p. 87). As a woman she cannot speak "masterfully." Unable to formulate her anger, Margret then lets her anger devour her. When she finally decides to confront Alex after learning of his affair, she rehearses the words and phrases she plans to use, since she is well aware of her inferiority in language vis-à-vis Alex:

> She had played through all variations of her big scene, which came to her often only after hours of deliberation, weighing word against word, gesture against gesture, and memorizing specific sentences, more precisely, specific questions, in their exact order. She didn't want to take the chance that she wouldn't know how to continue, that he would confuse her with something with which she

hadn't reckoned because of insufficient preparation, that he would gain the upper hand and put her off with the usual display. ("Bleiben lassen," pp. 103-104)

Despite this veneer of strength due to her careful rehearsal, when she confronts Alex, she chooses a pose of weakness. Her approach demonstrates her underlying lack of confidence inherent in her victim position. Alex's response demonstrates how women are discriminated against linguistically, a general phenomenon described by Senta Trömel-Plötz: "Discrimination often consists in how a woman is spoken to or not spoken to, how her contribution to conversation is dismissed, not heard, misunderstood, misquoted, interrupted, and ignored, how she is made ridiculous, patronized or dismissed and not least of all, how she is talked to."[38] As a typical male in control of even the pieces with which the game is played, Alex shows himself master of the situation, taking command with gestures and words, eschewing his guilt and placing it on Margret, refusing to take her seriously. When Margret fails to name her oppression, Frischmuth portrays the woman's ambivalent relationship to language, which must result from the current structure of male-female relationships.

Jordan (*Der Fall Franza*, The Case Franza) and Marek (*Requiem für Fanny Goldmann*, Requiem for Fanny Goldmann) use language to destroy women in the most devastating examples of male control of language in relationships. Ivan (*Malina*) is not involved in such destructive pursuits, but nonetheless he fails to accept the "I"'s perception of reality as legitimate and in effect rejects her reality. Appalled by the narrator's "obsession" with murder and death in her writing, Ivan dismisses a literature dealing with such topics. Ivan prescribes what the narrator should and should not write, denying her the legitimacy of her experience (*Werke*, III, 53-54).

Even Schwaiger's *Wie kommt das Salz ins Meer* (Why Is the Sea Salty), itself the gradual articulation process of a young woman, which marks a positive step towards establishing herself as an autonomous person, still shows an overriding problem with language. The narrator's struggle to assert herself is reflected in her difficulty articulating her anger and then not being taken seriously. She too states that as a woman her words are treated differently from a man's:

> He lets his hand wander, undoes, asks whether he can turn the light on, places pointed kisses on my skin which cannot protect itself because if a woman doesn't want to be kissed she has to justify it in detail and after she's done so, she gets a kiss for it because it's so touching when women try to explain something, because a woman's a woman. Men simply say no, and if they don't want to they don't have to. I say: No. The game begins. (*Wie kommt das Salz ins Meer*, p. 26)

The rules of society's game thus are so structured that Rolf cannot respect the narrator's perception of her own situation. Rather, he can manipulate her by pointing out how empty he perceives her words to be. "I can say nothing because he squeezes out everything that I confide in him. He gives me back the peel: Look, just so empty was your statement. Say something else, I want to test it. Look here, once again it's nothing" (*Wie kommt das*

Salz ins Meer, p. 38). She is thus trapped in a vicious circle in which her words and perceptions have no weight because her husband does not take her seriously, which is intensified by the fact that she initially does not take herself seriously. "My husband throws words out and they fall there where he wants them to. My words have no weight. They float murkily in space. I can catch them all again" (*Wie kommt das Salz ins Meer*, p. 79). However unsure this young woman is, she realizes that she does not want to be in a relationship with Rolf, and her conversations with herself make it possible for her to articulate her stance and leave the relationship. She can use words for herself but not as tools in the game.

As a slight variation, Jelinek describes in *Die Liebhaberinnen* both women and men who cannot articulate themselves. Thus, their inability serves to maintain capitalist and patriarchal systems in which traditional man/woman war games transpire. Not only is their own reality denied through their inability to articulate, but as Jelinek implies, the possibility for change can not exist until a group can define its oppression.

Conclusion

Three general patterns emerge in examining the male-female relationships in the works of the five writers, revealing the political nature of heterosexual relationships and the interaction between public and private spheres in the positive development of women's struggle in the relationships. First, in Frischmuth's "Bleiben lassen" (Let It Be) and "Baum des vergessenen Hundes" (Tree of the Forgotten Dog), Haushofer's *Wir töten Stella* (We're Killing Stella) and *Die Mansarde* (The Attic), and Jelinek's *Die Liebhaberinnen* (Women in Love), the female protagonists find themselves in unhappy relationships. Second, in Haushofer's *Die Tapetentür* (The Wallpapered Door) and Bachmann's *Todesarten* (Types of Death) the women are either "murdered" or emotionally crippled in a relationship that eventually dissolves. Third, in Haushofer's *Eine Handvoll Leben* (A Handful of Life), Schwaiger's *Wie kommt das Salz ins Meer* (Why Is the Sea Salty), and Frischmuth's "Unzeit" (Bad Timing), *Amy oder die Metamorphose* (Amy or the Metamorphosis), *Kai und die Liebe zu den Modellen* (Kai and the Love of Models), and *Bindungen* (Bonds) the women successfully terminate their marriage/love relationships. The critique of male-female relationships implies the need for radical changes in society; however, women who do break off their relationships choose individual solutions improving their situation, but making no changes in the general status of women.

Why some women are able to break off emotionally unsatisfactory relationships and others cannot is not always clear. It depends in part on women's real options, the individual personalities of the fictional characters, and the situations of the writers themselves. But the war all five writers specify is conducted in similar terms: whether the men are labelled fascists (*Der Fall Franza*, The Case Franza) or murderers (*Wir töten Stella*), or are seen merely as victims of the socialization process like Rolf (*Wie kommt das Salz ins Meer*), or Klemens (*Kai und die Liebe zu den Modellen*), men still are at an advantage in the love and marriage relationships that develop into war-like situations because of the male-centeredness of society. The female protagonists expect personal enrichment from love and/or marriage. This ranges from the mystical healing power that Bachmann's "I" in *Malina* hopes for to the true partnership that Amy Stern desires in Frischmuth's last two novels of her trilogy. The men, on the other hand, view the liaisons in terms which make impossible the type of relationship the women desire. They often view their wives as their possessions, as does Richard in Haushofer's *Wir töten Stella* or Theo in Frischmuth's "Baum des vergessenen Hundes." In extreme cases, such as in Bachmann's *Der Fall Franza* or in Haushofer's *Wir töten Stella*, the male protagonists appear compelled to destroy women. Because of unfulfilled expectations, suffering is an integral element in the female protagonists' love experience. The men, on the other hand, do not place the same importance on relationships, and do not, therefore, suffer to the same degree as the women, if at all. Rather than the "mutual vulnerability" that Firestone defines as an essential component of a healthy egalitarian relationship, the relationships in the fiction of these five authors are seen in terms of gamesmanship, role-playing, or out-and-out war. The rules, script, or battle plan are defined by the male, and the female often has to second-guess him to keep up with the action.

The women's economic dependence on their husbands is another card the men hold in the game against their wives. From the earlier works (Haushofer's *Wir töten Stella*) to the later works (Jelinek's *Die Liebhaberinnen*), the male is always more economically independent. The writers point out that the women's weaker economic position, often directly related to the women's reticence to leave or avoid a relationship, is yet another means of controlling women in the war described.

When the basis of the marriage dissolves and the women remain married, they often choose socially acceptable outlets to vent their dissatisfaction. As in the cases of Anna (Haushofer's *Wir töten Stella*) and Margret (Frischmuth's "Bleiben lassen"), they direct their dissatisfaction inward, harming no one but themselves. The men, on the other hand, continue with their lives, ignoring the problems of the women. Only after the women articulate both their own behavior and that of their partners do the women have a chance in the battle. The struggle developing out of their reflections allows them the critical distance they need to examine their behavior and seek alternatives. Coinciding with the critical process is the women's identification with other women. The female protagonists thus make the first step toward leaving their isolation behind.

Parallel to the war, violence, and struggle in the dynamic of the relationship, is the war, violence, and struggle present in language. When the female protagonists cannot articulate their problems, it appears nonexistent in the eyes of the rest of the world. When they speak, the female protagonists often find that their words do not have the same weight as men's, and they must struggle to be taken seriously. At the point at which they articulate their feelings, such as in the case of Schwaiger's narrator in *Wie kommt das Salz ins Meer*, the seeds of rebellion are sewn.

Although the protagonists of such works as Schwaiger's *Wie kommt das Salz ins Meer* and Frischmuth's *Kai und die Liebe zu den Modellen* find the strength to leave their relationships, the prospect of new relationships without the manipulations is not forthcoming. No male protagonists have undergone a comparable metamorphosis, and prospects of the elimination of the male advantage in heterosexual relationships are dim.

Notes

1.   Ingeborg Bachmann, *Werke*, 4 vols. (Munich: Piper, 1982), III, p. 236. All further references to Bachmann's works appear in the text.

2.   Kate Millett, *Sexual Politics* (Garden City, New York: Doubleday and Company, Inc., 1970), p. 23. See also Zillah R. Eisenstein, *The Radical Future of Liberal Feminism* (New York, London: Longman, 1981), p. 19.

3.   Examples of this theme can be found in:

Jean Jacques Rousseau, *Emile*, trans. Barbara Foxley (London: J. M. Dent and Sons, 1911), originally published 1762;

Johann Wolfgang von Goethe, *Wilhelm Meisters Lehrjahre*, in *Werke*, VII, 5th ed. (Hamburg: C. Wegner Verlag, 1962), originally published 1795-1796;

Johann Wolfgang von Goethe, *Die Leiden des jungen Werther*, in *Werke*, VI (Hamburg: C. Wegner Verlag, 1951), originally published 1774;

Friedrich Schlegel, *Lucinde*, in Hans Eichner, ed., *Dichtungen*, V (Munich, Paderborn, Vienna: Ferdinand Schöningh, 1962), originally published 1799;

Novalis, *Heinrich von Ofterdingen*, in Paul Kluckhohn and Richard Samuel, eds., *Schriften*, I (Stuttgart: W. Kohlhammer Verlag, 1960), originally published 1802.

For a discussion of the female as complement, particularly in the eighteenth century, see Sylvia Bovenschen, *Die imaginierte Weiblichkeit: Exemplarische Untersuchungen zu kulturgeschichtlichen und literarischen Präsentationsformen des Weiblichen* (Frankfurt am Main: Suhrkamp, 1979).

4.   See Heidi Rosenbaum, *Formen der Familie* (Frankfurt am Main: Suhrkamp, 1982), pp. 285-293, for a discussion of the development of marriage for love among the bourgeoisie in the eighteenth century.

5.   Margret Eifler, "Ingeborg Bachmann: Malina," *Modern Austrian Literature*, 12, No. 3/4 (1979), 379.

6.   Marlen Haushofer, *Die Tapetentür* (Hamburg, Vienna: Paul Zsolnay Verlag, 1957), p. 85. All further references appear in the text.

7.   Ingeborg Bachmann, *Wir müssen wahre Sätze finden: Gespräche und Interviews*, Christine Koschel and Inge von Weidenbaum, eds. (Munich, Zurich: Piper Verlag, 1983), p. 109.

8.   The "I"'s use of language to describe herself and her feelings when it is clear that her relationship with Ivan is dying is reminiscent of Christ's Passion. See the *Werke*, III, 173.

9.   Elfriede Jelinek, *Die Liebhaberinnen* (Reinbek bei Hamburg: Rowohlt, 1975), p. 21. All further references appear in the text.

10.   Simone de Beauvoir, *The Second Sex*, H. M. Parshley, trans. and ed. (New York: Vintage-Random House, 1974), pp. 713-714.

11.   Tobe Joyce Levin, "Political Ideology and Aesthetics in Neo-Feminist German Fiction: Verena Stefan, Elfriede Jelinek, Margot Schroeder," Diss. Cornell University 1979. See particularly, chapter three for her discussion of *Die Liebhaberinnen*. Here she discusses the connection between capitalism and the ideology of love. Particularly interesting is the connection Levin draws between the book's content and its formal appearance on p. 190, where she states, "On the cover we find the dress, the veil, the flowers, the cake, and the pork roast. In the text we find the hatred, the brutality, the economic compulsion behind the pageantry."

12. For a more general discussion of the connections between the media and patriarchal structures, see Jelinek's essay "Die endlose Unschuldigkeit," in *Die endlose Unschuldigkeit* (Munich: Schwiftinger Galerie-Verlag, 1980), pp. 49-82.

13. Marlen Haushofer, *Wir töten Stella* (Vienna: Bergland Verlag, 1958), p. 28. All further references appear in the text.

14. Barbara Frischmuth, *Rückkehr zum verläufigen Ausgangs-punkt/Haschen nach Wind* (Munich: Deutscher Taschenbuch Verlag, 1978), p. 127. All further references to "Baum des vergessenen Hundes" and "Bleiben lassen," also in the collection, appear in the text. *Haschen nach Wind*, a collection of four stories, was first published by Residenz Verlag in 1974.

15. de Beauvoir, pp. 742-743.

16. Ingeborg Bachmann, "Gier," in Hans Höller, ed., *Der Dunkle Schatten, dem ich schon seit Anfang folge* (Vienna, Munich: Löcker Verlag, 1982), pp. 17-61. Ingeborg Bachmann, *Werke*, III contains the unfinished novel cycle and an explanation of how the editors came to choose *Todesarten* as the title of the cycle.

17. Bachmann, *Wir müssen wahre Sätze finden*, p. 93.

18. Ellen Summerfield, *Ingeborg Bachmann: Die Auflösung der Figur in ihrem Roman* Malina (Bonn: Bouvier Verlag Herbert Grundmann, 1976), p. 44.

19. Some explanation for the motivation behind the murder/suicide appears on a would-be publicity flyer: "His [Rapatz's] greed is greed for money, power, possession of women, life. However, this greed destroys the people who are in his power and it also destroys him in the end." Quoted in Höller, *Der dunkle Schatten*, p. 61.

20. Christa Gürtler, in her article " 'Der Fall Franza': Eine Reise durch eine Krankheit und ein Buch über ein Verbrechen," in *Der dunkle Schatten*, p. 75, writes, "Franza's attacks, trembling, convulsions, escape from the body, demonstrate quite clearly the connection with her lack of speech."

21. Brigitte Schwaiger, *Wie kommt das Salz ins Meer* (Vienna, Hamburg: Paul Zsolnay Verlag, 1977), p. 157. All further references appear in the text.

22. Barbara Frischmuth, *Kai und die Liebe zu den Modellen* (Salzburg, Vienna: Residenz Verlag, 1979), p. 111. All further references appear in the text.

23. Susan Brownmiller, *Against our Will: Men, Women and Rape* (New York: Simon and Schuster, 1975), p. 360.

24. Bachmann, *Wir müssen wahre Sätze finden*, p. 144.

25. For a discussion of fascism as a personal as well as a political phenomenon, see Klaus Theweleit, *Männerphantasien* (Rowohlt: Reinbek bei Hamburg, 1980), I, especially pp. 226-227 (originally published by Roter Stern Verlag of Frankfurt am Main, 1977). The first of two volumes has appeared in English as *Male Fantasies*, trans. Stephen Conway (Minneapolis: University of Minnesota Press, 1987).

26. See Bachmann's introduction to a piece she read from *Der Fall Franza* concerning fascism gone underground and the role of literature in exposing it, *Werke*, III, 341-343.

27. Jacqueline Vansant, "Gespräch mit Elfriede Jelinek," *Deutsche Bücher*, 15, No. 1 (1985), 5.

28. Shulamith Firestone, *The Dialectic of Sex* (New York: Bantam, 1972), p. 130.

29. Evelyn Torton Beck and Biddy Martin, "Westdeutsche Frauenliteratur der siebziger Jahre," in Paul Michael Lützeler and Egon Schwarz, eds., *Deutsche Literatur in der Bundesrepublik seit 1965* (Königstein/Ts.: Athenäum, 1980), p. 140.

30. *The Random House College Dictionary* (New York, Toronto: Random House, 1973), p. 821.

31. de Beauvoir, p. 147.

32. de Beauvoir, p. 724.

33. Marlen Haushofer, *Eine Handvoll Leben* (Vienna: Paul Zsolnay Verlag, 1955), p. 129. All further references appear in the text.

34. Marlen Haushofer, *Die Mansarde* (Hamburg, Dusseldorf: Claassen, 1969), pp. 8-9.

35. Sandra Frieden, "The Left-Handed Compliment: Perspectives and Stereotypes in Criticism," in Susan L. Cocalis and Kay Goodman, eds., *Beyond the Eternal Feminine: Critical essays on Women and German Literature* (Stuttgart: Akademischer Verlag-Hans-Dieter Heinz, 1982), p. 317.

36. Barbara Frischmuth, *Amy oder die Metamorphose* (Salzburg, Vienna: Residenz Verlag, 1978), p. 176.

37. de Beauvoir, p. 737.

38. Senta Trömel-Plötz, *Frauensprache: Sprache der Veränderung* (Frankfurt am Main: Fischer, 1982), p. 37. See also Luise F. Pusch, *Das Deutsche als Männersprache* (Frankfurt am Main: Suhrkamp, 1984) and Senta Trömel-Plötz, ed., *Gewalt durch Sprache* (Frankfurt am Main: Fischer Taschenbuch Verlag, 1985).

5

Only Contrasts:
Relationships between Women

"the women discover nothing in common among themselves, only contrasts."

Elfriede Jelinek, *Die Liebhaberinnen*, (Women in Love), p. 24.

In contrast to the emphasis placed on the relationships between women and men, the number of pages the five writers devote to friendship and love relationships between women is indeed sparse. As chapters three and four demonstrate, when the fictional women center their lives around men, they find it either impossible or almost impossible to establish a healthy sense of self; they experience love and marriage relationships with men as singularly negative; and they develop a negative attitude toward their own sex. This being the case, in most of the works relationships between women are rarely presented, as was shown in chapter four. Only when the women cease to center their world around men, when they cultivate independence and develop a more affirmative opinion of the female sex, is a basis for lasting friendship and political solidarity imaginable.

With its rejection of traditional sex-roles and the expression of women's lives as a legitimate topic of literature, the women's movement provided the basis for the affirmation of positive relationships between females and established the importance of female solidarity. However in the literature of the five Austrian women under consideration here, a simple transformation from negative relationships to solely positive relationships cannot be found. In fact, even after the mid-seventies there are relatively few works with women's friendships or alliances central to the narrative.[1] This lack in Austrian literature is all the more striking when one considers the number of books from the two Germanies in which female friendships or love relationships play an important role. Examples include Christa Reinig's *Entmannung* (Emasculation), Verena Stefan's *Häutungen* (Shedding), Margot Schroeder's *Ich stehe meine Frau* (Act like a Woman), Christa Wolf's *Nachdenken über Christa T.* (The Quest for Christa T.), and Irmtraud Morgner's *Leben und Abenteuer der Trobadora Beatriz nach Zeugnissen ihrer Spielfrau Laura* (Life and Adventures of the Troubadour Beatriz according to her Minstrel Laura).[2] In contrast, within Austrian literature Frischmuth's trilogy is more or less the only major work with an explicitly positive portrayal of lasting female relationships. There exists, moreover, a difference between the portrayal of both rivalry and friendship between women in the works of Haushofer and Bachmann, as compared to portrayals of those emotions in Frischmuth and Jelinek. In the earlier works of all the authors, there is an implied critique of female rivalry and in their later works, an explicit critique.

Women's Ambivalent Feelings Toward Their Own Sex

In their treatment of women's ambivalence toward their own sex, Haushofer and Bachmann describe conditions prohibitive to female alliances in fictional situations in which their women are typically uncomfortable with traditional sex-roles and do not identify with other women, while still being critical of the male world. The characters are aware that they have grown up in a world in which their sex has been degraded and women's lives trivialized, a world with which they do not and cannot identify. However since they remain critical of the male world they suffer extreme isolation. The critical view of the male world thus indicates a "muted" consciousness on the part of the authors—"muted," because they were only able to protest, but not break out of the situation, as shown in the previous chapter. These portrayals perhaps reflect the situations in which the writers themselves were caught: they were writing essentially in a vacuum, as both the reviews and booksales would indicate; they, too, found themselves similarly isolated from the public visibility.

Although the portrayal of the women's ambivalent feelings does not form the center of any of the novels, the phenomenon represents a transitional phase from total acceptance of the male-centered world to a critical stance towards it, and as such captures the typical feelings of many women of the fifties and sixties. The authors do not provide solutions, but at least their critical stance toward the male-centered world points to the directions in which the typical woman would have to go to break down her isolation.

In Haushofer's *Eine Handvoll Leben* (1955, A Handful of Life) and *Die Tapetentür* (1957, The Wallpapered Door), the protagonists suffer because they identify more with men than with women, realizing at the same time that by virtue of their sex they will never be "full-fledged" members of the men's world for reasons shown in the last chapter. Annette (*Die Tapetentür*) writes in her diary of her uneasiness with women:

> At exclusive ladies' gatherings I am sometimes overcome by a fear of my own sex. It appears to me then that I could more easily bear to drink and play cards all night with smugglers, and I would feel safer and more comfortable in their company. Taking these judging glances and saccharine insults is more than I can bear, since I can't pay them back in kind. I know why many women are like that and not otherwise and my sympathy and understanding should be stronger than my fear and aversion.[3]

Although Annette senses the reason for her general dislike of women in the conditioning of society, she feels that there is no possibility to break down this barrier, which leads to little desire on her part to even try to do so.

Again the man/woman dichotomy has ripple effects into the purely female sphere.

Similarly Elisabeth Pfluger/Betty Russel in Haushofer's *Eine Handvoll Leben* (1955, A Handful of Life) feels more at ease with men than with women:

> That was one of the reasons why she had always felt more secure in dealing with men. They may have lied, too, but only with their mouths. Their bodies betrayed them, and Betty was sometimes surprised that it had not yet occurred to any of them to cover up their tracks as women do, with artificial scents and make-up.[4]

Betty thus also criticizes women's behavior as a means of hiding, finding it both detestable and foreign, just like an evil game. What she fails to realize is that women are forced into this position, and she does not ask why they feel compelled to cover up their true selves. She does not criticize the "ideal of beauty," which is held up to women by and for men. Rather she views this as women's effort to cover up their true selves, which in actuality they have not been allowed to develop. Therefore she has turned her internalization of male ideology against other women, in a profound ambivalence.

The feeling of such a female outsider from both the male and the female world is also captured in the description of the female protagonists' relationships to language in Haushofer's *Eine Handvoll Leben* (A Handful of Life) and Bachmann's short story "Ein Schritt nach Gomorrha" (1963, "A Step towards Gomorrah"), relationships acting as a metaphor for their position in society. Elisabeth/Betty, because of her desire to survive and gain personally, learns to be flexible and speak the language of men:

> Only much later did she comprehend and begin to learn everything about which one could talk with men. Her knowledge was, it is true, only superficial, but it was enough to understand the jargon of businessmen, politicians, and artists. She had the reputation of being a woman with whom one could talk like a man and from this time on her endeavors were crowned with some success. (*Eine Handvoll Leben*, p. 132)

Elisabeth/Betty does not use her skill to undermine the system and communicate with both women and men, but rather supports it and thereby separates herself from other women. She becomes the "token" woman in the "men's club," only tenuously connected with either group.

Similarly in Bachmann's "Ein Schritt nach Gomorrha," Charlotte observes her relationship to language and considers herself an outsider to both sexes:

> The language of men, insofar as it was applied to women, had been bad enough already and doubtful; but the language of women was even worse, more undignified—she had been shocked by it ever since she had seen through her mother, later through her sisters, girlfriends, and the wives of her men friends and had discovered that absolutely nothing, no insight, no observation corresponded to

this language, to the frivolous or pious maxims, the jumble of judgments and opinions or the sighed lament.

Charlotte liked looking at women; they frequently moved her or they pleased her visually, but so far as possible she avoided talking to them. She felt separated from them, from their language, their suffering, their heart.[5]

Again, in this early Austrian feminist work, it is women's language much more than men's that repulses Charlotte. She cannot identify with either women's trivialities or with men's brutalities, perhaps because she recognizes in it only the stereotypes she rejects.

Both Elisabeth/Betty and Charlotte display traits common to many women who cannot identify with their own sex or who view themselves as being outside or above other women. This attitude supports the male-centered system outlined in the previous chapter, isolating women from each other and hindering an analysis of their position in society as female individuals. However this women's critical view of society represents a first step in the transition towards a more far-reaching criticism or an "articulated" consciousness, which would take place later in the seventies.

Rivalry between Women

Ambivalence is the result when a female dismisses other females. Rivalry, in contrast, results when other women are acknowledged but concomitantly perceived as threats to the other's status. Both Haushofer and Jelinek examine female rivalry, each from a perspective that reflects the time in which their works were written. Haushofer's approach suggests an implicit criticism of rivalry; Jelinek's, an explicit one.

In her works *Wir töten Stella* (1958, We're Killing Stella) and *Die Tapetentür* (1957, The Wallpapered Door), Haushofer depicts what I term a "subversive rivalry." The "other women" in *Wir töten Stella* (an eighteen-year-old girl) and in *Die Tapetentür* (Gregor's first wife) act as agents who spur the protagonists to reflect on their own situations, prompting them to be critical of either their husbands' or their own behavior. Whereas the protagonists think they oppose the other women, neither the protagonist nor the reader really views one woman as wronged, with the other as interloper and the man as the sought-after prize. Instead, Haushofer as the author points to the necessity of breaking down the barriers between women and discovering commonalities between them. This type of rivalry thus serves to subvert the male system, which encourages a blind rivalry among women and discourages them from seeing commonalities among themselves.

In *Wir töten Stella* Stella, true to her name, throws further light on Anna's situation. Through Stella's intrusion, the fragile balance of the household is upset. Stella lives with her mother's schoolmate Anna and her family for the period of her commercial course, and her very presence disturbs or subverts the traditional male-centered family. Anna states, "Our household is arranged in such a manner that it doesn't tolerate an intruder or even a guest."[6] Anna, however, quickly adjusts to Stella's presence and returns to her "normal" life, even though the author has set up a situation in which another woman comes between a woman and her husband. Here, the wife Anna does not feel threatened by her husband's affair with Stella,

because neither Anna's existence nor her way of life is threatened.   In
actuality nothing in Anna's life has changed except that Richard finds his
next lover, Stella, in his own home.   Indeed not until after Stella's death,
which Anna is convinced was suicide, does Anna's normal routine change.
Stella's death thus acts as the catalyst that initiates Anna's critical
reflections which become the basis of the book.

In terms of Stella's death, Anna is not negatively disposed toward Stella.
She truly desires to help her, and even feels responsible because her
insistence that Richard take Stella to a party marked the beginning of the
affair.   But they never become allies and remain tacit rivals.   However it is
not until after Stella's suicide that Anna reaches a new awareness of her
own situation, her powerlessness, and the potential bond they were unable to
form.   Stella's death, more than her life, thus upsets Anna's life.   Her death
produces a split between Anna and her son Wolfgang, more dear to her than
her husband Richard.   "Stella will always stand between me and Wolfgang.
The time of childlike tenderness and trust is over.   Wolfgang loathes his
father and feels contempt for me because of my cowardice" (*Wir töten Stella*,
p. 12).   The parents' actions have destroyed the fragile balance within the
family and have exposed Anna's weakness, and their child must necessarily
evaluate them negatively.

In terms of her own image in the relationship, Anna had been
deceiving herself before Stella's death but can now no longer stand the
self-deception.   Finally she condemns her own behavior and sees herself as
having been ruined by Richard.   "Life with Richard has corrupted me and
made me useless" (*Wir töten Stella*, p. 33).   Anna believes that her
relationship with Richard has made her incapable of either really helping
Stella (that is, outside of aiding her entrance into a modified traditional
relationship) or of viewing her as an ally (in building a new set of social
rules based on women's needs).   Dagmar Lorenz, drawing on de Beauvoir,
points out:

> Haushofer, like de Beauvoir, considers the social conditions under
> which such an occurrence can happen: the wife is indeed blackmailed
> and betrayed by her husband, but is tied to her husband and
> sufficiently corrupted by the institution of marriage and her resulting
> economic dependency that she became too comfortable for rebellion,
> and would rather put up a good front, although inwardly her
> husband has become strange to her.[7]

This is a classic case of social and economic repression that keeps women
apart and marriages together.   Anna has been totally isolated through her
marriage with Richard and has built up a self-protective wall.   "I felt
genuine distress at the sight of her beautiful face, possessed by a wild, silent
pain, but I didn't wish to break through the wall which still separated me
from this pain" (*Wir töten Stella*, p. 43).   Such a move would have been
dangerous, for she would have been confronted by her own pain, and her
self-image in the relationship would have been destroyed.   She recognizes her
own cowardice, however, and cannot continue to tell herself that she has
done this solely for Wolfgang.

In a third area of subversion, Stella's death not only causes Anna to
condemn her own and Richard's behavior as a couple, but also to compare

herself with Stella as an individual. Anna feels that she is just as dead as Stella, because her life has been basically that of a robot: she fulfills her duties, is the good wife and mother. In Stella's rejection by Richard, Anna relives her own rejection and can externalize her situation to become conscious of it. "I knew what was going on inside her. Wild with longing and desperation, she waited at least to see Richard, to hear his voice, and to catch a glimpse of him. I could sense the humiliation which she had behind her and which still lay before her" (*Wir töten Stella*, p. 41). As she sits writing Stella's story, Anna realizes that it is as much her story as it is Stella's. "I would prefer it if I could trade places with her and I didn't have to sit here and write her wretched story, which is also my wretched story" (*Wir töten Stella*, p. 8). This awareness comes too late to help Stella, so Anna is left alone, without even the illusions she had previously. "Once everything was good and orderly and then someone snarled the threads" (*Wir töten Stella*, p. 51). Anna finally realizes that she has failed to reach out and help this young girl, who was then destroyed by her husband. Haushofer has taken a typical situation of a man between two women and used it only to shatter one woman's illusions about her life and not to present alternatives. Because of the world in which she lives, taking action is not a viable alternative. The only action that had been open to Anna was that of helping Stella, but that was destroyed by Stella's suicide. After Stella's death Anna is condemned to a life of painful awareness and inaction.

In Haushofer's *Die Tapetentür* (1957, The Wallpapered Door) and Bachmann's *Der Fall Franza*, (The Case Franza, written in the sixties and seventies, published posthumously) both protagonists see a connection between themselves and their husbands' former wives, which shows another facet of female relationships. Annette in *Die Tapetentür* feels an affinity, rather than jealousy or rivalry, between herself and Gregor's first wife. She empathizes with her predecessor's fate, as does Franza in Bachmann's *Der Fall Franza.* Unfortunately for the women, their consciousness of the connections comes at a point when it cannot help them. The rivalry implicit in the situation is subverted by the women's consciousness of their common status, but their too-late recognition of their bonds with their predecessors condemns them to awareness without the opportunity for action.

In *Die Liebhaberinnen* (Women in Love) Jelinek portrays a deadly variant of the rivalry between women: an economic one. Her depiction is informed by her stance as a Marxist feminist and her conscious use of fiction to critique society. In *Die Liebhaberinnen* Jelinek writes, ". . . the women discover nothing in common among themselves, only contrasts."[8] The society in which Jelinek's women live forces them to see only contrasts (*Gegensätze*) between themselves and other women, but Jelinek, through her narrative technique and use of market terminology to describe human relationships, manages to point to reasons for the lack of solidarity among women. The dialectic between individuals and the market economy reveals the devastating effects of rivalry among women.

The novel *Die Liebhaberinnen* divided into thirty-four mini-chapters, including a forward and epilogue, focuses on the lives of Brigitte and Paula and their relationships to their future husbands. The novel ends where it begins, in a bra factory. Brigitte has escaped the factory, whereas Paula, after she is discovered prostituting herself, loses her children and becomes an unskilled, emotionally bankrupt worker there. Their two stories form a dialectic, a series of contrasts and comparisons, which reveal the inner workings of the stresses to which they are subjected as women, and which turns women into rivals.   Chapters alternate between Brigitte and Paula until the chapter "brigittes weiteres schicksal" (Brigitte's further fate), in which the narrator contrasts and compares the situation of both women and their desire to marry in order to ensure their material existence.   The climax of the book is "HOCHZEIT" (wedding), after which the narrative concludes, chapters again alternating between Brigitte's and Paula's story.   Typically, in the chapter "HOCHZEIT" (wedding), Jelinek uses the same phrases to describe both couples, underlining the commonality of the experience, particularly for the two women, and the significance marriage has for both of them:

> brigitte has finally found a true complement to her life: a partner in joy and sorrow.
> paula has finally found a true complement to her life: a partner in joy and sorrow.
> many relatives have come to heinz and brigitte's.
> many relatives have come to erich and paula's.
> heinz and brigitte's wedding is very moving and solemn.
> erich and paula's wedding is very moving and solemn.
> brigitte is very, very happy.
> paula is very, very happy.
> brigitte has succeeded.
> paula has succeeded. (*Die Liebhaberinnen*, p. 106)

With this use of language, Jelinek points out that although the consequences of each marriage will be different, similar mechanisms are working in both:

> paula hung her fate on erich, which will yet be like a millstone hung around her neck.
> brigitte hung her fate on heinz, which was right and will yield her her own business as well as a beautiful car.
> purely by chance, paula was unlucky and will suffer a very bad downfall.
> purely by chance, brigitte was lucky and will experience a comet-like rise. (*Die Liebhaberinnen*, p. 108)

Their fate is determined by the men they attach themselves to; Brigitte is lucky, but Paula is less fortunate.   Although sharing a parallel fate, they are potential rivals in the marriage game.

Using terminology usually applied to critiquing capitalism rather than to discussing interpersonal relationships, Jelinek connects capitalism with patriarchy.   In her analysis she thus presents clear reasons for female rivalry and for the lack of female solidarity seen in all the women's works.   Women find themselves "commodities" (*Waren*) in a flooded market, where the quality of their existence depends on their ability to sell themselves to the desired male "buyer."   Their only capital is their bodies, with a value that fluctuates like any other product on the free market:

> brigitte has a body to offer.

> besides brigitte's body there are yet many other bodies being cast
> on the market. the one thing which brigitte has going for her on
> this path is the cosmetic industry and the textile industry.
>   brigitte has breasts, thighs, legs, hips, and a cunt.
>   the others have them, too, sometimes of even better quality. (*Die
> Liebhaberinnen*, p. 12)

In order to get the most return for the product "body," women must invest
in the hope of making themselves the most attractive piece of goods. Jelinek
also points out, however, that no matter how much a woman invests in the
venture to "catch a man," the market is fickle:

> for that brigitte invested much, her entire physical and mental
> capacities.
>   for that paula invested much, her entire physical and mental
> capacities.
>   luck and success are favorable to brigitte.
>   luck and success are not favorable to paula. (*Die Liebhaberinnen*,
> p. 108)

The fictional women's ability to bear children at the proper time has a
tremendous effect on their market value; they are not important as
individuals but as vessels. Paula's value, on the other hand, is reduced
because of her reproductive organs. Fifteen years old, pregnant, and unable
to convince Erich to marry her, she becomes spoiled goods and her market
value plunges:

> paula's poor stomach, which soon will be swollen up fat so that
> for the same amount of money one could get a lot more kilograms
> of paula, is being auctioned, but nobody wants it. that would be
> an enormous increase of value for a pig. for paula it's a sign that
> she was easy, too easy and is now that much harder to dispose of.
>   no one wants the contents of paula's stomach alone to raise and
> love; no one wants paula as a person, with or without the stomach.
> not even paula's outer skin finds a bidder. you can't sew a sofa
> pillow or rag rug out of her.
>   her head is not the subject. whoever takes paula's body and
> working power will receive paula's head as a gift. as a promotional
> item or "free gift." (*Die Liebhaberinnen*, pp. 78-79)

Evils compound themselves in this rivalry for the security of marriage: Paula
gives birth to a girl rather than a boy, which decreases her market value
even more.

    In a society in which human relations function like a capitalist
economy, competition among "goods" (women) results; for the "buyer" (men)
a desirable situation of devaluation of goods results, according to Jelinek's
analysis. The price is down and the competition is up. In a competitive
market overflowing with female bodies, competition, not identification; hate,
not love; arises between the sexes:

> the protected women despise the unprotected ones.

and the saleswomen hate the housewives in return because they are out of it all, while they still stand in the competitive market, and instead of varnished furniture still have to buy nylon stockings, pullovers and mini-skirts—as an investment.

yes, that adds up!

there is a general hating in the town which always grows, which infects everything, which stops for no one; the women discover nothing in common among themselves, only contrasts. (*Die Liebhaberinnen*, p. 24)

Rivalry and hatred between women thus exists on all levels in *Die Liebhaberinnen* (Women in Love), between the unprotected or unmarried and the protected or married women, between Brigitte and Susi (whom Brigitte views as her archenemy), between Brigitte and the secretary at work who identifies more with the male boss than with the female workers, between Paula and her mother (who wants Paula to have it as hard as she has), and between Brigitte and Heinz's mother (who considers Brigitte to be a bad investment for Heinz). The inability of the women to see behind the contrasts prevents analysis of female rivalry and perpetuates women's exploitation. If financial security is determined by the desired male, every woman who might steal this security is a potential threat.

As shown in the previous chapter, financial security is determined by the male the women attach themselves to. Thus it is inevitable that love and financial security must become inseparable for the women. Just as the terms *man*, *financial security*, and *love* are linked and become interchangeable, so do *woman*, *threat*, and *hate* become interchangeable. As Simone de Beauvoir writes of this general situation, "In a state of uncertainty, every woman is a rival, a danger. Love destroys the possibility of friendship with other women because the woman is shut off in her lover's universe; jealousy increases her isolation and thereby narrows her dependence."[9] Thus Jelinek's Brigitte naturally finds in Susi a threat to her financial security; yet, because of class difference, Susi does not view Brigitte as a threat in turn:

in brigitte's circles every bit of competition is hated. in brigitte's circles hate is written in capital letters. brigitte can't muster up any love for her kind, that has all been ruined.

in susi's circles the love which rules the entire world and before which hate should be silent rules. susi is very nice to b. because she is as indifferent to brigitte as to a piece of wood. brigitte hates susi like only something that wears a snow-white bathrobe can be hated. (*Die Liebhaberinnen*, p. 52)

Jelinek thus extends her analysis past a strictly feminist point of view to critique two aspects of social structure: class and patriarchy.

The inability of the women in *Die Liebhaberinnen* to identify with other women is related to "the ideology of the individual" which, as Zillah Eisenstein says, "assumes a competitive view of the individual."[10] Jelinek's women convince themselves that they alone will be the chosen woman, will get their prince, and will have their dreams come true:

paula dreams like all women about love.
all women, paula, too, dream about love.
many of her former schoolmates, many of her present colleagues
from work likewise dream about it, only each one strongly believes
that she alone will receive it. (*Die Liebhaberinnen*, p. 24)

The women stand together in the belief that each alone will be rewarded in love, and thereby isolate themselves from one another in this very belief. It is exactly this illusion Jelinek seeks to expose as the ultimate cause of female rivalry.

Friendships Among Women

Considering the examples cited above, it is not surprising that, in the literature before the second women's movement in the seventies, strong friendships between women either do not exist or they are not the central focus of the narrative. The major examples of friendships in earlier works are childhood friendships or relationships resulting from marriage, examples of which can be found in the works of Haushofer (1955-1968) and in Bachmann's "Das Gebell" (1972, "The Barking").

Although not a central focus, the friendships portrayed in Haushofer's works either provide an important link to the protagonist's past or offer a critique of women's position in society. In Haushofer's works the childhood friendships are destined to be broken off because of the pattern of women's lives. In her *Eine Handvoll Leben* (A Handful of Life), Betty realizes that she had never again found anyone as stimulating as Margot, her closest friend at boarding school. "She alone was my partner, thought Betty, surprised at this revelation" (*Eine Handvoll Leben*, p. 68). However, three factors interfere with their friendship. First, Margot falls in love with Elisabeth. "It made Elizabeth very happy until a disturbing incident occurred and Margot fell in love with her. It was incomprehensible and awful, but she didn't like Margot's body" (*Eine Handvoll Leben*, p. 70). In addition Elisabeth realizes that she cannot get too close to others if she feels her freedom is endangered. But most importantly, distance and separation from friends appears to lead to the dissolution of bonds: "The essential element in her relationships with other people was always destroyed by spatial distance" (*Eine Handvoll Leben*, p. 99). The "traditional" life of a woman, as seen by Haushofer, automatically leads in her fiction to the dissolution of friendships with other women. In traditional marriages, again, the women find their lives shaped by their husbands' lives and demands.

In a second example of this situation, Käthe's loyalty to her childhood friends provides Betty with the link to her past life as Elisabeth. Moreover Käthe marries Pfluger after Elisabeth's death/disappearance and feels closer to Elisabeth's son than to her own daughter. The narrator speculates, "For some reason or other Frau Käthe had always favored her stepson over her daughter. It may have been that she, like many women, didn't like girls, or that she continued to love her dead girlfriend in him" (*Eine Handvoll Leben*, p. 8). Käthe saves and neatly orders cards and photos of Elisabeth, thereby holding on to her lost friend the only way she can. Through the cards she opens up the door to Betty's past as Elizabeth.

In *Die Tapetentür* (1957, The Wallpapered Door), two female friends are mentioned, but only dealt with briefly. The relationship between

Annette and Martha, a friend she has not seen for six years, is a striking literary example of the lack of solidarity between women.   Martha, twenty-nine years old, with three children and a husband, lives in a two-bedroom apartment and, as Annette writes, "She is totally alienated from herself" (*Die Tapetentür*, p. 44)—that is, a typical fifties woman under a man's control.   But Annette is not moved enough to visit Martha anymore, even though she considers her a friend.   "Incidentally, I'm not going to visit Martha anymore: it would be senseless and could at best cause her pain.   My presence would probably remind her of the former Martha and that it shouldn't do" (*Die Tapetentür*, p. 46).   Instead of using her friendship as a means of support, Annette thus views it more as a reminder to Martha of her miserable situation.   However surprising Annette's behavior may seem, this passage exemplifies the situation of one woman and makes the reader aware of the stress some women faced at that time, and maybe still do.   Here again, friendships deteriorate with the passage of time.

Only in Frischmuth's trilogy, written in the more recent past, do the women develop deep friendships that also play a central role in the narrative.   In the trilogy (published 1976, 1978, and 1979) the friendships among women are more long-lasting and more positive than in any other works.   The protagonists are self-confident and not threatened by other women, viewing them as allies rather than as enemies.   In these positive portrayals, then, Frischmuth is consciously writing about the strength women can gain from friendships with women.

The first book, *Die Mystifikationen der Sophie Silber* (1976, The Mystification of Sophie Silber), contains   six chapters in which the life of fairies is intertwined with the history of the von Weitersleben family.   The women have for several generations had one female child each and refused to marry.   Sophie (von Weitersleben) Silber is the last of the female Weiterslebens and the first to have a son.   Her continuing friendship with the fairy, Amaryllis Sternwieser, is not designed to provide the reader with insight into female friendships, but rather to act as a device for bringing the two narrative strands together.   In the second and third books of the trilogy, after Amaryllis gives up her fairy form to become a human woman (Amy Stern), female friendships shift to the foreground.

In the second book, *Amy oder die Metamorphose* (1978, Amy or the Metamorphosis), almost half of the thirty-three episodes deal with Amy's friendships and interactions with women.   Amy Stern's world is comprised mostly of women: the restaurant where she works employs solely women; she becomes friends with a group of four women who come there; and she develops a friendship with Sophie Silber after she begins an affair with Sophie's son Klemens.   However, as Christa Gürtler writes:

> Barbara   Frischmuth   attempts   to   portray   an   abundance   of possibilities for women through conversations and stories by women. All too often, however, the figures take on model character and are hardly   drawn   as   individuals.   In   a   type   of   episode-technique, biography is juxtaposed to biography, all interspersed in the main plot without connections.[11]

This criticism maintains that the characters are prototypes, hardly real women.   But, although the reader is not presented with a detailed exposition of the relationships, Amy's friendships with Maya, Pola, Miranda, and Sophie Silber become important in her life in a way identifiable in the real world. The first time Amy meets Maya, Pola, and Miranda privately, for example, the conversations are largely monologues in which the others tell Amy about themselves and their problems. The reader learns how each has chosen her "art," or means of self-expression. Once Amy gets beyond just observing and becomes involved in life, the conversations become true dialogues. As Amy distances herself from her earlier fairy state and becomes more human, her need to talk about her own problems develops. In episodes twelve, seventeen, and twenty-one, the conversations are true exchanges with women for the first time. From that point on the conversations are no longer one-sided. Frischmuth thus presents a model on how to grow into reality, if you are a "non-human" woman—a life that may not be real at the start, but which gradually becomes so.

Amy's friendships with Maya and Pola provide the contrast between a productive friendship, both artistically and personally, and a nonproductive, disappointing female relationship. Maya is one of the two women with whom Amy actively seeks a friendship; the fact that they live in the same building facilitates both its development and maintenance. Whenever Maya and Amy meet, it is in Maya's apartment where Maya works on her art while talking to Amy. Their conversations revolve around creative work and personal problems and act as a stimulus for both women. Amy's and Maya's art each becomes intertwined with that of the other. For example, after Amy reads a story she wrote, she is surprised that Maya has paid such close attention. "On the contrary, your stories are in my drawings; don't you see how your arms and legs are developing more and more into fins?"[12] Their conversations thus allow them the opportunity to articulate problems. During a visit with Maya, Amy expresses for the first time her desire to give up medicine and work with words instead. Their conversations also include personal problems that are directly or indirectly related to their art. When Maya advises Amy to have an abortion, she emphasizes that it is virtually impossible for a woman to be both an artist and mother. Again, their exchanges stimulate and spur them both on, providing each with a sounding board and support.

Amy's relationship with Pola starts in a manner similar to that with Maya, but it remains nonproductive. The first time Pola and Amy meet alone, it is in a self-service restaurant in the city, and Pola expresses her ideas about her art, acting. With one exception, and in contrast to the homey atmosphere of Maya's workroom, their meetings are all chance. During one of their chance meetings, Pola happens to run into an old friend, Willi the midget, with whom she later falls in love. Men thus intrude into what should be women's time: the beginning of this affair marks the beginning of Pola's distancing from Amy and the other women. The last meeting that Pola and Amy have is marked by an underlying unpleasantness and disappointment. Amy reacts negatively to Pola's disclosure that she and Willi are going to use the name she had planned for her performing duo with Amy. "And the *Soft Eggs*? Amy Stern suddenly had an aversion to the black mocha and put her cup down" (*Amy oder die Metamorphose*, pp. 255-256). Pola also announces that she will no longer participate in the "Jockey-Game"; it appears inevitable that she will lose contact with Amy. "They had again hugged and kissed at length, sworn to each other to maintain contact, but all in all it had sounded very much like a farewell" (*Amy oder die Metamorphose*, p. 257).   The friendship does not appear strong enough to survive the intrusion of a man or Pola's change in lifestyle. Thus the contrasts between two types of women friends show the conditions under which women's friendship is possible, and that the men's world may still all-too-easily take over.

Amy's friendship with Sophie Silber provides both unexpected solidarity and a stable point between her relationships with other women and her male lover.   Sophie is able to remain objective concerning Amy's relationship with her son Klemens, because she did not rear him; and her solidarity with Amy as a person is possible because of her independent lifestyle.   Sophie has no stake in any of the traditional worlds in the novel.

In the third book of the trilogy, *Kai und die Liebe zu den Modellen* (1979, Kai and the Love of Models), female friendships continue to play a role, but, as reflected in the form of the book, relationships with others must fit into and not supersede Amy's relationship with her son Kai.   Each alternate chapter focuses on the adventures of Kai and his friends (two, four, six, eight); in the odd-numbered, extended chapters, Amy takes care of Kai, reflects on her work, her relationship with Klemens, and undertakes outings or talks with female friends.   Unlike Jelinek's dialectic between two women that shows rivalry, then, Frischmuth's dialectic between children's and women's worlds is productive for Amy's work.

Amy's friendships with Maya and Pola continue, but they each appear only once, and it is clear that they see each other rarely.   Sophie Silber also appears less frequently.   The new and major friend is Helene, Amy's editor, who has three main appearances in the book: the first time in chapter three, then after a movie in chapter seven, and finally in the last pages of the book.   Her first appearance gives Amy the opportunity to make several points clear to the reader.   After Helene begins to talk about women transforming their lives into literature, she states that she admires Amy for all she is able to do.   Amy, irritated, thinks to herself:

> And once again we're at exactly the same place I so hate to come to.   Instead of talking about how it could be, comfortable admiration is given out that I halfway manage the way things are.
> But I don't get anything out of that.   The sentence came out childishly stubborn.   I have no desire to complain.   I only know that there would be many possibilities if people cooperated more.[13]

For Amy, Helene looks backward.   Instead of being content with what she has achieved for herself, Amy makes a clear statement that it is now time to go beyond the stage of description and create new patterns in the society for both sexes.   Unable to find or create new patterns in the world of adults, Amy creates instead in the world of children—building for the future on the basis of her present.

The second point that is revealed in her meeting with Helene is Amy's rejection of lesbianism as a personal alternative, but her acceptance of it as an option other women might choose:

> Again and again I felt Helene's finger in the crook of my arm, her plea for closeness, which perhaps wasn't even meant for me

personally. What do I know about her? I don't believe at all that
she loves women. Perhaps it's only a fiction. There has been so
much written about the new dimensions which would result from it
for disappointed women. Only for disappointed? Is Helene
disappointed? Am I disappointed? . . .

I can imagine it, imagine very well how it is when women love
one another with a passion of exclusivity by which the power of the
feeling goes beyond all limitations. I can also imagine, however,
how one feels when one wants to try out love of another woman as
comfort for injuries, as a newly-opened possibility, in order to check
out the theory for its practical gain in pleasure. (*Kai und die Liebe
zu den Modellen*, p. 65)

The issue is not important to Frischmuth as a resolution, but only as a
problem. Amy does not resolve her physical discomfort with Helene, nor is
it ever revealed whether Helene is or is not lesbian.

Despite the depiction of positive aspects of women's friendships, the
three books of Frischmuth's trilogy do not contain a blueprint for a feminist
utopia. As positive as the exchange between the women is in the trilogy,
the friendships alone do not bring about larger political changes that could
have a greater impact on women's lives. Frischmuth does not show political
implications of female solidarity, but rather the importance of women in a
woman's life, and in building a new future for today's children by rejecting
old models.

Political Solidarity

The only work of the five women that demonstrates the political
potential in women's solidarity and friendship is Jelinek's radio play *Die
Bienenkönige* (The Bee Kings), which makes a statement on the political
strength of solidarity not just between women, but between exploited classes.
As Jelinek states of this utopian play:

It is a utopia of the possibility of the solidarity of the oppressed
class, in this case of the slave caste who is being bred by the
scientists and of the women, of the oppressed sex, of the oppressed
caste. The women are divided into groups. The one group of
women are the breeding cows, the mothers, who are actually lost
because they are the creations of the men and therefore have to
perish with them. It is, of course, quite cruel. The others are the
courtesans, the self-determined women who are freed from their
biology, then achieve liberation and revolt against the fathers. It is
a very contrived model of a society.[14]

In this science fiction, after the generator blows up, the female
survivors are divided into groups, depending on their ability to reproduce.
Those who are unable to have children serve as the colony prostitutes. The
men or "kings" rule over the women, and the sons, who become the workers
or drones, are enslaved just as the women are. Unable to rely on the
mothers for solidarity, the infertile females or courtesans seek aid elsewhere:

W 4: It's as if they [the childbearers] and the kings had one and the

same head.
W 5: Their brain is in their womb.
W 6: We can't expect any help from them.
W 4: They are going to kill us as soon as they have new young girls.
W 5: We have to ally ourselves with the sons.[15]

This is again a rivalry—Jelinek thus makes a strong statement concerning the unlikelihood of these women achieving solidarity with reactionary women, and the need of ordinary women to seek others in similar positions in order to reinforce their personal strengths:

W 6: We also have to kill their creations, the mothas.
W 5: They're women like we are.
W 4: But they think with the heads of the kings. The head has to die
      if you want to kill something.
W 6: We need allies, we need the sons. (*Die Bienenkönige*,
The Bee Kings, p. 43)

Jelinek also points out the necessity of finding existing bonds between seemingly different groups, whose similarities have been hidden by those in power in order to hinder the building of alliances against the existing system.

Lesbian Relationships

Perhaps even more noticeably absent from Austrian feminist literature than female friendships are love relationships between women. Unlike the Federal Republic of Germany, Austria has produced no well-known lesbian prose writers. Lesbianism is however at least peripherally acknowledged by all five of the Austrian writers under study. For example, in Haushofer's *Eine Handvoll Leben* (A Handful of Life), Margot, a secondary character, falls in love with Elisabeth. Although Haushofer does not pursue this aspect of the relationship, she also does not use the situation to condemn homosexuality. In *Die Tapetentür* (The Wallpapered Door) the reference to lesbianism is similarly brief; Haushofer thus more or less acknowledges the existence of lesbianism, but only as belonging to a realm different from that of the protagonist—not part of the lover's consciousness.

Frischmuth discusses lesbianism, too, once in *Die Mystifikationen der Sophie Silber* (The Mystification of Sophie Silber) and once in *Kai und die Liebe zu den Modellen* (Kai and the Love of Models), but in both cases very superficially. In *Die Mystifikationen* Amaryllis worries about how Sidonie von Weitersleben will carry on the tradition of having a baby and not marrying, since she is more interested in women than in men. Fate overcomes this difficulty: through a rather unlikely coincidence and the help of the carnival season, Sidonie pairs with a gay man whom she initially thinks is a woman. He, on the other hand, believes Sidonie to be a young man, and the birth of the next generation is secured. Again, homosexuality is neither the center of the narrative nor condemned.

In Bachmann's "Ein Schritt nach Gomorrha" ("A Step towards Gomorrah") the potential of a lesbian relationship is more explicitly discussed in the story which Karen Achberger describes as, "the story of destruction and creation, of death and salvation, from the breaking of old bonds and the coming of a new order, new knowledge, a new sex, a new race."[16] Charlotte rejects the old order and seeks to create a new one. Her vision for a lesbian relationship, however, does not appear to deviate from the repressive hierarchy in heterosexual relationships:

> She would be able to subjugate Mara, to guide and push her. She would have somebody who would tremble before her concerts, who would hold a warm jacket in readiness when she came out of the concert hall sweating, somebody for whom the only important thing was to take part in her life and for whom she was the measure of all things, somebody for whom it was more important to keep her linen in order, to turn back her bed, than to satisfy another ambition—somebody, above all, for whom it was more important to think with her thoughts than to have a thought of her own. (*The Thirtieth Year*, p. 125)

Although she is not able to think of new models, Charlotte still rejects the old order and will not accept a reversal of the old hierarchy. As Karen Achberger summarizes this situation:

> What Charlotte has in mind for her relationship to Mara—essentially a reversal of the dynamic of dominance and submission in her relationship to Franz—is clearly not to be read as a possible end in itself, but as an alienation effect, intended to cast a new light on the traditional heterosexual relationship as it exists in Charlotte's marriage.[17]

In the role reversal, Charlotte gains distance from her subjugation in the male-female relationship, which she ultimately rejects.

In Jelinek's latest play, *Krankheit oder die moderne Frau* (1984, Disease or the Modern Woman), two lesbian vampires are in the foreground.[18] Rather than depicting authentic experience, however, Jelinek uses these women for their symbolic value—they are repositories of male projections of the "female," and not intended to represent real women.

In the Austrian literature, then, lesbianism appears only on the periphery. It is not viewed as a logical consequence of a feminist stance that would point to the relationship between personal experience and art, nor identified as a necessary corollary to female friendships.

Conclusion

Although the dearth of women's friendships and lesbian relationships in the literature of the five Austrians under consideration is striking both in light of the number of pages they devote to problematic male-female relationships and the emergence of a body of literature in the two Germanies focusing on just these topics, a close examination of their literature indicates it would be false to conclude that they deal with the topic in a perfunctory manner. The earliest works, such as Haushofer's *Eine Handvoll Leben* (1955, A Handful of Life) or Bachmann's "Ein Schritt nach Gomorrha" (1963, "A Step towards Gomorrah") capture the ambivalence of women toward their own sex, while being critical of the male-centeredness of the society. Here the writers project their own feelings of isolation onto their female protagonists. This simultaneous ambivalence and criticism can be seen as a transitional stage toward a greater awareness of society's sexual politics.

From the earlier works such as Haushofer's *Wir töten Stella* (1958, We're Killing Stella) or Bachmann's *Der Fall Franza* (1966, The Case Franza) to the later works such as Jelinek's *Die Liebhaberinnen* (1975, Women in Love), rivalry between women is depicted as the primary dynamic in women's relationships to each other in a male-dominated society.[19] However the depiction of such rivalry is never used to affirm a system of male preference, but rather to undermine it by pointing out to the reader how the female protagonists are drawn into complicity with the males through such a dynamic. For example, Annette in Haushofer's *Die Tapetentür* (1957, The Wallpapered Door) and Franza in Bachmann's *Der Fall Franza* (The Case Franza) realize too late for themselves (but not for the reader) that they have more in common with their husbands' former wives than with their husbands. Jelinek's protagonists Brigitte and Paula in *Die Liebhaberinnen* (Women in Love) never discover their commonality with each other, perceiving only contrasts; however, the critical stance of the author points to the mechanisms that keep women apart and the consequences of encouraging rivalry.

Only in Frischmuth's trilogy (1976, 1978, and 1979) and Jelinek's *Die Bienenkönige* (1976, The Bee Kings) do the writers depict positive bonds between women. In both, such bonding provides support for women, allowing them to step out of their isolation, to view themselves as part of a whole, and in the case of the *Bienenkönige*, to take political action. Characteristic of the Austrian works is an implied critique of female rivalry in the earlier works, and an explicit one in the later works.

With this we are forced to realize that Austrian women's feminism is of a sort different from that represented in the two Germanies in particular and the women's movement in general, no matter how many commonalities in theme and interpretations we have been able to trace. It is the project of the concluding chapter, then, to try to tie together the threads we have discovered into a picture of one particular feminist movement in a real social and literary context.

Notes

1. See Liselotte Weingant, "Das Bild des Mannes im Frauenroman der Siebziger Jahre," Diss. University of Illinois at Urbana-Champaign 1981, pp. 90-91. She writes:

> The phenomenon of the female outsider, as Bachmann has presented over and over, can be considered typical for modern Austrian women's literature. Just as Bachmann's protagonists are lost loners, so are those of Marlen Haushofer, Friederike Mayröcker, Hilde Spiel, Marianne Fritz, Elfriede Jelinek, Barbara Frischmuth, and Brigitte Schwaiger. These figures act as if they were totally alone in this world, abandoned by their own sex, mistreated by the other sex. Each one sees herself confronted with situations which can happen only to her personally, a novelty in their problematic and a stress situation.

2. Christa Reinig, *Entmannung* (Dusseldorf: Verlag Eremiten Presse, c. 1976);

Verena Stefan, *Häutungen* (Munich: Verlag Frauenoffensive, 1975);

Margot Schroeder, *Ich stehe meine Frau* (Frankfurt am Main: Fischer Taschenbuch Verlag, 1975);

Christa Wolf, *Nachdenken über Christa T.* (Halle: Mitteldeutscher Verlag, 1968);

Irmtraud Morgner, *Leben und Abenteuer der Trobadora Beatriz nach Zeugnissen ihrer Spielfrau Laura* (Berlin, Weimar: Aufbau Verlag, 1974).

Other examples include:

Irmtraud Morgner, *Amanda: Ein Hexenroman* (Berlin, Weimar: Aufbau Verlag, 1983);

Christa Wolf, *Kindheitsmuster* (Berlin, Weimar: Aufbau Verlag, 1976);

Ingeborg Drewitz's *Gestern war Heute* (Dusseldorf: Claassen, 1975) is an example of a work in which mother-daughter relationships are central to the narrative.   They are not necessarily unproblematic, but certainly not destructive in the same sense as in Jelinek's *Die Klavierspielerin.*

American literature offers many examples of literature in which relationships between women are central:

Rita Mae Brown, *Rubyfruit Jungle* (Plainfield, Vermont: Daughters, Inc., 1973);

Rita Mae Brown, *Six of One* (New York: Harper and Row, 1978);

Toni Morrison, *Sula* (New York: Knopf, 1974);

Marge Piercy, *Small Changes* (New York: Fawcett, 1978);

Marge Piercy, *Woman on the Edge of Time* (New York: Knopf, 1976);

Alice Walker, *The Color Purple* (New York: Harcourt Brace Jovanovich, c. 1982).

3.   Marlen Haushofer, *Die Tapetentür* (Hamburg, Vienna: Paul Zsolnay Verlag, 1957), p. 48.

4.   Marlen Haushofer, *Eine Handvoll Leben* (Vienna: Paul Zsolnay Verlag, 1955), pp. 104-105.   All further references appear in the text.

5.   Ingeborg Bachmann, *The Thirtieth Year*, trans. Michael Bullock (New York: Alfred A. Knopf, 1964), p. 133.   All further references to Bachmann's works appear in the text.

6.   Marlen Haushofer, *Wir töten Stella* (Vienna: Bergland, 1958), p. 15.   All further references appear in the text.

7.   Dagmar   Lorenz,   "Biographie   und   Chiffre: Entwicklungsmöglichkeiten in der österreichischen Prosa nach 1945," Diss. University of Cincinnati 1974, p. 81.

8.   Elfriede Jelinek, *Die Liebhaberinnen* (Reinbek bei Hamburg: Rowohlt, 1975), p. 24.   All further references appear in the text.

9.   Simone de Beauvoir, *The Second Sex*, H. M. Parshley, trans. and ed. (New York: Vintage—Random House, 1974), p. 737.

10.   Zillah Eisenstein, *The Radical Future of Liberal Feminism* (New York, London: Longman, 1981), p. 5.

11.   Christa Gürtler, *Schreiben Frauen Anders?: Untersuchungen zu Ingeborg Bachmann und Barbara Frischmuth* (Stuttgart: Akademischer Verlag Hans-Dieter Heinz, 1983), p. 317.

12.   Barbara Frischmuth, *Amy oder die Metamorphose* (Salzburg, Vienna: Residenz Verlag, 1978), p. 246.   All further references appear in the text.

13.   Barbara Frischmuth, *Kai und die Liebe zu den Modellen* (Salzburg, Vienna: Residenz Verlag, 1979), p. 53.   All further references

appear in the text.

14.   Jacqueline Vansant, "Gespräch mit Elfriede Jelinek," *Deutsche Bücher*, 15, No. 1 (1985), 7.

15.   Elfriede Jelinek, "Die Bienenkönige," in *Was geschah, nachdem Nora ihren Mann verlassen hatte* (Munich: Deutscher Taschenbuch Verlag, 1982), p. 43. All further references appear in the text.

16.   Karen Achberger, "Bachmann und die Bibel: 'Ein Schritt nach Gomorrha' als weibliche Schöpfungsgeschichte," in Hans Höller, ed., *Der dunkle Schatten, dem ich schon seit Anfang folge* (Vienna, Munich: Löcker Verlag, 1982), p. 97.

17.   Achberger, p. 105.

18.   Elfriede Jelinek, "Krankheit oder die moderne Frau," in *manuskripte*, 23 (October 1984), 3-22.

19.   The editors of Bachmann's *Werke* write in *Werke*, III, 559: "The first and third chapters [*Der Fall Franza*] were originally published as a radio broadcast on the occasion of four public readings by Ingeborg Bachmann in Hamburg, Hannover, Berlin and Lübeck during March 22-25, 1966."

6

A Call for Change

"We are still isolated, wrapped in a veil of silence, yet soon, perhaps even here, it will be worth fighting for."

Marie-Thérèse Kerschbaumer,
Schwestern (Sisters), p. 35

As this study suggests, a literature has emerged and become established in Austria since the end of Nazi rule and World War II that focuses on and critiques women's subordinate position in that society. However, although they were actively involved in the literary scene of the immediate postwar years, it was not until the mid-fifties that women authors began to write about the conflicts and contradictions facing women in a male-centered world.[1] Understandably in the first ten years following the capitulation of the National Socialist regime and the end of the war, writers were concerned with rehabilitating literature and purging it of National Socialistic elements, rather than with dealing with specific feminist issues. Older writers, such as Heimito von Doderer (1896-1966), who had not fled Austria, sought the reestablishment of an Austrian literature with its roots in a uniquely Austrian past, distinct from a German tradition.[2] The émigrés, on the other hand, offered little help in revitalizing Austrian literature, because few of them returned to Austria in the immediate postwar years. One important exception, Hans Weigel, returned to Austria from his exile in Switzerland and acted as mentor and editor for many young writers, including Marlen Haushofer.

After World War II the younger generation of writers was seen as the hope for Austria's literary future.[3] Although not focusing on women's issues per se, for the first time in Austrian letters women took a respected and integral role in the literary production and the discussion revolving around the establishment of a new Austrian literature.[4] For example Ilse Aichinger's "Aufruf zum Mißtrauen," (A Call for Scepticism) which appeared in the periodical *Der Plan* in 1946 and called for clarity and honesty in writing, served as a manifesto for the young generation. In addition to Aichinger, Haushofer and Bachmann began writing and publishing in the early postwar years. Characteristically, however, their work in the early years of the

Second Republic dealt with either the experience of National Socialism, as in Aichinger's novel *Die größere Hoffnung* (1948, *Herod's Children*), existential themes, as in Bachmann's poetry, or the world through the eyes of children, as in Haushofer's prose work *Das fünfte Jahr* (1951, The Fifth Year).

Haushofer's novel *Eine Handvoll Leben* (A Handful of Life), published in 1955, marked a turning point not only in her own oeuvre, but in Austrian literature: the feminist point of view. Ingeborg Bachmann, whose collection of short stories *Das dreißigste Jahr* (1963, *The Thirtieth Year*) contains "Ein Schritt nach Gomorrha" ("A Step towards Gomorrah") and "Undine geht" ("Undine Goes") was the next writer to focus on similar themes.[5] Just as Haushofer and Bachmann did not initially write about women's subordinate position in society or of their exclusion from the symbolic order, neither did Frischmuth and Jelinek, who debuted as writers in 1968 and 1970, respectively. Only with Frischmuth's later collection of four short stories *Haschen nach Wind* (1974, Chasing the Wind) and Jelinek's *Die Liebhaberinnen* (1975, Women in Love) did the second generation of feminist writing emerge. Thereafter, however, both the public and writer expectations had paved the way for the acceptance of works written from a critical female perspective. Thus Brigitte Schwaiger's first novel *Wie kommt das Salz ins Meer* (1977, Why Is the Sea Salty) is written from the perspective of a woman who views critically male-female relationships and female socialization. Since 1974 almost every year has seen the publication of a new work by an Austrian woman writer that focuses on women's experiences in a male-centered world.

The emergence of a feminist voice or consciousness in Austrian literature of the Second Republic took place in two stages. During the first stage, authors such as Haushofer, Bachmann, Frischmuth, and Jelinek established themselves simply as writers, not writing either from a specifically female or from a feminist perspective. In the second stage, after having received recognition as writers of *niveau* from the literary establishment, the women developed a critical female perspective, scrutinizing in their works woman's position in a male-centered society. The mid-seventies in Austria produced an increase in literature from such a perspective. As a viable female voice was already present in the corpus of Austrian literature, Schwaiger and other writers debuting at this time did not go through a similar two-phase coming-to-consciousness, but rather wrote from this perspective in their first work.

Marlen Haushofer, Ingeborg Bachmann, Barbara Frischmuth, Elfriede Jelinek, and Brigitte Schwaiger, all members of the middle class, writing mainly for a middle-class audience, concentrate largely on the personal-pyschological and do not place their protagonists in a larger social context.[6] Unlike their counterparts in the two Germanies and in other Western countries, the five writers do not portray women in open opposition to the culture at large. With most of their works it would be very difficult to place the narrative in a historical framework.[7] The female protagonists are viewed in terms of their individual struggles.[8] In contrast, West German writers such as Ingeborg Drewitz, Luise Rinser, and Margot Schroeder use major political movements as a backdrop for their narrative or portray the involvement of a female protagonist in political or social action.

Only Jelinek deviates from this pattern, her critical position being informed by her political beliefs as a Marxist. In *Die Liebhaberinnen*

(Women in Love) and *Michael. Ein Jugendbuch für die Infantilgesellschaft* (Michael. A Youthbook for Infantile Society) and in many of her radio plays she is less interested in the psychology of the individual than in the model character and interchangeability of her protagonists in a system both capitalist and patriarchal. However, rather than depicting her characters within a distinguishable historical framework by referring to specific contemporary politics, she sets up confrontations that serve as models for the dynamics of a patriarchal and capitalist society, while at the same time experimenting with style.

The Austrian writers' depiction of fascism is the closest they come to discussing a general political phenomenon. However, fascism is located largely in interpersonal relationships, removed from a larger political context, such as Austria's fascist past.[9] As Bachmann herself writes, she chooses to expose a fascist mentality that has not disappeared with the removal of Nazi rule, but that has gone underground:

> I have often wondered—and probably you have, too—where the virus crime has gone to—it can't suddenly have disappeared from our world twenty years ago, simply because murder isn't being supported, demanded, decorated, and remembered with medals here. The massacres are over, but the murderers are still among us, often conjured up and sometimes found out, not all, but some, sentenced in trials. The existence of these murderers has been made known to all of us not only through more or less uneasy reporting, but also through literature.[10]

Bachmann uses explicit imagery, such as the gas chambers in the "I"'s dream in *Malina* or in Franza's in *Der Fall Franza* (The Case Franza). However she does not view male institutions as transmitters of fascism, but individual men. Similarly Haushofer locates and uncovers fascism in interpersonal relationships, politicizing the personal, but again leaving out the social dimension. For example Haushofer rarely mentions events connected with Nazi rule and Austria's role in the systematic extermination of Jews, political prisoners, and other "undesirables."[11] It is only in her portrayal of men as extremely destructive that any connection could be made to the mentality that dominated from 1938 to 1945 in Austria. In both cases it is the women who are victims and not active participants in history. In contrast writers of the same generation such as Ingeborg Drewitz (1923-1986, Federal Republic of Germany) and Christa Wolf (1929, German Democratic Republic) portray individual experiences during fascist rule and question the responsibility of male and female individuals in resisting National Socialism.

Another consequence of the absence of a larger social context in the Austrian women's depictions is the minor role played by work outside the home. Rarely is gainful employment viewed as a means of fulfillment and self-expression or transcendence. If the women are gainfully employed, it is often at highly individualized tasks, which do not help them overcome their isolation or seek alternatives to their situations. Haushofer's protagonists are educated housewives, working within the home. Or they are women such as the narrator of *Die Mansarde* (The Attic), who as an illustrator is consequently isolated by her work. Her individual craft does not allow her to develop interpersonal relationships.   It does comfort her, but that ironically only reinforces her isolation.

When women are in a large social context it is portrayed as peripheral, an implicit rather than present feature.   Haushofer's Annette in *Die Tapetentür* (The Wallpapered Door) refuses to give up her job because of her pregnancy.   Although the reader rarely sees Annette in her capacity as worker, she/he senses that Annette views her work as a key to independent identity.   Bachmann, too, has women characters who are professionals, but once again, the reader does not experience the women in their professional capacities.   Although Barbara Frischmuth has often portrayed women as professionals, only in her trilogy (*Die Mystifikationen der Sophie Silber*, The Mystification of Sophie Silber; *Amy oder die Metamorphose*, Amy or the Metamorphosis; and *Kai und die Liebe zu den Modellen*, Kai and the Love of Models) is the profession/craft women choose—an artistic profession (sculpting, writing)—seen as an integral element in self-expression and as an important component in establishing a female tradition.

In contrast Jelinek's fiction portrays gainful employment as another location of women's alienation rather than as a means of fulfillment.   In *Was geschah, nachdem Nora ihren Mann verlassen hatte?* (What Happened after Nora Left her Husband?), *Michael. Ein Jugendbuch für die Infantilgesellschaft* (Michael. A Youthbook for Infantile Society), and *Die Liebhaberinnen* (Women in Love) working-class women long for the possibility of working only within the home.   Otherwise they are faced with alienating work and a double work-load.

Almost totally missing from the fiction are female-female relationships (both love and friendship), which serve in the feminist literature of other countries as an alternative to relationships with men, a source of power, and a center of the narrative structure.[12] In contrast female friendships and coalitions appear to be an   important component in literature of both the Federal Republic of Germany and the German Democratic Republic.   East German writer Irmtraud Morgner in her montage novel *Leben und Abenteuer der Trobadora Beatriz nach Zeugnissen ihrer Spielfrau Laura* (Life and Adventures of the Troubadour Beatriz according to her Minstrel Laura) and her witch novel *Amanda* depicts female bonding that allows the women to step out of their isolation and find strength in a community of women.   West German Margot Schroeder in *Ich stehe meine Frau* (Act like a Woman) discusses the political expediency of forming female coalitions which may or may not be based on friendship.   Moreover, in West German women's fiction, lesbian relationships become a viable alternative to heterosexual relationships.   In Verena Stefan's *Häutungen* (Shedding), the heroine simultaneously sheds layers of socialization and rejects heterosexual relationships.   She withdraws from society with her lover to establish an egalitarian relationship.   In the fiction of Austrian women, the lack of female friendships seems to be indicative of women's continued isolation or alienation.   The relatively few references to lesbian relationships in Austrian literature, with the exception of Bachmann's "Ein Schritt nach Gomorrha" ("A Step towards Gomorrah") and Jelinek's *Krankheit oder die moderne Frau* (Disease or the Modern Woman), can be linked to the writers' own sexual preference.

The focus on the personal-psychological removed from a larger context may appear in contradiction to a literature which has political potential.

However the absence of a larger social dimension hints at the authors' alienation from their "culture, especially as that culture defined and circumscribed women," which they in turn project onto their characters.[13] The estrangement the authors themselves feel as women in a male-centered culture has no doubt shaped their prose. There appears to be total alienation from the public sphere, indicated by the absence of references to it, and a more immediately felt alienation from the private sphere, demonstrated by the writers' concern with it in their fiction.[14] Thus it is logical that the five writers do not place their narratives in a larger social context, but rather deal with conflicts women face in the private sphere, fighting the narrow definitions of "woman" and dealing with male-female relationships. This, as Evelyn Beck and Biddy Martin write, can be seen as the strength of their texts:

> The strength of these texts lies in the fact that they do not allow us to see the alienation and oppression of women as only an abstract and general problem which represents nothing more than a practical contradiction within a larger context. Instead, the texts force us to take notice of the innumerable details in which the oppression of women manifests itself concretely in their daily life.[15]

This study suggests that such texts locate women's oppression within the family and, more specifically, in male-female relationships, a microcosm of patriarchal structures. The absence of a social dimension, work outside the home, and female-female relationships is in stark contrast to the fiction of women writers in the two Germanies. Their writing underscores the Austrian writers' alienation from patriarchal Austrian society and it further suggests the failure of the public sphere to offer any alternatives for women. Austrian women's writing is an indictment of a system that tenaciously circumscribes women, defining them in relation to men rather than as autonomous beings. In substance it rallies the call for radical change.

Notes

1. Sigrid Schmid-Bortenschlager, "Beiträge österreichischer Schrift-stellerinnen zur Literatur seit 1945," in *Moderna Sprak*, 75, No. 2 (1981), 149-162.
    In her article Schmid-Bortenschlager discusses literature of all genres and themes written by Austrian women since World War II and comes up with a three-stage periodization:
    1) The period after the war was favorable for many women writers because of the overthrow of a regime that saw woman's destiny totally in terms of her biological role as mother;
    2) The fifties were conservative both politically and literarily and therefore not conducive to new women's writings;
    3) The late sixties and seventies were accompanied by a new climate favorable to new writers as a result of the student and women's movements.
    She focuses on literature in general and does not organize by topic. See particularly pp. 150-151 and 161.
2. Hilde Spiel, "Die österreichische literatur nach 1945," in *Die zeitgenössische Literatur Österreichs* (Zurich, Munich: Kindler Verlag, 1976),

pp. 49-62.

3.   Spiel, p. 61.

4.   To compare with women writers in the First Republic see Lynda J. King, "The Woman Question and Politics in Austrian Interwar Literature," in *German Studies Review* 6, No. 1 (1983), 75-100.   See especially pp. 81-82.

5.   Schmid-Bortenschlager views the period 1953 to 1965 (p. 161) as a time of relatively little production by women, but it is during that time that four out of the five Marlen Haushofer books dealt with here and Bachmann's *Das dreißigste Jahr* (with "Ein Schritt nach Gomorrha" and "Undine geht") appeared.

6.   Christa Gürtler, *Schreiben Frauen Anders?: Untersuchungen zu Ingeborg Bachmann und Barbara Frischmuth* (Stuttgart: Akademischer Verlag Hans-Dieter Heinz, 1983), p. 390, connects the focus on the individual in the works of Bachmann and Frischmuth to class: "Experience means for both writers to describe women of the middle class, writers, intellectuals; the social dimension of women's liberation hardly enters the picture."

7.   Wendelin Schmidt-Dengler in his article "Geschichten gegen die Geschichte. Gibt es das Österreichische in der österreichischen Literatur?" in *Modern Austrian Literature,* 17, No. 3/4 (1984), 149-157 discusses the focus on the individual as a general characteristic of Austrian literature and writes on p. 154: "One should ask whether this so frequent attempt to individualize universal history hasn't in itself led to that reproachful identifying feature of Austrian literature of the suppression of historical facts."

8.   Evelyn Beck and Biddy Martin, "Westdeutsche Frauenliteratur der siebziger Jahre," in Paul Michael Lützeler and Egon Schwarz, eds., *Deutsche Literatur in der Bundesrepublik seit 1965* (Königstein/Ts.:   Athenäum, 1980), p. 142.   They write:

> There are texts which concern themselves exclusively with the oppression of woman and the consequences without, however, pointing to a way out which goes beyond the individual leaving a repressive situation—for example, texts by Schwaiger, Heinrich, Peterson, and Walters.

9.   See Elisabeth Reichart's *Februar Schatten* (Vienna: Brandstätter, 1984).   Reichart's novel deals with a mother-daughter conflict, as well as the confrontation of a woman with Austria's fascist past.

10.   Ingeborg Bachmann, *Werke*, 4 vols.   (Munich: Piper, 1982), III, pp. 341-342.

11.   See Marlen Haushofer, *Die Tapetentür* (Hamburg, Vienna: Paul Zsolnay Verlag, 1957), pp. 46-47 and the short story "Die Willows," appearing in *Schreckliche Treue* (Hamburg, Dusseldorf: Claassen Verlag, 1968), pp. 133-146.

12.   Exceptions are Marie-Thérèse Kerschbaumer's, *Schwestern* (Olten, Freiburg im Breisgau: Walter Verlag, 1982) and Elisabeth Reichart's *Februar Schatten.*

13.   Sandra M. Gilbert and Susan Gubar, *The Madwoman in the Attic: The Woman Writer and the Nineteenth-Century Literary Imagination* (New Haven and London: Yale University Press, 1979), p. 117.   Gilbert and Gubar discuss the narrow parameters of Jane Austen fiction in terms of

alienation, and this appears to be an appropriate explanation for a similar phenomenon in the works of the five Austrian writers.

14.   Beck and Martin, p. 136 discuss women's alienation in the family and its literary consequences.

15.   Beck and Martin, p. 137.

Biographical Background

Marlen Haushofer (1920-1970)

Born Marie Helene Frauendorfer in the Upper Austrian town of Frauenstein on April 11, 1920, the daughter of a forester who ran a small farm with his wife, Marlen Haushofer has received the least acclaim of the five writers. She spent two years in an Ursuline convent in Linz in order to further her education, because possibilities for schooling were limited in Frauenstein; this proved to be an unpleasant experience, which has pervaded her work. The year following the *Anschluß* with Germany, she completed her high school work and did her compulsory work service (*Arbeitsdienst*) in Prussia. Returning in 1940 to Austria, Haushofer began her university studies in German literature, met and married Manfred Haushofer, and gave birth to her first son, Christian. Between 1940 and 1942 the family lived in Munich and Prague, returning to Vienna in 1942 where their son Manfred was born. In 1947 the family moved to Steyr, in Upper Austria where Dr. Manfred Haushofer set up a dental practice. In the years after World War II, Haushofer was one of a circle of writers who gravitated around author/critic Hans Weigel. He worked closely with Haushofer on texts, editing, suggesting names for works, and even prompting her to destroy a manuscript. In 1953 she and her husband were divorced, but continued to live together. They remarried in 1957. Her first work of any length, the novella *Das fünfte Jahr* (The Fifth Year), was published in 1951, and her first novel *Eine Handvoll Leben* (A Handful of Life), followed in 1955. Her production in the last 15 years of her life included numerous short stories, three novels, and a novella. Haushofer died in March 1970 of bone cancer. Isolation and the irreconcilability between the male and female worlds are major themes in Haushofer's works.

Ingeborg Bachmann (1926-1973)

The daughter of a teacher, Ingeborg Bachmann, born in Klagenfurt on June 25, 1926, began her university studies in 1945. She studied philosophy, German literature, and psychology at the Universities of Innsbruck, Graz, and Vienna. In 1950 she received her Ph.D. from the University of Vienna after submitting her dissertation on the reception of the works by existentialist Martin Heidegger. The *Gruppe 47* invited Bachmann to read in 1952, and in 1953 she received the *Gruppe 47* prize. Her volumes of poetry have received much critical acclaim, but not until recently has her prose been reviewed positively. It is in her prose that Bachmann writes most explicitly about women's problems, comparing sexual politics to fascism with little hope of change. Bachmann died in Rome on October 17, 1973 of burns received in a fire.

Barbara Frischmuth (b. 1941)

Born in Altaussee, Styria on July 5, 1941, the daughter of hotel owners and operators, Frischmuth is perhaps one of Austria's best-known living woman writers outside of Austrian borders. She briefly attended a Catholic boarding school; her experiences there would later serve as the basis for her first book, *Die Klosterschule* (The Convent School), published in 1968. After finishing her high school work at a public school, she began her study of Turkish and Hungarian at the *Dolmetschinstitut* in Graz. To further her language skills she spent one year in Turkey (1961) and one in Hungary (1963), and then continued her work in Oriental Studies at the University of Vienna. One of the early members of the avant-garde group of writers and artists in Graz known as the *Forum Stadtpark*, Frischmuth dealt to a large degree with a critique of language in her early works. Since her marriage, its dissolution, and the birth of her son, she has written more consciously from a woman's perspective and about women's lives. In addition to her many prose works, Frischmuth has written several radio plays, many critical essays, and numerous translations.

Elfriede Jelinek (b. 1946)

Born in Mürzzuschlag, Styria on October 20, 1946, the daughter of a Jewish chemist (father) and a personnel manager of a large concern (mother), Jelinek grew up in Vienna, where she studied art history and theater at the University of Vienna and organ at the Vienna Conservatory, where she received a degree in 1970. After recovery from a nervous breakdown at age eighteen, she began to write seriously. Jelinek's first novel, *wir sind lockvögel baby!* (we are decoys, baby!), in which she satirizes comics and *Trivialliteratur* (trivial literature), displays an affinity with the *Wiener Gruppe* through her use of experimental language and cut-up texts. She also considers herself greatly influenced by the "Eastern Jewish tradition." In Jelinek's works there is little, if any, identification between the writer and her literary figures; in this fashion she attempts to avoid what she describes as *larmoyance*, a trait she finds in much writing by women.   Jelinek's corpus of works contains not only her novels, but also numerous radio plays, essays in newspapers and journals, and dramas.

Brigitte Schwaiger (b. 1949)

The second of four daughters, Schwaiger was born in Freistadt, Upper Austria on April 6, 1949.   Her mother is a housewife, and her father was a general practitioner.   Before beginning to write Schwaiger pursued a variety of career possibilities: she studied acting, painting, pedagogy, and philosophy, worked as a secretary in a publishing house, and acted in a cellar theater in Linz.   In 1968 she moved to Spain, where she painted and gave language instruction.   There she married a Spanish army officer, from whom she separated after two years of marriage, later obtaining a divorce.   After her separation she returned to Austria, where she initially studied at the *Pädagogische Akademie* in Linz for three semesters.   Her first book, *Wie kommt das Salz ins Meer* (Why is the Sea Salty), was the first Austrian best-seller to deal explicitly with feminist themes.   In addition to her longer prose she has written plays and short stories.

References

Ingeborg Bachmann

"The Barking," in Elizabeth Rütschi Herrmann and Edna Huttenmaier Spitz, eds., *German Women Writers of the Twentieth Century*, trans. Ingeborg Day (New York: Pergamon Press, 1978), pp. 78-86.

"Gier" (Greed), in *Der dunkle Schatten, dem ich schon seit Anfang folge* (The Dark Shadow I Have Been Following from the Beginning) (Vienna, Munich: Löcker Verlag, 1982), pp. 17-69. Fragment.

The Thirtieth Year, trans. Michael Bulloch (New York: Alfred A. Knopf), 1964.

Werke (Works) 4 vols., Christine Koschel, Inge von Weidenbaum, and Clemens Muenster, eds. (Munich, Zurich: Piper Verlag), 1982.

Barbara Frischmuth

Amy oder die Metamorphose (Amy or the Metamorphosis) (Salzburg, Vienna: Residenz Verlag), 1978.

Bindungen (Bonds) (Salzburg, Vienna: Residenz Verlag), 1980.

Entzug—ein Menetekel der zärtlichsten Art (Withdrawal—A Warning of the Most Tender Kind) 2nd edition (Pfaffenweiler: Pfaffenweiler Presse, 1979). Graphiken von Heinz Treiber.

Die Frau im Mond (The Woman on the Moon) (Salzburg, Vienna: Residenz Verlag), 1982.

Kai und die Liebe zu den Modellen (Kai and the Love of Models) (Salzburg, Vienna: Residenz Verlag), 1979.

Die Klosterschule (The Convent School) (Frankfurt am Main: Suhrkamp, 1968).

Die Mystifikationen der Sophie Silber (The Mystification of Sophie Silber) (Salzburg: Residenz Verlag), 1976.

Rückkehr zum vorläufigen Ausgangspunkt / Haschen nach Wind (Return to the Provisional Starting Point / Chasing the Wind) (Munich: Deutscher Taschenbuch Verlag, 1978).

Marlen Haushofer

Das fünfte Jahr (The Fifth Year) (Vienna: Jungbrunnen, 1951).

Eine Handvoll Leben (A Handful of Life) (Vienna: Paul Zsolnay Verlag, 1955).

Himmel, der nirgendwo endet (Never-Ending Heaven) (Gütersloh: Mohn, 1966).

Haushofer, Marlen. "Die Höhle" (The Cave), in *Hoffnung und Erfüllung* (Hope and Fulfillment) (Graz, Vienna: Stiasny Bücherei, 1960), pp. 109-112.

Lebenslänglich (For Life) (Graz: Stiasny Verlag, 1966). Short stories selected and introduced by Oskar Jan Tauschinski.

Die Mansarde (The Attic) (Hamburg: Claassen, 1969).

Schreckliche Treue (Terrible Fidelity) (Hamburg: Claassen, 1968).

Die Tapetentür (The Wallpapered Door) (Vienna: Paul Zsolnay Verlag, 1957).

Die Vergißmeinnichtquelle (The Forget-Me-Not Spring) (Vienna: Bergland, 1956).

Die Wand (The Wall) (Gütersloh: Mohn, 1963).

Wir töten Stella (We're Killing Stella) (Vienna: Bergland, 1958).

Elfriede Jelinek

"Die Bienenkönige" (The Bee Kings), in Helga Geyer-Ryan, ed., *Was geschah, nachdem Nora ihren Mann verlassen hatte?* (What Happened after Nora Left her Husband?) (Munich: Deutscher Taschenbuch Verlag, 1982).

"Clara S.: musikalische Tragödie" (Clara S: Musical Tragedy), *manuskripte*, 21, No. 72 (1981), 3-21.

Die endlose Unschuldigkeit: Prosa—Hörspiel—Essay (The Endless
    Innocentness: Prose—Radio Play—Essay) (Munich: Schwiftinger Galerie-
    Verlag, 1980).

Die Klavierspielerin (The Piano Player) (Reinbek bei Hamburg: Rowohlt,
    1983).

"Krankheit oder die moderne Frau" (Disease or the Modern Woman),
    manuskripte, 23 (October 1984), 3-22.

Die Liebhaberinnen (Women in Love) (Reinbek bei Hamburg: Rowohlt,
    1975). Excerpts appear in English translation in the Altbach et al.
    anthology *German Feminism* under the title "take paula for example."

"Was geschah, nachdem Nora ihren Mann verlassen hatte?" in Helga Geyer-
    Ryan, ed., *Was geschah, nachdem Nora ihren Mann verlassen hatte?*
    (What Happened after Nora Left Her Husband?) (Munich: Deutscher
    Taschenbuch Verlag, 1982), pp. 170-205.

wir sind lockvögel baby! (we are decoys, baby!) (Reinbek bei Hamburg:
    Rowohlt, 1970).

Brigitte Schwaiger

Lange Abwesenheit (The Long Absence) (Vienna, Hamburg: Paul Zsolnay
    Verlag, 1980).

Mein spanisches Dorf (My Spanish Village) (Vienna, Hamburg: Paul Zsolnay
    Verlag, 1978).

Wie kommt das Salz ins Meer (Why is the Sea Salty) (Vienna, Hamburg:
    Paul Zsolnay Verlag, 1977).

Further Primary Literature

Aichinger, Ilse. "Aufruf zum Mißtrauen" (Call for Skepticism), in Klaus
    Wagenbach, and Winfried Stephan and Michael Krüger, eds., *Vaterland,
    Muttersprache. Deutsche Schriftsteller und ihr Staat seit 1945* (Berlin:
    Verlag Klaus Wagenbach, 1979), pp. 40-41. The text originally appeared
    in *Der Plan* (The Plan) July 1946.

———. *Die größere Hoffnung* (Herod's Children) (Amsterdam: Bermann-
    Fischer, 1948).

———. *Herod's Children*, trans. Cornelia Schaeffer (New York:
    Atheneum, 1963).

Brown, Rita Mae. *Rubyfruit Jungle* (Plainfield, Vermont: Daughters, Inc.,
    1973).

———. *Six of One* (New York: Harper and Row, 1978).

Piercy, Marge. *Small Changes* (New York: Fawcett, 1978).

————. *Woman on the Edge of Time* (New York: Knopf, 1976).

Reichart, Elisabeth. *Februar Schatten* (February Shadow) (Vienna: Brandstätter, 1984).

Reinig, Christa. *Entmannung* (Emasculation) (Dusseldorf: Verlag Eremiten Presse, 1976).

Rousseau, Jean Jacques. *Emile,* trans. Barbara Foxley (London: J. M. Dent and Sons, 1911). Originally published 1762.

Schlegel, Friedrich. "Lucinde" in Hans Eichner, ed., *Dichtungen* (Literary Works) (Munich, Paderborn, Vienna: Ferdinand Schöningh, 1962). Originally published 1799.

Schroeder, Margot. *Ich stehe meine Frau* (Act Like a Woman) (Frankfurt am Main: Fischer Taschenbuch Verlag), 1975. Excerpts appear in English translation in the Altbach et al. anthology *German Feminism* under the title "Take It Like a Woman."

Stefan, Verena. *Häutungen* (Shedding) (Munich: Verlag Frauenoffensive, 1975).

————. *Shedding,* trans. Johanna Moore and Beth Weckmueller (New York: Daughters Co., 1978).

Walker, Alice. *The Color Purple* (New York: Harcourt Brace Jovanovich, 1982).

Wolf, Christa. *Kindheitsmuster* (Patterns of Childhood) (Berlin, Weimar: Aufbau Verlag, 1976).

————. *Nachdenken über Christa T* (The Quest for Christa T) (Halle: Mitteldeutscher Verlag, 1968).

————. *Patterns of Childhood,* trans. Ursele Molinaro and Hedwig Rappolt (New York: Farrar, Straus, and Girioux, 1984).

————. *The Quest for Christa T,* trans. Christopher Middleton (New York: Farrar, Straus, and Girioux, 1971).

Secondary References

Abel, Elisabeth. *Writing and Sexual Difference* (Chicago: The University of Chicago Press), 1982.

Abraham, Ulf. "Topos und Utopie: Die Romane der Marlen Haushofer" (Topos and Utopia: The Novels of Marlen Haushofer), *Adalbert-Stifter-Institut des Landes Ober Österreich. Vierteljahresschrift* (The Adalbert Stifter Institute of Upper Austria. Quarterly), 35 (1988), 53-83.

Achberger, Karen. "Beyond Patriarchy: Ingeborg Bachmann and Fairytales," *Modern Austrian Literature,* 18, No. 3/4 (1985), 211-222.

Adrian, Sylvia. "Im Brachland der Gefühle: Ein Rückblick auf die Literatur über Vaterfiguren" (In the Fallow Land of Feelings: A Survey of Literature about Father Figures), in *Deutsche Literatur 1981: Ein Jahresüberblick* (German Literature 1981: A Year in Review) (Stuttgart: Reclam, 1982), pp. 241-247.

Altbach, Edith Hoshino, Jeanette Clausen, Dagmar Schultz, and Naomi Stephan, eds. *German Feminism: Readings in Politics and Literature* (Albany, New York: State University of New York Press), 1984.

Andraschko, Elisabeth and Alois Ecker. "Frauen im Lehrberuf" (Women in the Teaching Profession), *Erziehung und Unterricht* (Education and Instruction), 132, No. 4 (1982), 295-309.

Arbeitsgruppe Frauenmaul. *Ich hab' Dir keinen Rosengarten versprochen . . .: Das Bild der Frau in vier österreichischen Tageszeitungen—eine Dokumentation* (I Never Promised You a Rose Garden: The Image of Woman in Four Austrian Dailies—A Documentation) (Vienna: Frischfleisch und Löwenmaul, 1978).

Arnold, Heinz Ludwig, ed. *TEXT + KRITIK: Ingeborg Bachmann*, (Text and Critique: Ingeborg Bachmann), 6 (1971, 1980—4th edition).

Austrian People's Party. *Salzburger Programm* (Salzburg Platform) (Vienna: Vereinigung für politische Bildung), 1980.

Autorinnen-Gruppe Universität Wien. *Das ewige Klischee* (The Eternal Cliché) (Vienna, Cologne, Graz: Hermann Böhlaus Nachfolger, 1981).

Baden, Hans Jürgen. "Eros und Erlösung: Das Weltbild von Ingeborg Bachmann" (Eros and Salvation: Ingeborg Bachmann's World View), in *Poesie und Theologie* (Poetry and Theology) (Hamburg: Agentur des Rauhen Hauses, 1971), pp. 79-98.

Bail, Gabriele. *Weibliche Identität: Ingeborg Bachmanns "Malina"* (Female Identity: Ingeborg Bachmann's *Malina*) (Göttingen: edition herodot), 1984.

Bargil, Marianne. "Berufliche Rollenvorstellungen von Lehrlingen" (Apprentices' Conceptions of Professional Roles), *Erziehung und Unterricht* (Education and Instruction), 132, No. 4 (1982), 320-323.

Bartsch, Kurt, Dietmar Goltschnigg, and Gerhard Melzer. *Für und wider eine österreichische Literatur* (For and Against an Austrian Literature) (Königstein/Ts.: Athenäum), 1982.

Basil, Otto, Herbert Eisenreich, and Ivar Ivask. *Das große Erbe* (The Great Inheritance) (Graz, Vienna: Stiasny Verlag, 1962).

Bauer, Roger. "Österreichische Literatur oder Literatur aus Österreich?" (Austrian Literature or Literature from Austria?), in Robert A. Kann and Friedrich Prinz, eds., *Deutschland und Österreich* (Germany and Austria) (Vienna, Munich: Jugend und Volk, 1980), pp. 264-287.

de Beauvoir, Simone. *The Second Sex,* trans. and ed. H. M. Parshley (New York: Vintage-Random House, 1974).

Beck, Evelyn Torton and Patricia Russian. "Die Schriften der modernen Frauenbewegung" (The Writings of the Modern Women's Movement), in Jost Hermand, ed., *Neues Handbuch der Literaturwissenschaft* (The New Handbook of Literary Studies) (Wiesbaden: Akademische Verlagsgesellschaft Athenaion, 1979), pp. 357-386.

Beck, Evelyn Torton and Biddy Martin. "Westdeutsche Frauenliteratur der siebziger Jahre" (West German Women's Literature of the Seventies), in Paul Michael Lützeler and Egon Schwarz, eds., *Deutsche Literatur in der Bundesrepublik seit 1965* (German Literature in the Federal Republic since 1965) (Königstein/Ts.: Athenäum, 1980), pp. 135-149.

Becker-Cantarino, Barbara. "Stimmen des 'zweiten Geschlechts': die neue Politik und Literatur der Frauen" (Voices of the Second Sex: The New Politics and Literature of Women), in *Propyläen Geschichte der Literatur* (Proplyäen's History of Literature), 6 (Berlin: Propyläen Verlag, 1982).

Berchtold, Klaus, ed. *Österreichische Parteiprogramme 1868-1966* (Austrian Party Platforms 1868-1966) (Vienna: Verlag für Geschichte und Politik, 1967).

Berger, John. *Ways of Seeing* (London, Middlesex: British Broadcasting Corporation and Penguin Books, 1972).

Berger, Karin. *Zwischen Eintopf und Fließband: Frauenarbeit und Frauenbild im Faschismus, Österreich 1938-1945* (Between Stew and Conveyor Belt: Women's Work and the Image of Women in Fascism, Austria 1938-1945) (Vienna: Verlag für Gesellschaftskritik, 1984).

Berger, Maria. "Braucht Österreich ein Antidiskriminierungsgesetz?" (Does Austria Need an Anti-Discrimination Law?), in *Frau und Recht* (Women and the Law) (Vienna: Bundespressedienst, 1981), pp. 9-13.

Beyer, Johanna, Franziska Lamott, and Birgit Meyer. *Frauenhandlexikon: Stichworte zur Selbstbestimmung* (Women's Dictionary: Key Words to Self-Determination) (Munich: Verlag C. H. Beck, 1983).

Bock, G. and B. Duden. "Arbeit aus Liebe—Liebe als Arbeit: Zur Entstehung der Hausarbeit im Kapitalismus" (Work for Love—Love as Work: Concerning the Rise of Housework in Capitalism), in *Frauen und Wissenschaft: Beiträge zur Berliner Sommeruniversität für Frauen, Juli 1976* (Women and Scholarship: Contributions to the Berlin Summer University for Women) (Berlin: Courage Verlag, 1977), pp. 118-199.

Boedefeld, Gerda. "Alleinsein ist eine gute Sache" (Being Alone is a Good Thing), *Brigitte,* No. 27 (24 December 1971), 61-63.

Boesso, Anna. *Barbara Frischmuth,* Doctoral dissertation, Universita degli Studi di Padova, 1982.

Bovenschen, Silvia. *Die imaginierte Weiblichkeit: Exemplarische Untersuchungen zu kulturgeschichtlichen und literarischen Präsentationsformen des Weiblichen* (Imagined Feminity: Exemplary Investigations of Cultural-Historical and Literary Representation Forms of the Female) (Frankfurt am Main: Suhrkamp Verlag, 1979).

_____. "Is There a Feminine Aesthetic?" in Gisela Ecker, ed., *Feminist Aesthetics,* trans. Harriet Anderson (Boston: Beacon Press, 1985), pp. 23-50.

_____. "Über die Frage: Gibt es eine weibliche Ästhetik?" (Is There a Feminine Aesthetic?), *Ästhetik und Kommunikation* (Aesthetics and Communication), Jahrgang 7 Heft 25 (Sept. 1976), 60-75.

Brandstaller, Trautl. *Frauen in Österreich: Bilanz und Ausblick* (Mid Decade 1980: Review and Evaluation) (Vienna: Bundespressedienst, 1981).

_____. *Mid Decade 1980: Review and Evaluation,* trans. Angelika Loskot (Vienna: Bundespressedienst, 1981).

von Bredow, Wilfried and Hans-Friedrich Foltin. *Zwiespältige Zufluchten* (Ambiguous Refuges) (Berlin, Bonn: Verlag J. H. W. Dietz Nachfolger, 1981).

Bridenthal, Renate, Atina Grossmann, and Marion Kaplan, eds. *When Biology Became Destiny: Women in Weimar and Nazi Germany* (New York: Monthly Review Press, 1984).

Brownmiller, Susan. *Against our Will: Men, Women and Rape* (New York: Simon and Schuster, 1975).

Cella, Ingrid. " 'Das Rätsel Weib' und die Literatur: Feminismus, feministische Ästhetik und die neue Frauenliteratur in Österreich" ('The Puzzle Woman' and Literature: Feminism, a Feminist Aesthetic, and the New Women's Literature), in Herbert Zeman, ed., *Studien zur österreichischen Erzählliteratur der Gegenwart* (Studies of Contemporary Austrian Prose) *Amsterdamer Beiträge zur neueren Germanistik*, Vol. 14 (Amsterdam: Rodopi, 1982), pp. 189-228.

Chesler, Phyllis. *Women and Madness* (New York: Avon, 1973).

Chodorow, Nancy. *The Reproduction of Mothering: Psychoanalysis and the Sociology of Gender* (Berkeley, Los Angeles, London: University of California Press, 1978).

Cornillon, Susan Koppelman. *Images of Women in Fiction: Feminist Perspectives* (Bowling Green: Bowling Green University Popular Press, 1972). Revised edition 1973.

Crews, Elisabeth Thompson. *Wort und Wahrheit: Das Problem der Sprache in der Prosa Ingeborg Bachmanns,* (Word and Truth: The Problem of Language in Ingeborg Bachmann's Prose), Doctoral dissertation, University of Minnesota, 1977.

Daviau, Donald G. "Barbara Frischmuth" in David G. Daviau, ed., *Major Figures of Contemporary Austrian Literature* (New York: Peter Lang, 1987), pp. 185-206.

_____. "Das junge und das jüngste Wien" (The Young and Youngest Vienna), in Wolfgang Paulsen, ed., *Österreichische Gegenwart: Die moderne Literatur und ihr Verhältnis zur Tradition* (The Austrian Present: Modern Literature and its Relationship to Tradition) (Bern: Francke Verlag, 1980).

Dohnal, Johanna. Letter to author, 13 April 1984.

_____. Personal interview, 29 October 1986.

_____. *Sozialdemokratie und Frauenbewegung (Historisch und Heute)* (Social Democracy and the Women's Movement—Historically and Today) (Vienna-Penzing: SPÖ, 1983).

_____. "Weg vom Klischee" (Away from the Cliché), *Erziehung und Unterricht* (Education and Instruction), 132, No. 4 (1982), 274-283.

Dor, Milo, ed. *Die Verbannten: Eine Anthologie* (The Banned: an Anthology) (Graz: Stiasny Verlag, 1962).

Eifler, Margret. "Ingeborg Bachmann: 'Malina'," *Modern Austrian Literature,* 12, No. 3/4 (1979), 373-391.

Eisenstein, Hester. *Contemporary Feminist Thought* (Boston: G. K. Hall and Co., 1983).

Eisenstein, Hester and Alice Jardine. *The Future of Difference* (Boston: G. K. Hall and Co., 1980).

Eisenstein, Zillah R. *Capitalist Patriarchy and the Case for Socialist Feminism* (New York, London: Monthly Review Press, 1979).

_____. *The Radical Future of Liberal Feminism* (New York, London: Longman, 1981).

Emmerich, Wolfgang. "Identität und Geschlechtertausch. Notizen zur Selbstdarstellung der Frau in der neuen DDR-Literatur" (Identity and Sex Change. Notes on the Self-Representation of Women in the New Literature of the GDR), *Basis: Jahresbuch für deutsche Gegenwartsliteratur* (Basis: Yearbook for Contemporary German Literature), 8 (1978), 127-154.

Ernst, Gustav and Klaus Wagenbach, eds. *Tintenfisch 16: Literatur in Österreich* (Octopus 16: Literature in Austria) (Berlin: Verlag Klaus Wagenbach, 1979).

Ezergailis, Inta. *Women Writers—The Divided Self: Analysis of novels by Christa Wolf, Ingeborg Bachmann, Doris Lessing, and others* (Bonn: Bouvier Verlag Herbert Grundmann, 1982).

Feigl, Susanne. *Women in Austria 1975-1985* (Vienna: Staatssekretariat für allgemeine Frauenfragen, 1985).

Ferguson, Mary Anne. *Images of Women in Literature* (Boston: Houghton Mifflin, 1973).

Firestone, Shulamith. *The Dialectic of Sex* (New York: Bantam, 1972).

Fischer, Ernst. *Die Entstehung des österreichischen Volkscharakters* (The Development of the Austrian National Character) Vol. 2 of *Schriftenreihe "Neues Österreich"* (Series "New Austria") (Vienna: "Neues Österreich" Zeitungs- und Verlagsgesellschaft, 1945).

Fliedl, Konstanze. "Die melancholische Insel. Zum Werk Marlen Haushofers" (The Melancholy Island: The Works of Marlen Haushofer), *Adalbert-Stifter-Institut des Landes Ober Österreich. Vierteljahresschrift* (The Adalbert Stifter Institute of Upper Austria. Quarterly), 35 (1988), 35-51.

Foreman, Ann. *Femininity as Alienation: Women and the Family in Marxism and Psychoanalysis* (London: Pluto Press, 1977).

Franck, Barbara. *Ich schau'in den Spiegel und sehe meine Mutter* (I Look in the Mirror and See My Mother) (Hamburg: Hoffmann und Campe, 1979).

Frankfurter, Johannes. "Elfriede Jelinek und die Kunst des Ekelns" (Elfriede Jelinek and the Art of Revulsion), *Neue Zeit* (New Time), (7 July 1983), 15.

Freud, Sigmund. *Drei Abhandlungen zur Sexualtheorie: Die sexuellen Abirrungen* (Three Essays on Sexuality) Vol. 5 of *Gesammelte Werke* (The Collected Works) (London: Imago Publishing Co., Ltd., 1945).

_____. "Female Sexuality," in *The Future of an Illusion: Civilizaton and Its Discontents and Other Works,* in *The Complete Psychological Works of Sigmund Freud*, translated under the general editorship of James Strachey, Vol. XXI (London: Hogarth Press and Institute of Psycho-Analysis, 1961), pp. 221-243.

_____. *The Interpretation of Dreams,* in *The Complete Psychological Works of Sigmund Freud*, translated under the general editorship of James Strachey, Vol. IV&V (London: Hogarth Press and Institute of Psycho-Analysis, 1953).

_____. *Jokes and Their Relation to the Unconscious* In *The Complete Psychological Works of Sigmund Freud* translated under the general editorship of James Strachey, Vol. VIII (London: Hogarth Press and Institute of Psycho-Analysis, 1960).

_____. *Psychopathologie des Alltagslebens* (Psychopathology of Everyday Life) Vol. 4 of *Gesammelte Schriften* (Collected Literature) (Leipzig, Vienna, Zurich: Internationaler Psychoanalytischer Verlag, 1924).

_____. *Psychopathology of Everyday Life,* in *The Complete Psychological Works of Sigmund Freud*, translated under the general editorship of James Strachey, Vol. VI (London: Hogarth Press and Institute of Psycho-Analysis, 1960).

_____. *Three Essays on Sexuality,* in *The Complete Psychological Works of Sigmund Freud* translated under the general editorship of James Strachey, Vol. VII (London: Hogarth Press and Institute of Psycho-Analysis, 1953).

_____. *Die Traumdeutung* (The Interpretation of Dreams) Vol. 2 of *Gesammelte Schriften* (The Collected Works) (Leipzig, Vienna, Zurich: Internationaler Psychoanalytischer Verlag, 1925). First published 1900 by Verlag Franz Deuticke, Leipzig and Vienna.

_____. "Über die weibliche Sexualität" (Female Sexuality), in *Werke aus den Jahren 1925-1931* , *Gesammelte Werke* (The Collected Works), Vol 14 (London: Imago Publishing Co., Ltd., 1948), pp. 517-537.

_____. *Der Witz und seine Bezeihung zum Unbewußten* (Jokes and Their Relation to the Unconscious) Vol. 9 of *Gesammelte Werke* (The Collected Works) (Leipzig, Vienna, Zurich: Internationaler Psychoanalytischer Verlag, 1925).

Frieden, Sandra. "Bachmann's 'Malina' and 'Todesarten': Subliminal Crimes" *The German Quarterly,* 56, No. 1 (January 1983), 61-73.

_____. "The Left-handed Compliment: Perspectives and Stereotypes in Criticism," in Susan L. Cocalis and Kay Goodman, eds., *Beyond the Eternal Feminine: Critical Essays on Women and German Literature* (Stuttgart: Akademischer Verlag Hans-Dieter Heinz, 1982), pp. 311-333.

Frischmuth, Barbara. "Denken Sie bitte nach, meine Damen!: Ringen um ein neues Weltmodel" (Ladies, Please Think about It: Striving for a New World Model), *Die Presse* (The Press), No. 8/9 (March 1975), 22.

_____. "Österreich—versuchsweise betrachtet" (Austria—Observed On a Trial Basis), in *Glückliches Österreich* (Happy Austria) (Salzburg, Vienna: Residenz Verlag, 1978), pp. 66-70.

_____. "Der Ort der Phantasie" (The Place of Fantasy), *Die Presse* (The Press), No. 9/10 (July 1977), 20.

_____. Personal interview, 25 February 1983.

_____. "Die stressere Hälfte" (The Half More Stressed), *Profil* (Profile), 29 March 1978, 51-53.

Führmann, Franz, Dietrich Simon, and Joachim Schreck. "Gedanken beim Lesen: Gespräch über Barbara Frischmuth" (Thoughts While Reading: A Conversation about Barbara Frischmuth), *Sinn und Form* (Meaning and Form), 28, No. 2 (March/April 1976), 423-436.

Gaudart, Dorothea. *The Status of Women in Austria* (Vienna: Austrian Federal Ministry of Social Affairs, 1976).

_____. "Die Stellung der Frau" (The Position of Women), in E. Bodzenta, ed., *Die österreichische Gesellschaft* (The Austrian Society) (Vienna, New York: Springer Verlag, 1972).

_____. "Women and Social Policy Decision-Making: The Case of
    Austria," in *Research Symposium on the Occasion of the International
    Women's Year—'Women and Decision-Making: A Social Policy Priority'*
    (Geneva: Bundesministerium für soziale Verwaltung, 1975).

_____ and Rose Marie Greve. *Die Frau in den Arbeitsbeziehungen:
    Rahmenpapier und analytische Zusammenfassung der Diskussionen eines
    Internationalen Symposiums* (Women in Work Relationships: Preliminary
    Paper and Analytical Summary of the Discussion of an International
    Symposium) (Vienna: Bundesministerium für sozial Verwaltung, 1978).

_____ and Wolfgang Schulz. *Mädchenerziehung wozu?* (Girls' Education:
    What for?) Vol. 1 in Agnes Niegl, ed., *Schriften zur Mädchen- und
    Frauenbildung* (Literature on the Education of Girls and Women)
    (Vienna: Österreichischer Bundesverlag für Unterricht Wissenschaft und
    Kunst, 1971).

"Gespräch mit Elfriede Jelinek vom Münchner
    Literaturarbeitskreis."(Conversation with Elfriede Jelinek by the Munich
    Literary Study Group), *mamas pfirsiche* (mama's peach), 9/10 (Fall
    1978), 170-180.

Gilbert, Sandra M. and Susan Gubar. *The Madwoman in the Attic* (New
    Haven, London: Yale University Press, 1980).

Göttner-Abendroth, Heide. *Die tanzende Göttin: Prinzipien einer
    matriarchalen Ästhetik* (The Dancing Goddess: Principles of a
    Matriarchal Aesthetic) (Munich: Frauenoffensive, 1982). Excerpts
    appear in English in the Altbach et al. anthology *German Feminism*
    under the title "Nine Principles of a Matriarchal Aesthetic."

Gornick, Vivian and Barbara K. Moran. *Woman in Sexist Society* (New
    York, London: Basic Books, Inc., 1971).

Grieser, Dietmar. *Dietmar Grieser über Frischmuth,* (Dietmar Grieser on
    Frischmuth), *Österreichische Phonothek* (Austrian Phonotheque), Tape
    number 760250.

Gürtler, Christa. *Schreiben Frauen Anders?: Untersuchungen zu Ingeborg
    Bachmann und Barbara Frischmuth* (Do Women Write Differently?
    Analyses of Ingeborg Bachmann and Barbara Frischmuth) (Stuttgart:
    Akademischer Verlag Hans-Dieter Heinz, 1983).

Haberland, Paul M. "The Role of Art in the Writings of Barbara
    Frischmuth," *Modern Austrian Literature,* 14, No. 1/2 (1981), 85-96.

Hacker, Hanna. "Staatsbürgerinnen" (Female Citizens), in Franz Kadmoska,
    ed., *Aufbruch und Untergang* (Emergence and Decline) (Vienna,
    Munich, Zurich: Europa Verlag, 1981), pp. 225-245.

Haller, M. *Die Frau in der Gesellschaft,* (Women in Society), Doctoral
    dissertation, Universität Wien, 1975.

Hammer, Signe. *Mothers and Daughters: Daughters and Mothers* (New
    York: Signet, 1975).

Hapkemeyer, Andreas. *Die Sprachthematik in der späten Prosa Ingeborg Bachmanns*, (The Thematic of Language in Ingeborg Bachmann's Late Prose), Doctoral dissertation, Universität Innsbruck, 1981.

Harris, Judith May. *Modes of Domination: The Social Dimension in Ingeborg Bachmann's Fiction*, Doctoral dissertation, University of California, Berkeley, 1983.

Helczmanovski, H. "Geburtenzuwachs and Geburtenrückgang nach der amtlichen Bevölkerungsstatistik Österreichs" (Rise and Fall of the Birth Rate According to the Official Austrian Population Statistics), in *Die amtliche Statistik in Österreich, gestern—heute—morgen* (Official Austrian Statistics: Yesterday—Today—Tomorrow) (Vienna: Österreichisches Statistisches Zentralamt, 1977).

Herte, Christlieb. "Anmerkungen zur österreichischen Literatur" (Observations concerning Austrian Literature), *Weimarer Beiträge* (Weimar Essays), 27, No. 6 (1981), 129-158.

Hieden, Helga. *Die Frau in der Gesellschaft* (Women in Society) (Vienna: Verlag für Geschichte und Politik, 1983).

————. "Die gesellschaftliche Stellung der Frau im Schulsystem: ein Beitrag zur geschlechtsspezifischen Erziehung?" (Women's Societal Position in the School System: A Contribution to Sex-Specific Education?), *Erziehung und Unterricht* (Education and Instruction), 132, No. 4 (1982), 283-295.

Höller, Hans, ed. *Der dunkle Schatten, dem ich schon seit Anfang folge* (The Dark Shadow I Have Been Following from the Beginning) (Vienna, Munich: Löcker Verlag, 1983).

Ingeborg Bachmann: das Werk von dem frühesten Gedichten bis zum "Todesarten"-Zyklus (Ingeborg Bachmann: Her Literature from the Earliest Poems to the Cycle "Types of Death") (Frankfurt am Mainz: Athenäum, 1987).

Hofmeister, Donna. "Access Routes into Postmodernism: Interviews with Innerhofer, Jelinek, Rosei, and Wolfgruber" *Modern Austrian Literature*, 20, No. 2 (1987), 97-130.

Hofmüller, Gertha. "Was bedeutet der Frauenausschluβ für die Rechtsentwicklung?" (What Does the Women's Committee Mean for Legal Development?), in *Frau und Recht* (Women and the Law) (Vienna: Bundespressedienst, 1981), pp. 14-19.

Horsley, Ritta Jo. "Re-reading 'Undine geht': Bachmann and Feminist Theory," *Modern Austrian Literature*, 18, No. 3/4 (1985), 223-238.

Irigaray, Luce. *Speculum of the Other Woman,* trans. Gillian C. Gill (Ithaca: Cornell University Press, 1985). This originally appeared as *Speculum de l'autre femme* (Paris: Les Editions de Minuit, 1974).

Jauβ, Hans Robert. "Literaturgeschichte als Provokation," in *Literaturgeschichte als Provokation* (Literary History as a Challenge to Literary Theory) trans. Elizabeth Benzinger (Frankfurt am Main: Suhrkamp, 1974), pp. 144-207.

_____. "Literary History as a Challenge to Literary Theory," *New Literary History*, 2 (1970), 7-37.

Jelinek, Elfriede. *Elfriede Jelinek liest ihr "Nora"*, (Elfriede Jelinek reads her *Nora*), *Österreichische Phonothek* (Austrian Phonotheque) tape number T 2501. (April 17, 1978),

_____. *Elfriede Jelinek spricht über Elfriede Gerstl*, (Elfriede Jelinek Talks about Elfriede Gerstl), *Österreichische Phonothek* (Austrian Phonotheque) tape number 760163. (April 8, 1976),

_____. "Der ewige Kampf: Zwei Arsenleichen (weibl.) in der Literatur" (The Eternal Battle: Two Arsenic Corpses (fem.) in Literature), *Wespennest* (Wasp's Nest), 44 (1981), 32-36.

_____. "Frauenbewegung und Frauenkultur" (The Women's Movement and Women's Culture), *Volkstimme* (The People's Voice), (22 July , 1978).

_____. Personal interview, 19 September 1983.

Johnston, William M. *The Austrian Mind: An Intellectual and Social History* (Berkeley, Los Angeles, London: University of California Press, 1972).

Jurgensen, Manfred. *Deutsche Frauenautoren der Gegenwart* (Contemporary German Women Writers) (Bern: Francke Verlag, 1983).

_____. *Frauenliteratur: Autorinnen—Perspektiven—Konzepten* (Women's Literature: Authors—Perspectives—Concepts) (Frankfurt: Peter Lang Verlag, 1983).

_____. *Ingeborg Bachmann: Die neue Sprache* (Ingeborg Bachmann: The New Language) (Frankfurt am Main: Peter Lang Verlag, 1981).

Kapfer, Dr. Hans, ed. *Das allgemeine bürgerliche Gesetzbuch*, (The Civil Code), (Vienna: Manzsche Verlags- und Universitätsbuchhandlung), 1980, Manzsche Taschenausgabe. Neue Reihe österreichische Gesetze, Band 2.

Karl, Elfriede. "Foreword," in *Familienplanung 1975* (Family Planning 1975) (Vienna: Österreichische Gesellschaft für Familienplanung, 1975).

Kathrein, Karin. "Bücher, Pferde und ein Ehemann: 'Presse'-Gespräch mit der Schriftstellerin Barbara Frischmuth" (Books, Horses, and a Husband: Conversation with Barbara Frischmuth), *Die Presse* (The Press), No. 18/19 (December 1971), 7.

Key, Mary Ritchie. *Male/Female Language* (Metuchen, N. J.: Scarecrow Press, 1975).

Kienlechner, Toni.   "Gespräch mit Ingeborg Bachmann: 19 März 1972"
    (Conversation with Ingeborg Bachmann), *Die Brücke. Kärntner
    Kulturzeitschrift 1* (The Bridge.   Carinthian Cultural Magazine), (1975),
    98-104.

King, Lynda J.   "The Woman Question and Politics in Austrian Interwar
    Literature," *German Studies Review,* 6, No. 1 (1983), 75-100.

Klaar, Dr. Helene.   *Was tue ich, wenn . . . es zur Scheidung kommt?*
    (What Do I Do If It Comes to a Divorce?) (Vienna:
    Bundespressedienst, 1982).

Klaus, Wolfgang. *Barbara Frischmuth liest Sophie Silber mit Gespräch und
    Einführung von Dr. Wolfgang Klaus,* (Barbara Frischmuth Reads *Sophie
    Silber* with a Conversation and an Introduction by Dr. Wolfgang
    Klaus), *Österreichische Phonothek* (Austrian Phonoteque) Tape number
    760307.

Klein-Löw, Dr. Stella. Personal interview, 2 November 1984.

Kolodny, Annette.   "Some Notes on Defining a 'Feminist' Literary
    Criticism," in Cherl L. Brown and Karen Olsen, eds., *Feminist
    Criticisms* (Metuchen, N. J. and London: The Scarecrow Press, Inc.,
    1978), pp. 37-58.

Kommunikationswoche der Wiener Frauenkooperative. *Schulfunk: Dichter
    interpretieren Gedichte. Folge 23,* (Educational Broadcasting: Poets
    Interpret Poems.   Number 23), *Österreichische Phonothek* (Austrian
    Phonotheque), Tape number T 2544,

Kreuz, H. and H. Fürnschuß. *Chancen der Weiterbildung* (Chances of
    Continuing Education) Agnes Niegl, ed. (Vienna: Österreichischer
    Bundesverlag, 1971).

Laing, R. D.   *The Divided Self* (Chicago: Quadrangle Books, 1960).

Lebeda, Andreas. *Konstanz und Wandel im Prosawerk Barbara Frischmuths*
    (Constancy and Change in the Prose of Barbara Frischmuth),   Master's
    thesis, Universität Salzburg, September 1981.

Lenk, Elisabeth.   "The Self-reflecting Woman," in Gisela Ecker, ed., *Feminist
    Aesthetics* (Boston: Beacon Press, 1986), pp. 51-58.

_____.   "Die sich selbst verdoppelnde Frau" (The Self-reflecting Woman),
    Ästhetik und Kommunikation, 7, No. 25 (September 1976), 84-87.

Lennox, Sara.   "In the Cemetery of the Murdered Daughters: Ingeborg
    Bachmann's 'Malina'," *Studies in Twentieth Century Literature,* 5, No. 1
    (Fall 1980), 75-105.

Levin, Tobe Joyce. *Political Ideology and Aesthetics in Neo-feminist German
    Fiction: Verena Stefan, Elfriede Jelinek, Margot Schroeder,*   Doctoral
    dissertation, Cornell University, August 1979.

Linhoff, Ursula. *Die neue Frauenbewegung: USA—Europa seit 1968* (The New Women's Movement: USA—Europe since 1968) (Köln: Kiepenheuer and Witsch), 1975.

Lippard, Lucy R. *From the Center: Feminist Essays on Women's Art* (New York: Dutton, 1976).

Löffler, Sigrid. "Der sensible Vampir" (The Sensitive Vampire), *Emma*, (October 1985), 33-36.

Lorenz, Dagmar C. G. *Biographie und Chiffre: Entwicklungsmöglichkeiten in der österreichischen Prosa nach 1945, dargestellt an den Beispielen Marlen Haushofer und Ilse Aichinger*, (Biography and Code: Possibilities of Development in Austrian Prose after 1945 Exemplified by Marlen Haushofer and Ilse Aichinger), Doctoral dissertation, University of Cincinnati, 1974.

_____. "Creativity and Imagination in the Work of Barbara Frischmuth," in Marianne Burkhard and Edith Walstein, eds., *Women in German Yearbook 2* (Lanham, New York, and London: University Press of America, 1986), pp. 37-56.

_____. "Ein Definitionsproblem: Österreichische Literatur" (A Problem of Definition: Austrian Literature), *Modern Austrian Literature*, 12, No. 2 (1979), 1-21.

_____. "Ein Interview: Barbara Frischmuth" (An Interview: Barbara Frischmuth), in Marianne Burkhard and Edith Waldstein, eds., *Women in German Yearbook 2* (New York: University Press of America, 1986).

_____. "Marlen Haushofer—eine Feministin aus Österreich" (Marlen Haushofer—A Feminist from Austria), *Modern Austrian Literature*, 12, No. 3/4 (1979), 171-191.

von der Lühe, Irmela, ed. *Entwürfe von Frauen in der Literatur des zwanzigsten Jahrhunderts* (Literary Blueprints by Women in the Twentieth Century) (Berlin: Argument-Verlag, 1982).

_____. "Schreiben und Leben: Der Fall Ingeborg Bachmann" (To Write and Live: The Case of Ingeborg Bachmann), in *Feministiche Literaturwissenschaft* (Feminist Literary Studies) (Berlin: Argument Verlag, 1984), pp. 43-53. Dokumentation der Tagung in Hamburg vom Mai 1983. Argument-Sonderband.

Malek, Stefan. "Ein politisches Stück, ein Stück übers Kapital" (A Political Play, A Play about Capital), *Kleine Zeitung* (The Little Newspaper), (6 October 1979), 20.

Mansour, Dina. *Die Frauengestalten im Erzählwerk von Barbara Frischmuth* (Female Figures in the Prose of Barbara Frischmuth), Master's thesis, University of Cairo, 1983.

Maritsch, Renate. "Die Berufswahl der Mädchen—für die Zukunft entscheidend" (Girls' Choice of Profession—Decisive for the Future), *Erziehung und Unterricht* (Education and Instruction), 132, No. 4 (1982), 324-326.

Marks, Elaine and Isabelle de Courtivon. *New French Feminisms* (New York: Schocken Books, 1981).

McConnell-Ginet, Sally, Ruth Borker, and Nelly Furman, eds. *Women and Language in Literature and Society* (New York: Praeger, 1980).

Meise, Helga. "Einige Gedanken über Krieg und Liebe" (Some Thoughts about War and Love), *Frauenforschungsprojekt Marburg* (Marburg Women's Research Project), 13, (September 1980), 101-108.

Menschik, Jutta. *Feminismus* (Feminism) (Köln: Paul-Rugenstein, 1977).

Millett, Kate. *Sexual Politics* (London: Rupert Hart-Davis, 1969).

Mitchell, Juliet. *Woman's Estate* (New York: Pantheon Books, Random House, 1971).

Mitterauer, Michael. "Geschlechtsrollenerziehung und Lehrerausbildung an den Hochschulen" (Gender-Role Education and Teacher-Training at the University Level), *Erziehung und Unterricht* (Education and Instruction), 132, No. 4 (1982), 315-320.

_____ and Reinhard Sieder. *The European Family: Patriarchy to Partnership from the Middle Ages to the Present* (Oxford: Basil Blackwell, 1982). First published as *Vom Patriarchat zur Partnerschaft: Zum Strukturwandel der Familie* (Munich: C. H. Beck, 1977).

Möhrmann, Renate. "Feministische Ansätze in der Germanistik seit 1945" (Feminist Beginnings in German Studies since 1945), in Magdalena Heuser, ed., *Frauen—Sprache—Literatur: Fachwissenschaftliche Forschungsansätze und didaktische Modelle und Erfahrungsberichte für den Deutschunterricht* (Women—Language—Literature: Specialized Research and Didactic Models and Reports of Personal Experience for the Instruction of German) (Paderborn: Ferdinand Schöningh, 1982), pp. 91-115.

_____. "Feministische Trends in der deutschen Gegenwarsliteratur" (Feminist Trends in Contemporary German Literature), in Manfred Durzak, ed., *Deutsche Gegenwartsliteratur: Ausgangspositionen und aktuelle Entwicklungen* (German Contemporary Literature: Starting Points and Current Developments) (Stuttgart: Reclam, 1981), pp. 336-358.

Moers, Ellen. *Literary Women* (Garden City, New York: Doubleday, 1976).

Müller, Sylvia. *Die Lehrpläne an Österreichs Allgemeinbildenden Höheren Schulen qvon 1848 bis zur Gegenwart*, (The Curricula at Austrian Secondary Schools from 1848 to the Present), Doctoral dissertation, Universität Salzburg, 1970.

Münz, R. and H. Wimmer. "Erfahrungen in Familienberatungsstellen: Ein Vergleich der Situation in Kärnten, Tirol und Wien" (Experiences in Family Counseling Centers: A Comparison of the Situation in Carinthia, the Tyrol, and Vienna), *Österreichische Zeitschrift für Soziologie* (Austrian Journal for Sociology), No. 3-4 (1977), 116-123.

Münz, Rainer and Jürgen M. Pelikan. *Geburt oder Abtreibung* (Birth or Abortion) (Vienna: Jugend und Volk, 1978).

Nagel, Wolfgang. "Auf der Flucht zu sich selbst" (The Escape to One's Self), *Zeit-Magazin* (Time-Magazine), No. 37 (1978), 14-20.

Oesterreichisches Statistisches Zentralamt.   12, Tabellenband I (Demographischer Teil): *Ergebnisse der Volkszählungen vom 1. Juni 1951* (Results of the Census from June 1, 1951) (Vienna: Druck und Kommissionsverlag der österreichischen Staatsdruckerei, 1953).

Ozer, Irma J. *The Treatment of the Maladjusted Protagonist in the Fiction of Ingeborg Bachmann and Christa Wolf*, Doctoral dissertation, New York University, 1986.

Paulsen, Wolfgang, ed. *Die Frau als Heldin und Autorin* (Woman as Heroine and Author) (Bern: Franke Verlag, 1979).

Pichl, Robert. "Rhetorisches bei Ingeborg Bachmann. Zu den redenden Namen im 'Simultan'" (Ingeborg Bachmann's Rhetorical Figures: About the Rhetorical Names in "Simultaneous"), *Akten des sechsten Internationalen Germanisten-Kongresses Basel* (Records of the Sixth International Congress of Germanists in Basel), (1980), 301f.

_____. "Voraussetzungen und Problemhorizont der gegenwärtigen Ingeborg-Bachmann-Forschung" (Premises and Problems of Contemporary Study of Ingeborg Bachmann), *Jahrbuch der Grillparzergesellschaft* (Yearbook of the Grillparzer Society), 3, No. 14 (1980), 89.

_____. "Das Werk Ingeborg Bachmanns: Probleme und Aufgaben" (Ingeborg Bachmann's Writings: Problems and Tasks), *Literaturwissenschaftliches Jahrbuch* (Yearbook of Literary Study), 17 (1976), 373-385.

Polheim, Karl Konrad. *Literatur aus Österreich. Österreichische Literatur: Ein Bonner Symposium* (Literature from Austria. Austrian Literature: A Symposium in Bonn) (Bonn: Bouvier Verlag Herbert Grundmann, 1981).

Puknus, Heinz, ed. *Neue Literatur der Frauen* (New Women's Literature) (Munich: Verlag C. H. Beck, 1980).

Pusch, Luise F. *Das Deutsche als Männersprache* (German as a Languge of Men) (Frankfurt am Main: Suhrkamp, 1984).

_____, ed. *Feminismus: Inspektion der Herrenkultur* (Feminism: Examination of the Master Culture) (Frankfurt am Main: Suhrkamp, 1983).

The Random House College Dictionary (New York, Toronto: Random House, 1973).

Ranftl-Guggenberger, Doris. "Rollenfixierungen im Kinderbuch des Vorschulalters" (Role Fixation in the Childrens' Book of the Pre-Schooler), *Erziehung und Unterricht* (Education and Instruction), No. 4 (1982), 327-343.

Raschauer, Dr. Bernhard, ed. *Bundesverfassungsrecht*, (Constitutional Law), (Munich: Wilhelm Goldmann Verlag). This edition contains the law as of 1 October 1975.

Rechberger, Maria. "Die Stellung der Frau in Schule und Familie" (The Position of Women in School and Family), *Erziehung und Unterricht* (Education and Instruction), 132, No. 4 (1982), 344-348.

Reik, Theodor. *Masochism in Modern Man* trans. Margaret H. Beigel and Gertrud M. Kurth (New York: Farrar, Strauss, and Company, 1941).

Rich, Adrienne. *Of Woman Born: Motherhood as Experience and Institution* (New York: W. W. Norton and Co., 1976).

Rigler, Edith. *Frauenleitbild und Frauenarbeit in Österreich* (Women's Role Model and Women's Work in Austria) (Vienna: Verlag für Geschichte und Politik, 1976).

Rohrbaugh, Joanna Bunker. *Women: Psychology's Puzzle* (New York: Basic Books, 1979).

Roβmann, Andreas. "Brigitte Schwaiger: Wie kommt das Salz ins Meer" (Brigitte Schwaiger: Why Is the Sea Salty), *Text und Kritik* (Text and Critique), No. 126/127 (July/August 1978), 422-423.

Rowbotham, Sheila. *Woman's Consciousness, Man's World* (Middlesex: Penguin Books, 1971).

Ruiss, Gerhard and J. A. Vyoral. *Zur Situation junger österreichischer Autoren: Eine Bestandsaufnahme der gegenwärtigen österreichischen Literaturszene* (On the Situation of Young Austrian Authors: A Stocktaking of the Contemporary Austrian Literary Scene) (Vienna: Autorenkooperative, 1978).

Sartori, Paola. *Barbara Frischmuth—'Haschen nach Wind': Vier Frauenschicksale*, (Barbara Frischmuth—*Haschen nach Wind*: The Fates of Four Women), Doctoral dissertation, Universita degli Studi die Venezia, 1979.

Sauter, Josef-Hermann. "Interviews mit Barbara Frischmuth, Elfriede Jelinek, Michael Scharang" (Interviews with Barbara Frischmuth, Elfriede Jelinek, Michael Scharang), *Weimarer Beiträge* (Weimar Essays), 27, No. 6 (1981), 99-128.

Scheibe, Susanne. *Schreiben als Antwort auf den Abschied: Eine Untersuchung zu Ingeborg Bachmanns "Malina" unter Berücksichtigung des Romans von Emma Santos "Ich habe Emma S. getötet"* (Writing as an Answer to Parting: A Study of Ingeborg Bachmann's *Malina* in Light of the Novel by Emma Santos *I Killed Emma S.*) (Frankfurt am Main: Haap und Herchen Verlag, 1983).

Schenk, Herrad. *Die feministische Herausforderung: 150 Jahre Frauenbewegung in Deutschland* (The Feminist Challenge) (Munich: Verlag C. H. Beck, 1980).

Schmid-Bortenschlager, Sigrid. "Beiträge österreichischer Schriftstellerinnen zur Literatur seit 1945" (Contributions of Austrian Women Writers to Literature since 1945), *Moderna Sprak* (Modern Language), 75, No. 2 (1981), 149-162.

_____. "Spiegelszenen bei Bachmann: Ansätze einer psychoanalytischen Interpretation" (Mirror Scenes in Bachmann's Literature: Attempts at a Psycho-Analytical Interpretation), *Modern Austrian Literature,* 18, No. 3/4 (1985), 39-52.

Schmidt-Dengler, Wendelin. "Geschichten gegen die Geschichte. Gibt es das Österreichische in der österreichischen Literatur?" (Stories against History. Is There an Austrian Essence in Austrian Literature?), *Modern Austrian Literature,* 17, No. 3/4 (1984), 149-157.

Schmölzer, Hilde. *Frau sein und schreiben: Österreichische Schriftstellerinnen definieren sich selbst* (To Be a Woman and Write: Women Writers Define Themselves) (Vienna: Österreichischer Bundesverlag, 1982).

Scholes, Robert. *Semiotics and Interpretation* (New Haven, London: Yale University Press, 1982).

_____. *Structuralism in Literature* (New Haven, London: Yale University Press, 1975).

Schulz, Wolfgang. "Daten zur Situation der Frau in Österreich" (Information on the Situation of Women in Austria), in *Die Situation der Frau in der Männergesellschaft* (The Situation of Women in Male Society) (Vienna: Österreichische Gesellschaft für Politik), n. d.

Schwaiger, Brigitte. Personal interview, 8 April 1983.

Schwarz, Egon. "Was ist österreichische Literatur? Das Beispiel H. C. Artmanns und Helmut Qualtingers" (What is Austrian Literature? The Example of H. C. Artmann and Helmut Qualtinger), in Kurt Bartsch, Dietmar Goltschnigg, and Gerhard Melzer, eds., *Für und Wider eine österreichische Literatur* (For and Against an Austrian Literature) (Königstein/Ts.: Athenäum, 1982), pp. 130-151.

_____. "What Is Austrian Literature? The Example of H. C. Artmann and Helmut Qualtinger," in Reinhold Grimm, Peter Spycher, and Richard A. Zipser, eds., *From Kafka and Dada to Brecht and Beyond* (Madison: The University of Wisconsin Press, 1982), pp. 63-83.

Serke, Jürgen. *Frauen schreiben* (Women Writing) (Frankfurt am Main: Fischer Tascherbuch Verlag, 1982). Originally Sternbuch 1979.

————. "Der Vater ist tot, es lebe der Vater" (Father Is Dead, Long Live Father), *Stern* (Star), No. 14 (27 March 1980), 242-252.

Shainess, Natalie. *Sweet Suffering* (Indianapolis, New York: Bobbs-Merrill Company, Inc., 1984).

Showalter, Elaine. *A Literature of their Own* (Princeton, N. J.: Princeton University Press, c. 1977).

Sozialistische Partei Österreich. *Jahrbuch 1978: Bericht an den 24. ordentlichen Bundesparteitag der SPÖ, Wien-Konzerthaus 18.-20. Mai 1978* (Yearbook 1978: Report on the Twentieth Regular Party Convention of the SPÖ, Vienna Concert Hall May 18-20, 1978) (Vienna: Sozialistische Partei Österreich, 1978).

Spiel, Hilde, ed. *Kindlers Literaturgeschichte der Gegenwart: Die zeitgenössische Literatur Österreichs* (Kindler's Literary History of the Present: Austrian Contemporary Literature) (Zurich, Munich: Kindler Verlag, 1976).

Staatssekretariat für allgemeine Frauenfragen. *Frauenbericht* (Women's Report) (Vienna: Bundespressedienst, 1975).

————. *Mehr tun für die Frauen im Bundesdienst* (Do More for the Women in the Civil Service) (Vienna: Bundespressedienst, 1981).

————. *Patriachat 1981 oder: der Geschlechterkampf um Partnerschaft im Haushalt* (Patriarchy 1981 or The Fight Between the Sexes for Partnership in Housekeeping) (Vienna: Bundespressedienst, 1981).

Stadler, Karl. *Austria* (London: Benn, 1971).

Steiger, Robert. *"Malina"—Versuch einer Deutung des Romans von Ingeborg Bachmann* (An attempt to Interpret Ingeborg Bachmann's Novel *Malina*) (Heidelberg: Carl Winter Universitätsverlag, 1978).

Stumm, Reinhardt. "Vater—lieber Vater: Thema mit Variationen in neuen Büchern" (Father—Dear Father: Theme and Variations in Recent Books), *Die Zeit* (Time), (15 February 1980), 25-26.

Suchy, Victor. *Literatur in Österreich von 1945 bis 1970* (Literature in Austria from 1945 to 1970) (Vienna: Dokumentationsstelle für neuere österreichische Literatur), 1971.

Summerfield, Ellen. *Die Auflösung der Figur in Ingeborg Bachmann*, (Character Dissolution in Ingeborg Bachmann), Doctoral dissertation, University of Connecticut, 1975.

————. *Ingeborg Bachmann: Die Auflösung der Figur in ihrem Roman 'Malina'* (Ingeborg Bachmann: Character Dissolution in Her Novel *Malina*) (Bonn: Bouvier Verlag Herbert Grundmann), 1976.

Szinovacz, M. *Educational and Occupational Aspirations in Women* (Vienna: Institut für Soziologie, 1971).

Theweleit, Klaus. *Männerphantasien* (Male Fantasies) Vol. 1 (Reinbek bei Hamburg: Rowohlt, 1982). Copyright 1977 by Verlag Roter Stern, Frankfurt am Main.

————. *Male Fantasies,* trans. Stephan Conway (Minneapolis: University of Minnesota Press, 1987).

Thorne, Barrie and Nancy Henley, eds. *Language and Sex: Difference and Dominance* (Rowley, Massachusetts: Newberry House, 1975).

Trömel-Plötz, Senta. *Frauensprache: Sprache der Veränderung* (Women's Language: Language of Change) (Frankfurt am Main: Fischer Taschenbuch Verlag, 1982).

————, ed. *Gewalt durch Sprache* (Violence through Language) (Frankfurt am Main: Fischer Taschenbuch Verlag, 1985).

Tubach, Sally Patterson. *Female Homoeroticism in German Literature and Culture,* Doctoral dissertation, University of California, Berkeley, 1980.

Vansant, Jacqueline. "Gespräch mit Elfriede Jelinek" (Conversation with Elfriede Jelinek), *Deutsche Bücher* 15, No. 1 (1985), 1-9.

Venske, Regula. " 'Vielleicht, daß ein sehr entferntes Auge eine geheime Schrift aus diesem Splitterwerk enträtseln könnte . . .': Zur Kritik der Rezeption Marlen Haushofers" (Perhaps a Very Distant Eye Could Decipher the Secret Writing from the Fragment...: To a Critique of the Reception of Marlen Haushofer), in *"Oder war da manchmal noch etwas anderes?": Texte zu Marlen Haushofer* (Was There Still Sometimes Something Else: Texts About Marlen Haushofer) (Frankfurt am Main: Verlag Neue Kritik, 1986), pp. 43-66.

de Vin, Daniel. "Schreibstunden: Brigitte Schwaiger im Gespräch" (Writing Lessons: A Conversation with Brigitte Schwaiger), *Germanistische Mitteilungen* (German Studies' Reports), 17 (1983), 27-50.

Weber, Albrecht. " 'Das Gebell' in Interpretationen zu Ingeborg Bachmann" ("The Barking" in Interpretations for German Instruction), in Rupert Hirschenauer and Albrecht Weber, eds., *Interpretationen zum Deutschunterricht* (Munich: R. Oldenbourg Verlag, 1976), pp. 110-124.

Weber, Norbert. *Das gesellschaftlich Vermittelte der Romane österreichischer Schriftsteller seit 1970* (That Which Is Mediated by Society in the Novels of Austrian Writers since 1970) (Frankfurt am Main: Peter Lang Verlag, 1980).

Weigel, Sigrid. "Overcoming Absence: Contemporary German Women's Literature," *New German Critique,* 11, No. 2 (Spring-Summer, 1984), 3-22.

————, ed. *TEXT + KRITIK: Ingeborg Bachmann* (Text and Critique: Ingeborg Bachmann) (Munich: edition text und kritik, 1984).

_____. " 'Woman Begins Relating to Herself': Contemporary German Women's Literature," *New German Critique,* 11, No. 1 (Winter 1984), 53-94.

Weinberg, Thomas and G. W. Levi Kamel. *S & M: Studies in Sadomasochism* (Buffalo: Prometheus Books, 1983).

Weingant, Liselotte. *Das Bild des Mannes im Frauenroman der Siebziger Jahre,* (The Image of Man in the Women's Novel of the Seventies), Doctoral dissertation, University of Illinois at Urbana-Champaign, 1981.

_____. "Brigitte Schwaiger, 'Lange Abwesenheit' " (Brigitte Schwaiger "Long Absence"), *Modern Austrian Literature,* 15, No. 2 (1982), 91-93.

Weinzierl, Erika. *Emanzipation?: Österreichische Frauen im zwanzigsten Jahrhundert* (Emancipation? Austrian Women in the Twentieth Century) (Vienna, Munich: Jugend und Volk, 1975).

_____ and Kurt Skalnik, eds. *Österreich: Die Zweite Republik* (Austria: The Second Republic) (Graz: Verlag Styria, 1972).

_____ and Kurt Skalnik, eds. *Österreich 1918-1938: Geschichte der Ersten Republik* (Austria 1918-1938: History of the First Republic) (Graz: Styria, 1983).

Weiß, Walter and Sigrid Schmid, eds. *Zwischenbilanz: Eine Anthologie österreichischer Gegenwartsliteratur* (An Interim Statement: An Anthology of Contemporary Austrian Literature) (Salzburg: Residenz Verlag, 1976).

Wimmer, H. *Partnerschaft und Familienplanung: Eine empirische Untersuchung in Wien,* (Partnership and Family Planning: An Empirical Study in Vienna), Doctoral dissertation, Universität Wien, 1977.

Wirsing, Sybille. "Ingeborg Bachmann: Simultan" (Ingeborg Bachmann: Simultaneous), *Neue deutsche Hefte* (New German Notebooks), 19, No. 4 (1972), 149-151.

Witte, Bernd. "Schmerzton Ingeborg Bachmann: Perspektiven einer feministischen Literatur" (Painful Sound Ingeborg Bachmann: Perspectives of a Feminist Literature), *die horen* (The Horae), 28, No. 132 (Fall 1983), 76-82.

Wolf, Christa. "Truth That Can Be Faced: Ingeborg Bachmann's Prose" in *The Reader and the Writer,* trans. Joan Becker (New York: Signet, 1977).

_____. "Die zumutbare Wahrheit: Prosa der Ingeborg Bachmann" (Truth That Can Be Faced: Ingeborg Bachmann's Prose), in *Lesen und Schreiben: Aufsätze und Prosastücke* (The Reader and the Writer: Essays, Sketches, Memories) (Darmstadt: Luchterhand, 1972), pp. 121-134.

Index

About the Author

JACQUELINE VANSANT is a Visiting Assistant Professor at Hamilton College, Clinton, New York. She is the author of numerous scholarly papers and reviews, and has contributed articles to *Deutsche Bucher* and *Der weiblichen Zahmung*.